Charleston Conference Proceedings 2004

MGEN
MR943

Charleston Conference Proceedings 2004

Edited by Rosann Bazirjian, Vicky Speck, and Beth R. Bernhardt

Katina Strauch, Series Editor

Westport, Connecticut • London

b 30482239

Z
731
.C46
2004

Library of Congress Cataloging-in-Publication Data

Charleston Conference (24th : 2004 : Charleston, S.C.)
  Charleston Conference proceedings, 2004 / edited by Rosann Bazirjian, Vicky Speck, and Beth R. Bernhardt.
      p. cm.
    Includes bibliographical references and index.
    ISBN 1-59158-339-X (pbk. : alk. paper)
    1. Library science—United States—Congresses. 2. Libraries—Information technology—United States—Congresses. 3. Collection development (Libraries) —United States—Congresses. 4. Serial librarianship—United States—Congresses. 5. Libraries and electronic publishing—United States—Congresses. 6. Libraries and booksellers—United States—Congresses. 7. Acquisitions (Libraries)—Costs—United States—Congresses. 8. Cataloging of electronic journals—United States—Congresses. 9. Books—United States—History—Congresses. I. Bazirjian, Rosann. II. Speck, Vicky H. III. Bernhardt, Beth R. IV. Title.
Z672.5.C53 2004
020.973—dc22   2005028603

British Library Cataloguing in Publication Data is available.

Copyright © 2006 by Libraries Unlimited

All rights reserved. No portion of this book may be reproduced, by any process or technique, without the express written consent of the publisher.

Library of Congress Catalog Number: 2005028603
ISBN: 1-59158-339-X

First published in 2006

Libraries Unlimited, 88 Post Road West, Westport, CT 06881
A Member of the Greenwood Publishing Group, Inc.
www.lu.com

Printed in the United States of America

The paper used in this book complies with the Permanent Paper Standard issued by the National Information Standards Organization (Z39.48-1984).

10 9 8 7 6 5 4 3 2 1

Table of Contents

The Book

Technology

Personnel Issues

Budget/Fiscal Matters

Robert Alan, Head of the Serials Department, The Pennsylvania State University Libraries, University Park

Books and the Internet: Buying, Selling, and Libraries

Buying Books Consortially—From the Big Deal to Open Access

MARC Records for E-Journals

The Charleston Conference turned 24 in November 2004. What began as an informal gathering of barely 20 people in the commons room of a dorm on the College of Charleston campus has grown to an international meeting of professional librarians, publishers, vendors, aggregators, consultants, and others who work together every day to solve problems and talk through issues related to the publication and acquisition of scholarly information. The work we do has changed dramatically since 1980, back when the IBM correcting Selectric typewriter was the machine of choice and there was no e-mail or World Wide Web. Still, the Conference keeps attracting professionals to gather and discuss informally the issues and problems that consume us.

The theme of the 2004 Charleston Conference was "All the World's a Serial," pointing out the tendency of online products to update their offerings and assign continuing prices to their items. Gone are the days of the static monograph that is rarely, if ever, updated. Along with the exciting possibilities that this brings for information delivery come budgetary concerns and concerns about the support infrastructures that must be put in place to bring this about and to allow for the linking of online content.

This volume is divided into nine sections: Collection Development, Journals, The Book, Technology, Personnel Issues, Budget/Fiscal Matters, Books and the Internet, Buying Books Consortially, and MARC Records for E-Journals. These sections represent the state of the art in acquisitions and collection development in 2004 and 2005.

This volume was expertly compiled, refereed, and edited by Rosann Bazirjian, Vicky Speck, and Beth Bernhardt. We owe them our special thanks for preserving the content of a valuable Conference and dialogue among professionals. Thanks are also due to Julia Warner and Sharon DeJohn of Libraries Unlimited.

We look forward to seeing you in Charleston November 2–5, 2005! In the meantime, visit our Web site at http://www.katina.info/conference. See you soon!

Katina Strauch
kstrauch@comcast.net

Preface and Acknowledgments

The Charleston Conference continues to be a major event for information exchange among librarians, vendors, and publishers. Almost everyone who has ever attended the Charleston Conference tells us how informative and thought-provoking the sessions continue to be. The Conference provides a collegial atmosphere in which librarians can talk freely and directly with publishers and vendors about issues facing them and their libraries. All this interaction occurs in the wonderful city of Charleston, South Carolina. This is the fifth year that Rosann Bazirjian and Vicky Speck have put together the proceedings from the Conference, and the first year for Beth Bernhardt. We are pleased to share some of the learning experience that we, and other attendees, had at the conference.

The theme of the 2004 Charleston Conference was "All the World's a Serial." While not all presenters prepared written versions of their remarks, enough did so that we are able to include an overview of such subjects as evaluating electronic resources, the history of the book, open access, the future of the book, pay-per-view, digital archiving, book buying over the Internet, developing consortia, e-journals, and MARC record issues. All of these topics are of great interest to librarians and can be looked at from numerous viewpoints.

Katina Strauch, founder of the Conference, continues to serve as an inspiration to us. Her enthusiasm for the Conference and the proceedings was motivating. We hope you, the reader, find the contributions as informative as we did and that they encourage the continuation of the ongoing dialogue among librarians, publishers, and vendors that can only enhance the learning and research experience for the ultimate user.

Signed,

Co-Editors of the 24th Charleston Conference proceedings

Rosann Bazirjian, University Librarian, University of North Carolina at Greensboro

Vicky H. Speck, Editorial Director, Serials, ABC-CLIO

Beth R. Bernhardt, Electronic Journals/Document Delivery Librarian, University of North Carolina at Greensboro

Introduction

When you think of the Charleston Conference you think of collection development. With the growth of electronic resources, collection development librarians find themselves looking for ways to accurately evaluate these resources. Several 2004 presentations dealt with ways to do this. Other topics important to collection development that were presented are how researchers use books, dealing with gifts, scholarship and reference publishing, acquiring resources for new programs, and knowledge management.

Collection Development

INTERDISCIPLINARY SCHOLARSHIP AND REFERENCE PUBLISHING

Karen Christensen, CEO, Berkshire Publishing Group, Great Barrington, Massachusetts

This chapter is about the growing demand for interdisciplinary scholarship and the practical difficulties involved in creating, marketing, and managing interdisciplinary publications. Exploring the relationships between various major areas of human endeavor is nothing new, and the best-known discussion is perhaps that about "the two cultures," started by scientist and writer C. P. Snow. Snow's Cambridge lecture "The Two Cultures," given in 1959, discussed the differences between scientific and artistic cultures and what these differences meant for education and society. The topic has inspired hundreds of articles, books, and Web sites. It is a perennial debate, and one of particular importance today as developments in science and technology have increasing impact on every aspect of life and on the well-being of the planet we live on.

This debate has been of particular interest to me since I was a student at the University of California Santa Barbara (UCSB). I was studying literature but took a history of science class, then physics, and soon found myself writing a feature article for the alumni magazine about the Institute for Theoretical Physics, spending weeks with physicists including Lee Smolin, whose recent *The Life of the Cosmos* has been widely reviewed and is known for applying principles of biological evolution to cosmology.

The panel here brought me together with Sarah Pritchard, University Librarian at UCSB, and Rolf Janke from Sage Publications in nearby Thousand Oaks, so it did feel like coming full circle, to explore a topic that has become all the more important and complex in the last two decades.

For many, interdisciplinary efforts should span this divide. But to a large extent, interdisciplinary efforts have been equated with only a few of the possible areas, such as women's studies and Latino studies. I was startled, as a publisher who has produced some uniquely interdisciplinary projects, to find that at Yankee Book Peddler the "interdisciplinary" tag wouldn't apply to anything we do because the list of fields is restricted to ethnic or minority studies. And it remains very difficult to have a work cataloged under a variety of disciplines under the LOC CIP system. When the book or database gets to the library, librarians face considerable challenges in seeing that it reaches all its potential users in different fields.

Rolf Janke, vice president and publisher at Sage Reference, and David Levinson, Ph.D., cultural anthropologist, Berkshire's president, and editor of a number of major interdisciplinary reference works including Berkshire's *Encyclopedia of Crime & Punishment* and the *Encyclopedia of Marriage and the Family,* were active panel participants, sharing stories from their experience on different projects. They particularly focused on the *Encyclopedia of Leadership,* which Sage published and Berkshire Levinson created and directed, working with leadership scholars in fields ranging from political science and history to psychology and education. (It's perhaps worth noting that these established fields were once emerging, interdisciplinary fields, too.)

We had hoped to have David Christian, a professor of history at San Diego State University and author of *Maps of Time: An Introduction to Big History* (University of California Press, 2004) with us to offer a perspective broader—bigger—than perhaps any other interdisciplinary endeavor. Big history brings together history and the sciences, from archeology to biology, astronomy to ecology. *Maps of Time,* wrote William H. McNeill, "unites natural history and human history in a single, grand, and intelligible narrative." Both McNeill and Christian are profoundly interested in the relationship between history and science, which truly reflects the dilemma of the "two cultures." They see history becoming more scientific as science becomes more historical (and cultural, too) in its understanding.

The texts below incorporate ideas raised in the panel and subsequent discussions with the audience, looking at library challenges, scholarly challenges, and human/cognitive challenges in interdisciplinary scholarship and publishing.

The Librarian's Perspective

Sarah M. Pritchard, University of California-Santa Barbara

I come to this topic with the perspective of a librarian doing reference and collection development in the field of women's studies, and my career has been shaped by the excitement, diversity, and challenges presented by interdisciplinary scholarship.

These issues have evolved from the time when women's studies was still emerging into the academy from its political foundations and thus struggling for intellectual legitimacy as well as redefining content and terminology.

Not all interdisciplinary fields emerge in the same way, and the nature of the trajectory is one of the issues to look at in understanding, as a field grows, how its literature evolves at the levels of primary, secondary, and tertiary sources, the last of which is where I place reference works, indexes, and the like

If a new interdisciplinary topic is derived directly from well-established existing academic fields, for example as with many interdisciplinary subfields in the sciences, then it is somewhat easier to piggyback on existing resources and then get the new work integrated into standard tools. It subsequently becomes readily apparent when there is so much literature that the topic merits an independent identity.

But if the field is evolving from social movements or activities occurring initially outside of academia, there are difficult hurdles of legitimacy and quality to overcome before one even gets to the more practical problems of library selection, budgeting, or cataloging. Just getting the work to be seen in academic contexts takes some active work on the part of those who create, publish, and archive it. In the case of women's studies, it not only had activist political roots; its key tenets implied that traditional categories and terminology and canonical works were themselves incomplete and suspect; you couldn't just "add women and stir."

People want to assign each interdisciplinary field somehow to its parents. Is it a social science, a science, or what? The definition of interdisciplinary itself is debated among academics, but in fact the details of the blending of scholarly methodologies and core concepts may not matter so much as the extent to which the work falls in between our hidebound ways of categorizing. Whether it is the schedules of library classification or the standard lineup of academic departments, we have a series of existing buckets into which our work has to fit, and it is simply because of the principles of standardization, of least effort and cost, that we are going to try to force everything into those molds. In libraries we need to allocate the materials budget, arrange the collections physically, and assign subject responsibility to various librarians—we want an easy way to deal with all this.

As a field evolves, however, there are points at which we may need to change or expand, and we tend to do that as we are "pushed" by the emergence of the literature itself and the research demands of the faculty. There are two trends or tendencies that I have observed in this evolutionary process.

First is the debate over a separate versus an integrated approach. In the academy, this plays out at the departmental level, and in the library it comes down to decisions about budgeting and physical arrangement. There are advantages and disadvantages to each, and in fact one gets complaints either way. There are political implications; what does the choice say about the nature and visibility of the field? Authors and faculty themselves don't agree on the best strategy, and it shifts over time within the same institution. Handling the budget is especially problematic. A new field usually starts off at a disadvantage because it just gets allocated a small amount of money that then grows incrementally, slowly. Meanwhile the people selecting for the large traditional areas may think they no longer need to worry about that new area, so they stop buying! And yet there is often soon too much for the small new budget, and the person monitoring that field must go around nagging and cadging funds across the range of other relevant categories. On the other hand, if there is no separate line there are indeed some titles that never seem quite to fit, so they fall between the conceptual cracks and nobody buys them.

The second tendency is the movement from the fringes to the mainstream; this is related to the separate/integrated dynamic but not the same; the two trends can mesh or not. Publishing companies may play a unique role in legitimizing a field and moving it more to the center, with dedicated journals, monograph series, bibliographies, and textbooks. By the time there are large formal reference indexes and databases about a topic, we're home free! In women's studies, for example, the early sources were largely mimeographed book lists, newsletters produced in someone's kitchen, and self-published books that never got reviewed in *Choice*. Librarians worked early on with both independent and mainstream publishers to get good reference sources, inclusion in abstracting and indexing services, upgrading of periodicals, retrospective reprints, microform collections, and the like. This was invaluable in building the corpus of literature that we now (almost) take for granted.

Library solutions to the challenges of interdisciplinarity range from the informal to formal. Of course we want to be responsive to the growth of new topics and the interests of students and faculty, but there are issues of costs in acquisitions, cataloging, space, and staff. Libraries can do what is quick and simple first, while seeing whether a topic is just a small subfield or something growing into a major program and reshaping the terminology of research. Levels of treatment include the following, from simplest to most complex and heavily supported:

- Finding aids, book displays, and Web pages.

- Profiling in approval and vendor plans, and assigning as a field to the librarian in one of the "parent" disciplines.

- Enhanced cataloging—adding local headings and metadata. This is expensive, since it is nonstandardized. It's less and less common, unfortunately, but specialized thesauri were for a time the direction of choice in specialty fields. Now in the era of Google, people mistakenly think controlled vocabularies are no longer so much needed.

- Library instruction targeted to the difficulties of a new field; not only the paucity of reference sources but the need to rediscover or re-evaluate older and primary sources.

- Separate physical collections—for the entire collection, or just reference works.

- A full-time subject specialist librarian, with active faculty outreach.

One way or another, it takes some individual librarian tracking both faculty interests and publishing trends to detect and monitor the growth of an interdisciplinary area. Some fields will just not be on our radar screen, especially in smaller institutions or those with fairly traditional academic programs. There is probably a good market for a publisher or jobber who wants to help libraries play "catch-up" on an interdisciplinary field that they missed!

The Publisher's Perspective

Karen Christensen

Interdisciplinary publishing isn't easy, but it has been Berkshire's focus since early days, perhaps because our partnership is interdisciplinary. I studied English and comparative literature and have been writing about environmental issues and community for the last 10 years. I also have a great interest in science generally and in emerging technologies. David Levinson, on the other hand, is a cultural anthropologist who has done much work in psychology and criminology. Each of us brings a set of interests and expertise to our publishing, and we've consciously developed a network of scholarly advisors from other disciplines.

As Sarah has explained, librarians generally relish interdisciplinary thinking and publications but struggle with the practicalities involved in managing them and making them readily accessible to students. We publishers, too, face practical difficulties in developing—and marketing—interdisciplinary projects.

First, there's the task of recruiting and managing a group of contributors from many disciplines. Even when these scholars quickly recognize the value of a major interdisciplinary publication in their field, as they did with Berkshire's *Encyclopedia of Community,* for example, they often do not know one another, have different perspectives on what matters most, and use different terminology.

Second, the effort of directing their writing, reviewing and editing articles, and finalizing content is far more challenging in interdisciplinary scholarship than when working within an established field with clear boundaries. (Interdisciplinary fields, new or developing, do not have established boundaries; one of the roles of a major reference work, such as our *Encyclopedia of World Environmental History,* is to put an interdisciplinary field on the map, and to define it for those both inside and out.) Much staff time and expertise is required to create works that are integrated and consistent.

Third, existing systems for categorizing publications, both at the Library of Congress and in distributor and library databases, often do not allow for even the simplest of cross- and interdisciplinary tagging. For example, the *Berkshire Encyclopedia of Human-Computer Interaction* is both computer science and social science; that's the nature of the new but well-established field of human–computer interaction. This work had to be tagged as *human* and *computer,* but in almost every case we could choose only one. (We chose *computer,* but realize that means people in psychology, sociology, and philosophy may never find it.)

Finally, it's more difficult to find the particular person who is ready to make a purchase decision. We know that we're creating publications that a considerable community of scholars, students, and professionals want, and reviewers are always enthusiastic about the interdisciplinary coverage. (Have you ever seen a work criticized for being interdisciplinary?) But as Sarah explains, it's often difficult to know just who within the library is responsible for buying a book or encyclopedia in an interdisciplinary field.

Nonetheless, interdisciplinary scholarship continues to be highly valued (a quick Google search of "interdisciplinary scholarship," in fact, makes this blazingly clear), and the fascinating project before us is to make it easier to understand and navigate, both in the library itself and in individual databases and other publications. A variety of technologies may be helpful (human–computer interaction comes in here), from mapping tools to wikis. Berkshire will be experimenting with wikis for its new projects and continuing this discussion about interdisciplinary scholarship on its blog,[1] and perhaps even in a wiki that will enable publishers, librarians, aggregators, and scholars to create an open dialogue about this vital, transformative approach to knowledge creation.

Note

1. See *The Two Cultures (and More)*, February 16, 2005 [Online], available: http://www.berkshirepublishing.com/blog.

GIFT MATERIALS: A CASE STUDY

Mary E. (Tinker) Massey, Library Technical Assistant, University of South Carolina, Columbia

Our session started with an overview of gift problems and policies. A general outline was presented to the group for establishing a policy statement. It was noted that polling of university Web sites showed about 10% of the institutions not accepting in-kind donations for their collections, while 10% accepted everything they could get and 80% have some special arrangements for acceptance of materials. Those examples were presented and discussed in the group regarding their acceptance policies and strategies. Part of this discussion was about the current IRS regulations pertaining to gifts and donations. Everyone was warned against doing on-site evaluations of donations, and to definitely follow the IRS regulations precisely.

The second part of the session dealt with the management of the process. At the University of South Carolina (USC), we had established some local notes (590) that are keyword accessible, to display the donor's name and the holding area for the material (example: Box 19). At the session we showed how this information could be and has been used to give patrons access to the materials (even before cataloging), has bolstered the giving incentives for donors, allows administrators to examine massive gifts and how they have been integrated into the system, and controls information for collection management personnel.

We also explained how changes in ILS systems prompted an additional local note for the record number in the old system. A further local note (980) has been used for the state accountant, enabling that person to determine the purchasing status. We all agreed that gifts are not free, and that the most recent studies have shown them to cost the receiving institution about $45 per item for processing into their collections.

An informal poll in the room revealed that most people attending had some educational basis for being able to deal with the processing of gifts. Those who didn't have that background, were able to learn much of what they needed from others in the field or from experience. Some have considered taking an additional course in collection management. They responded that the handout with the bibliography would be helpful. At USC, the music librarian teaches a course in librarianship that covers the basic problems and solutions in handling donations.

The basic utilization of 590 fields in the bibliographic records to tender information about the materials in the collections from donations has given the library a new way to encourage gifts, use materials not previously available to patrons, and manage a previously unruly group of items. The bane of our existence has come to be almost a pleasure during these poor economic times.

THE ICEBERG PROBLEM, OR IS THE INVESTMENT IN OUR COLLECTIONS VISIBLE TO PATRONS?

Ezra Schwartz , Principal Consultant, Art & Tech, Inc., Chicago, Illinois

> *For every complex problem, there is a solution that is simple, neat, and wrong.*—H. L. Mencken

A collection is a potential, a discovery waiting to happen. Since digital collections are only accessible through their user interfaces, the role of the user interface as a facilitator of discovery cannot be overestimated. It appears, however, that while academic electronic collections have grown exponentially—and often as a result of significant institutional investment—the utilization rates for many of these collections remain lower than expected. Computers and broadband networks are ubiquitous, patrons are computer savvy, and researchers are excited about the potential of electronic resources—what then stands in the way of greater utilization of electronic scholarly collections?

Driven by substantial industry investment, significant advances in e-commerce over the last few years have dramatically changed users' expectations for usability and quick gratification during online sessions. Many libraries, on the other hand, are facing shrinking budgets and diminishing resources just as the rising popularity of commercial research tools makes the success of academic collections increasingly contingent on enabling quick and easy access to the wealth of resources they offer. For collection developers, this situation suggests the need to take a closer look at the user interfaces that provide access to their collections.

Of Icebergs and Penguins

Icebergs are a good metaphor for the relationship between collections and the user interface. Like icebergs, most collections are largely invisible. The user interface, or the tip of the iceberg, does not reflect the actual scope or depth of the submerged mass. Some collection portals attempt to attract patrons by using gimmicky interface designs intended to create a contemporary look—these are the penguins of our metaphor. Still, server log analyses, used like the underwater equipment necessary to explore the submerged mass, often reveal that only a small chunk of the collection is ever used. Analyses of inter-library loan requests support the frustrating realization that patrons remain unaware of much of the content available in the collection.

The iceberg problem can be framed as follows: What can be done to facilitate interaction patterns that help patrons realize the discovery potential of the available electronic resources and, by extension, justify current and future investment in the collection? I believe that the answer is in the user interface. In what follows, I further explore the conceptual and strategic relationship between the user interface and collection utilization.

Utilization, along with *usability* and *accessibility*, are no longer the obscure jargon of narrowly technical discussions. Increasingly, these terms permeate the electronic resources discourse. Yet the topics they represent often remain only loosely connected to the efforts of many collection developers. This is understandable given the traditional separation between content and containers, or the collection and the technology that makes it available. Organizational structures often reflect and reinforce the boundaries between content and technology, making it difficult to establish effective communication between decision makers on both sides. The resulting disconnect between the visible and submerged parts of the collection "iceberg" can lead not only to decreased utilization, but also, and more problematically, to an inversion in the relationship between collection development and improved usability and accessibility.

Connecting Tip and Base

Collection developers often conceptualize the value of their collections for patrons in terms of quality and scope. From this perspective, the collection development process tends to focus on uniqueness and growth. To achieve uniqueness, collection developers use their domain expertise to guide the direction of further investment in subscriptions and other electronic resources, with the intention of creating collections that are unique in quality and strength. Growth is related to richness and wealth of content concentration—two central factors in making any collection authoritative and influential in its particular domain. The centrality of growth (whether highly focused, widely inclusive, or both) as a means to increase the appeal of the collection is further highlighted by the unprecedented availability of new content and an apparently matching increase in demand. Uniqueness and growth are inherent in the mission of collections and constitute key motivators for collection developers.

Yet despite being key attributes of collection development, uniqueness and growth become problematic when considered from the perspective of the delivery and consumption medium for electronic collections—the Web. To explain this point, I first examine the role of growth using the concept of "zero sum gains," which I borrow from economics. Zero sum gains means that in some circumstances, the value of continued investment can diminish to the point of becoming meaningless. With billions of pages indexed on various search engines, the Web is a medium to which the concept of zero sum gains clearly applies—especially from the perspective of the end-user. Growth is meaningful only if the end-user realizes that an increasingly large number of resources are available in the collection. Consequently, it is quite possible to invest in the growth of a collection without attaining a comparable expansion of its utilization.

Uniqueness too is a complicated construct given the pace at which competing alternatives emerge on the Web. The comodification of information on the Web inevitably implies susceptibility to high substitution rates. In other words, the cost of switching from one Web site to another is minimal to the end-user. To understand how the low cost of switching affects the relationship among uniqueness, investment, and utilization, let us contrast electronic collections with brick and mortar ones.

In traditional museums or special libraries, we can see uniqueness in action. For example, the availability of a Vermeer masterpiece in a certain museum makes that institution a unique destination for Vermeer fans and scholars. Yet the availability of a digital impression of the same Vermeer masterpiece in numerous digital collections does not make any of them a unique destination. On the contrary, each of these collections runs the risk of becoming interchangeable with all the others.

I am not suggesting that considerations of utilization, accessibility, and usability displace uniqueness and growth as guiding concepts and motivating principles in the process of collection development. Rather, I would like to integrate the two perspectives represented by these concepts. Much like the two differently positioned but nonetheless inseparable parts of the iceberg, a scholarly electronic collection and its user interface constitute a single entity. In the remainder of this chapter I consider how we can implement an integrative framework—one that can facilitate a dynamic interaction between the development of content and user interface—in the discourse on electronic collections. I propose that we begin with a closer look at the patron, or the *user* in the user interface construct.

Know Thy Patron

Classifying users too generically is a mistake that I initially made when I became director of interface design for some of the industry's most sophisticated products. At that time, I came up with "GRUF scenarios," scenarios for **g**raduate students, **r**esearch assistants, **u**ndergraduates, and **f**aculty. I assigned broadly construed attributes to each of these patron groups. For example, undergraduates were designated—based more on media portrayals than empirical examination—as logging onto the system at midnight, after an evening of partying, and in desperate need of finishing a term paper by 8:00 A.M. The tendency to pigeonhole the needs of patrons is similar to the inclination to make assumptions that classify patron groups by level of sophistication in system use or familiarity with approaches to research and use of advanced search features.

GRUF scenarios are currently widespread in our field, but they do not capture the relationship between patrons and the unique characteristics of Web sites, nor do they adequately explain the process of interaction with Web sites. The Web browser frames a homogenous interaction pattern as patrons continuously link from one site to another, and the overall experience is more like surfing TV channels than using software. In this context, *who* the patron is no longer defines the search process. Whether he or she is an undergraduate novice or an experienced scholar, the proprietary relationship between patron and resource, which can be seen as unique and external to the Web, has been transformed into an interaction that is inherently Web-based and shaped by the navigation process.

I revisit common patron-classification patterns in order to suggest a shift from focusing on irrelevant assumptions about patrons and their motivations to an analysis of action-driving attributes. The task, rather than the individual, is at the center of this approach, and our concern should be with task parameters, such as prioritization, complexity, frequency, and vocabulary. A detailed discussion of the scenario building (or use case) methodology suggested by this analysis is beyond the scope of this chapter. Nonetheless, it is clear that a more precise perspective on patron–collection interaction is needed.

Seek and You Shall Find

There is mounting pressure on everyone involved in the development of user interfaces for library portals to replicate the interaction models employed by commercial portals and search engines. Aiming to increase patron traffic and resource utilization rates, this approach seems to make sense and match patrons' feedback. However, a closer analysis of the strategic goals and interaction patterns that drive the user interface in the business and commercial domains reveals that effective user interface design for scholarly collections requires a different approach.

The guiding strategic motivation in the user interfaces of commercial portals and search engines is to facilitate action, or more specifically, transaction. The faster a user can transition from typing a query into a search field to typing a number in a credit card field, the happier are both customer and business. Not surprisingly, "Seek and you shall find" has been the catchphrase of successful search engine vendors (viz. Google's public offering in 2004). This maxim encapsulates the main thrust of successful interaction within the commercial domain: Task A (seek) directly leads to outcome B (find). This interaction model is vectorial—its directionality is governed by the wish to achieve a single outcome.

Based on the vectorial interaction model, successful commercial search engines eliminate the vast landscape of the Web by providing patrons with a relevant result to their search query quickly—on the first results screen and often in the top record. The fact that these search engines simultaneously provide an entirely unusable result-set of hundreds of thousands of records further emphasizes the underlying goal of providing the single relevant match for the search. Given a result-set of workable dimensions (e.g., 25 links), the user would have been likely to explore it, but the paradoxical combination of results presented by the commercial search engines does not offer the user real choices. Rather, it conditions the user to view the action of searching and its outcome as inseparable, providing an instantly gratifying experience packaged as a volitional choice process.

Different from the "seek and you shall find" vectorial model is a model of user–collection interaction characterized by the phrase "seek *so you can* find." Here, the relationship between task A (seek) and task B (find) is more reciprocal and dynamic. It suggests a spiral interaction model in which the outcome emerges as a synthesis enabled by the search process. Whereas the vectorial interaction model works well for commercial search engines, I believe that the spiral interaction model is more appropriate for the academic and scholarly domains.

Commercial search engines help users find a needle in a haystack—and this has never been easier. Google's ability is amazing even to those who understand its underlying technology. Nonetheless, finding a needle in a haystack (vectorial model) is not, in fact, such a big deal when you have the right equipment—a magnet in the case of this analogy. Only the needle attaches to the magnet, while the haystack becomes immaterial. Most research and academic electronic collections, on the other hand, are serving patrons who are interested in finding a piece of hay in the haystack (spiral model). The magnet becomes useless; the key functions of assigning relevancy and ranking of information become dependent on human capacities such as critical evaluation, synthesis, and decision making.

New Ideas Long Forgotten

In *The Memory Palace of Matteo Ricci*, Jonathan Spence[1] describes a memory system devised by a sixteenth-century Italian Jesuit priest. Matteo Ricci's goal was to find a way to store in one's head the sum of all human knowledge, so he suggested the following idea: Depending on how much one wants to remember, one can build in one's head virtual urban centers of various sizes. These imaginary cities should be complete with fully furnished palaces, homes, public meeting places, and so on. Each one of these imagined spaces would serve as a memory location to reference a piece of knowledge. It would be possible "to walk" through this vast mental construct to access this or that item or bit of information. Five centuries later, I find Matteo Ricci's idea fantastically intriguing and completely relevant to the discussion about the relationship among patrons, scholarly collections, and user interfaces.

It is entirely possible that the key to greater utilization of electronic resources may be in user interfaces that support the spiral interaction model by allowing dynamic visualization of information and enabling presentation that supports both near and associated contextualization. Consider, for example, the following common problem, which was aptly illustrated by Judy Luther, an industry veteran, in a recent panel discussion on emerging visualization tools. According to Luther, patrons often comment that they "have found all these other books on the shelf that weren't in the catalog," but could not "find the book that was (in the catalogue)." "I guess the catalog was wrong," is a common conclusion.[2] These comments underscore the significance of contextualization. They also highlight the weakness of vectorial interaction with scholarly electronic resources, in which pinpointed searches eliminate the context of knowledge—a context that can be accessible in a memory palace or through familiarity with the library stacks.

Some current attempts to develop user interfaces that provide better support for interaction with and synthesis of vast amounts of information are beginning to tackle the issues raised in this chapter. These efforts focus on creating highly visual and interactive presentations of datasets. Their user interfaces relate clusters of shapes in various sizes and colors to subjects of knowledge within a disciple or across disciplines. While the results of this approach to interface design can be esthetically appealing and entertaining, some fundamental issues remain unresolved, including productivity and accessibility for visually impaired patrons.

Other directions are suggested by grassroots efforts originating in institutions that attempt to find local solutions to the iceberg problems of utilization, accessibility, and usability. An excellent example is the Results Navigator developed at the University of Rochester and recently described by Stanley Wilder as an "open-source interface for managing diverse metadata."[3] Instead of the literal approach to visualization presented above, this tool enables contextualization of information by implementing FRBR, a cataloging protocol that "reveals relationships among works that would otherwise not be possible. For example, a search for Shakespeare and Tempest would return sites grouped into editions of the play, criticism about it, films, opera, and so on."[4]

Conclusion

Icebergs dissolve over time—their size diminishes until they finally melt away—and so will the iceberg problem discussed here. Collections will become highly visible through the implementation of user interfaces developed with industry standards and metadata protocols. These interfaces will support interaction models that fit the unique requirements of their patrons for knowledge synthesis through interactive and accessible direct manipulation.

Attempts to develop such interfaces are on the way, but workable solutions for this significant challenge may take some time to realize. In the meantime, collection developers should be aware of the inherent ties between the collection and its user interface and seek an active role in guiding the development and future direction of the user interfaces serving their collections. An investment in the tip of the iceberg now can save the entire collection from sinking into invisibility.

Notes

1. J. D. Spence, *The Memory Palace of Matteo Ricci* (New York: Penguin Books, 1984).

2. Judy Luther, "Visible Content . . . Transparent Libraries" (paper presented at the Charleston Conference, November 5, 2004). Cited here by permission of the author. Judy Luther is an industry consultant, author, speaker, and futurist with 35 years' experience as a librarian, publisher, vendor, and information consumer.

3. Stanley Wilder, "The University of Rochester Results Navigator" (paper presented at the Charleston Conference, November 5, 2004). Cited here by permission of the author. Stanley Wilder is associate dean, University of Rochester Libraries.

4. Ibid.

KNOWLEDGE MANAGEMENT: AN EVOLUTION

Geraldine M. Benson, Government Documents Librarian, Millersville University, Pennsylvania
Irene Risser, Collection Development Librarian, Millersville University, Pennsylvania

The knowledge management presentation reviewed the evolution of collection development and collection management into the current theory of knowledge management. Discussion revealed that librarians are well versed in and actively living the theories and philosophy of knowledge management in their professional responsibilities, although not always referring to their experiences in knowledge management terms. Judging from the participation, librarians and student librarians from solo pharmaceutical libraries, research libraries, an ALA degree-granting institution, and medium-sized academic libraries speak and work within the realms of active knowledge management as discussed in the presentation.

The session leaders introduced a discussion guide called Academic Library X (see p. 25). The Library X discussion presented topics dealing with library budget allocations, reflecting the dilemma of being a repository as well as a gateway given current budget constraints in higher education. The group applied concepts of knowledge management to the discussion and their decisions in response to the common issue of budget constraints and libraries. The discussion moved to the further implication of succession planning for librarians dealing with organizational change in relationship to intellectual capital and knowledge management.

The knowledge management presentation reviewed three current factors in the evolution of collection development and collection management into knowledge management (the management and support of expertise): budget constrictions, changed research use of libraries, and the information technology revolution. This study reviews evolutionary shifts and dilemmas of collection development and management (the management of collections of data and information) in academic libraries that are centered on changed organizational structures and arrangements of information in the digital age.

Implications of the origins and philosophical foundations of knowledge management for the information professions include changes in education and training, leadership and stewardship, expertise, cultural and social issues, and consumers. The use of intellectual capital, taken from models of business, industry, and science, to be successful and effective requires changed organizational structures needing a shared information knowledge culture created by collaboration, trust, and harmony. Policies and strategies for shared vision and communications in the digital library, coupled with the reality of reduced budgets, the inclusion of electronic databases, the status of tangible collections, and new methods to access information by differently trained users, are supported with a suggested list of references.

The study actively researched the most far-reaching transitions in current academic librarianship: organizational change, scholarly information, digital libraries, personnel expertise and leadership, and budgetary allocations. The mutual exchange of information among academic librarians from various library types, publishers, and vendors provided firsthand experience, expertise, and library points-of-view for library professionals in an era of enormous change.

Academic Library X

(Discussion Guide)

- Library Mission: To be an informative gateway, a "library without walls"

- Current base materials budget:

  $545,000 base + $76,835 carryover and 1-time allocation = $622,481 total

- Materials budget is allocated as follows:

  Subscription materials: $564,540 or 90% of $622,481
  $564,540 or 103% of the base budget of $545,000

- The library has an established course-integrated instruction program and liaison program.

- The primary undergraduate institution supported by Library X has an FTE enrollment of 7,500 UG and G students enrolled in liberal arts and education programs. Information literacy is one of the institution's educational goals for its students.

Discussion Topics:

- Evaluate this library's budget allocation.

- Does it or does it not support the library mission? Give examples.

- What would you change in terms of how the materials budget is currently allocated?

- How can an academic library today be both a repository with depth as well as a gateway with breadth in terms of information access and knowledge management given current budget constraints in higher education?

Bibliography

Blair, David. "Knowledge Management: Hype, Hope, or Help?" *Journal of the American Society for Information Science and Technology* 53, no. 12 2002): 1019–28.

Branin, Joseph. "Knowledge Management in Academic Libraries: Building the Knowledge Bank at the Ohio State University." *Journal of Library Administration* 39, no. 4 (2003): 41–56.

McInerney, Claire. "Knowledge Management and the Dynamic Nature of Knowledge." *Journal of the American Society for Information Science and Technology* 53, no. 12 (2002): 1009–18.

Montgomery, Carol H., and JoAnne Sparks. "The Transition to an Electronic Journal Collection: Managing the Organizational Changes." *Serials Review* 26, no. 3 (2000): 4–19.

THE ICEBERG AT ROCHESTER

Stanley Wilder, Associate Dean, University of Rochester, New York

In January, a group of us at the University of Rochester published an article in the *Charleston Observer* called "Serial Failure." The premise of "Serial Failure" is that students who use academic library Web sites to find articles fail miserably because our interfaces are too complex, too numerous, and too limited. In that article, we called serial failure the most important access-related problem in librarianship today.

But since that article came out, we've changed our minds. If we were writing the article today, we'd be *more likely* to call it "interface failure," because of our growing conviction that we can't focus on article databases *independently* of all the rest of our databases. Any silo is a bad silo and will obstruct use of *all* of our collections. Students will never look at our catalogs, for example, and just guess that they can find journal *titles* there but not journal *articles*. And they sure won't *intuit* which silo contains institutional repository articles, or image collections, or fill in the blank.

Some libraries view these distinctions as "teaching moments." Our library wishes that students never have to learn all these idiosyncratic, gloriously incompatible interfaces in the first place. We believe that those interfaces drive our communities away, and to such a degree that our bypassed collections don't feel like an access problem anymore; they feel like a collection development problem of the highest order. Collection development because it's about content: for the time being, Google searches don't deliver the high quality scholarly information that is available only by purchase, subscription, or lease. Woe unto the library that squanders *this* precious advantage by teaching obstacles instead of eliminating them. But I say also collection development by virtue of the stark economic reality that in the long term, we cannot hope to justify materials expenditures in the face of widespread *avoidance*.

But the situation is not desperate. Ezra Schwartz, Judy Luther, and I believe that users are certain to recognize and appreciate our superior collections, provided we can make it easy enough for them to *get* there in the first place. And each of us believes that exposing those collections is the work of the interface. Making interfaces better will require effort from everyone: libraries, vendors, and publishers. The rest of this chapter describes our own recent work at Rochester.

I have four brief examples of silo-busting technologies to describe. The first is very near production, the second is a proof of concept, the third is a grant proposal, and the fourth is a kind of throwaway experiment, the sort of thing that happens when we give our man Jeff three or four days to do whatever he wants.

All of our current interface work is based on the premise that the path *away* from difficult, silo-y databases leads directly to a metadata problem, one of managing clusters of incompatible formats: Dublin Core, MARS, and oceans of MARC. We can't make interfaces that break silos without technology that supports multiple metadata formats. METS is the most promising example. As Roy Tennant describes it, METS is a technology that works like a kind of wrapper, bundling up diverse metadata formats. We are nowhere near a METS infrastructure; my point is that managing multiple formats is where we're going.

My first example is a metasearch box as tailored for use in a course page. Almost all of Rochester's courses have pages like these, and our students LOVE them. And we love them to love them because it means we can give them only the most appropriate journal databases without making them choose. This change alone significantly increases the success rate of students. The box only does articles, but because it's a single interface to multiple databases, it's a big step in the right direction.

My second example is a proof of concept that relates to the formidable silo that is our catalog. This is CUIPID, which is an acronym for something, it hardly matters what. It is a test database that consists of about 1,300 bibliographic records and 1,500 item records, all relating to five authors, and all converted to XML format. There's nothing terribly revolutionary about this—there are fully functional XML catalogs out there already. But converting MARC records to XML feels like liberation to us, liberation from the tiresome and stupid limitations of our catalog. I don't mean this as a slam on Endeavor, because no ILS is designed to do the sort of things we want to do, especially integrating metadata from any source. CUIPID can do this easily. I'll give you one quick example: Where Voyager splits bib records into literally hundreds of impenetrable tables, the converted XML bib record is a single, manipulable flat file. Ahhh!

Cuipid 1
- main search screen for CUIPID.
- Google-like search box,
- 4 Choices each for searching and sorting

Cuipid 2
- title is misspelled

Cuipid 3
- 'Did You Mean' and link to search re-execution 'a tale of two cities'
- Initial article solved

Cuipid 4
- equivalent of Voyager Titles page. this is a de-duped list of title that match a keyword search for 'a tale of two cities'
- all editions of 'A Tale of Two Cities' are bundled into one search result. this is much different than in Voyager, where no such relation can be made, and each edition appears on the Titles list as a separate hit.

Cuipid 5
- Pick an edition and get the holdings.
- @ Voyager freedom—type of link indicator. Possibilities are endless.

Cuipid 6
- Donor record link example

Cuipid 7
- A map of the stacks, level 3.

Our librarians *love* CUIPID, and we're currently shopping for query software capable of managing our full catalog and the many millions of records it would represent.

But although CUIPID gives us an idea of how the interface might differ from Voyager, we're careful to say that the real value of the project will be to serve as the data infrastructure for our future search platform. CUIPID is the piece that breaks our MARC shackles, allowing us to manipulate MARC and any other metadata we choose.

The actual interface for the CUIPID infrastructure needs to wait for my third example, the grant proposal we called Results Navigator.

Results navigator is intended to be an open-source interface for managing diverse metadata. It will rest on our CUIPID XML infrastructure and will be FRBR-based, much like RLG's Red Light Green, FRBR being the cataloging protocol that reveals relationships among works that would otherwise not be possible. So, for example, searching for "shakespeare and tempest" would return cites grouped into editions of the play itself, criticism about it, films, opera, and so on.

Here are the features we think we can deliver in our projected two-year grant period:

- Simple search box—with few or no choices

- Forgiving—"did you mean," initial article, carrying over search strings

- Organizing content—ranking, grouping, filtering, collapsing

- Post-search manipulation—results returned with suggested refinements. Maybe "show me electronic only" or only recently published items, or "more like this."

- User-centered design—

- Endless iteration—

These are features, not metadata. What we're doing is easy and sharable, well within the capabilities of a modest-sized staff like ours, but just one library's efforts won't get us where we're going.

(The PowerPoint™ slides shown at this presentation can be found at http://www.katina. info/conference/.)

DATABASE EVALUATION: POLICY AND PROCESS

Stefanie DuBose, Head of Acquisitions, East Carolina University, Greenville
Joseph Thomas, Reference Librarian, East Carolina University, Greenville

Abstract

Many libraries are facing the challenge of increasing access to electronic resources with static, if not decreasing, materials budgets. Evaluations must be a collaborative mechanism for the acquisition, retention, and cancellation of electronic resources, and they require planning for policy and process before the evaluations themselves may be done. Collaboration and on-going communication are necessary among faculty and staff throughout the library before, during, and after an evaluation. The evaluation process must take into account the current and future curriculum/research needs of the parent institution, how the classes are delivered, and the budget constraints under which libraries operate. On a practical level, the process must reflect these concerns *and* include specific criteria regarding content, usability, curriculum needs, and vendors. (The presentation is available at http://personal.ecu.edu/thomasw/ DatabaseEval.htm.)

Database Evaluation

Database evaluation is a necessary part of collection development, an especially difficult part in light of the increasing pressure for libraries to provide research materials electronically during a time of static or decreasing materials budgets. Evaluations must provide a collaborative mechanism for the acquisition, retention, and cancellation of electronic resources, and they require at least three components addressed here: policy, procedure, and resource evaluation. Policy is approached as a way of setting the framework and rationale for decision making. The procedures involved in database evaluation include establishing a profile of the institution's users; creating a working balance across content, subject area, and budget; and developing evaluation criteria. Resource evaluation refers to the application of those evaluation criteria to the databases and analysis of the results.

Policies

Polices provide ways to ask and to answer the question "why." The term "policy" tends to make people nervous, so the focus should be on the purposes for having policies for database evaluation. Policies provide frameworks that guide decision making both in the short term and in the long term; these frameworks allow for the opportunity to think through the appropriate coverage balances the library needs to achieve for the content, subject area, and budgetary concerns that it has. The policy framework takes into account issues of coverage across and within disciplines and encourages ongoing collection analysis in order to develop and refine the short-term and long-term goals. One of the other primary reasons to consider policy is because policies provide a means of formulating explanations for what kinds of decisions the library must make before, during, and after the evaluation.

Process

Process, on the other hand, entails asking and answering the question "how." To answer "how" questions, librarians need to develop profiles of the library's stakeholders and curricula, work within the library's limits—those dreaded "b" words, budget and balance—and then decide how to conduct the evaluation itself. Creating ways to carry out the evaluation includes developing and applying criteria for evaluation and learning how to negotiate between the subject view and the big picture.

Profiles

Profiles of the university's stakeholders will help in the process of evaluating database subscriptions. Subject area liaisons will do these profiles to provide context for the information needs of the discipline and context for the institution's overall needs. Liaisons should consider curricula in their areas, paying particular attention to the degrees offered, accreditation standards, current and developing programs and courses, and distributed education initiatives. The faculty's and students' research needs should also be considered and should include not only current research and publishing, but also new and continuing grants.

Community outreach makes up another part of the profile: What partnerships exist between the parent institution and the surrounding community? East Carolina University, our institution, is affiliated with several local facilities and institutes. The Eastern Area Health Education Center is housed in the Laupus Library and provides education programs in partnership with other agencies and organizations to improve the health of the people of eastern North Carolina. East Carolina has a number of educational centers committed to recruiting teachers and enhancing the educational opportunities available to those living in the region. Most recently, the university has begun developing a center for tourism that combines community engagement with educational opportunities in researching sustainable tourism for North Carolina. Having the profile helps the subject librarians come together to see how their subject areas interact with the broader campus needs.

Budget and Balance

In order to target databases for new or canceled subscriptions, libraries must confront the "b" words: budget and balance. Having a target budget is necessary; the budget provides the basis for establishing priorities for expending funds and allows the library to track expenses. The overall goal is to work within the budget to find the appropriate level of support for the disciplines, based on the institution's needs. This is a balance issue in multiple dimensions, though, that is, balancing access to the literature of needed subject areas as well as balancing the allocations for resources within those subject areas. Prioritizing coverage of subject areas within available funds is a *negotiation* process—it will be different for each institution and must be worked out internally. For balance, profiles are crucial—the library must know what its faculty members and students are researching and teaching and what its parent institution's priorities and goals are, in order to achieve a working balance for the library's electronic collections. With the profiles, budget in hand, the next step is the evaluation criteria.

Evaluation Criteria

Developing evaluation criteria is an ongoing process, and the process itself is more important than the particular wording any institution chooses. During East Carolina's database evaluation project last year, the subject librarians developed together a set of criteria with four main components: usability, content, curriculum needs, and vendor criteria. (See Appendix 1.) Consider also the value of outside reviews and include them as part of the evaluation. Usability criteria focus primarily on the end-user's experience and include topics like ease of navigating the interface, search options, usage statistics and turn-aways, ease of off-campus use, and the database's Help documents. Usability criteria also include means of access, ease of access for off-campus users, OpenURL compliance, alerting options, and file formats for full text documents. Content refers to the coverage of the literature of the discipline and the reviewed database's fit within the array of the institution's subscriptions. Content criteria also consider full text and archival access issues, including embargoes and whether the library has access to this content in another format or through another database. Curriculum needs include current and planned programs and courses and distributed education needs. Input from teaching faculty, library service points, and inter-library loan is appropriate when considering curriculum needs. Vendor criteria focus on relations and support and include cost, database response time, timeliness of updates, vendor-provided training, and problem resolution. Reviews from *Choice*, the *Charleston Advisor*, or other sources are also taken into consideration.

Resource Evaluation

Resource evaluation refers to the application of evaluation criteria to each database and the analysis of individual evaluations to make decisions about the acquisition, retention, or cancellation of electronic resources. The East Carolina University libraries used the appended evaluation criteria to complete a database evaluation project during the spring and summer of 2003. The libraries' Electronic Resources Review Committee (ERRC) led this evaluation project. There were several concerns to address and procedures to develop for the application of the evaluation criteria and analysis of the results. One concern was rating the databases; liaison librarians wondered how to address variability among reviewers and across subject areas. One way to address reviewer variability was to have a norming session, during which one of the committee members demonstrated an evaluation of one of the databases, explaining step-by-step how she arrived at her conclusions. To address variability across subject areas, the subject librarians and ERRC had to rely on supporting current and developing curricula and research and finding the right balance of subject-area access for our university. In order to do this, each ERRC member headed a group of liaisons who were chosen by broad discipline—arts and sciences, social sciences, sciences, selected interdisciplinary subjects, and reference.

Each group evaluated a corresponding group of databases and discussed the evaluations and impact of maintaining or deselecting certain titles. The groups then made recommendations for cancellation, maintenance, or selection of new subscriptions to cover their subject areas. The ERRC took the groups' recommendations into consideration when providing final recommendations to library administration. After administrative decisions were made, subscription changes began in June and continued into the fall of 2004.

Resource evaluation allows subject librarians to see how their subject fits within broader discipline coverage and how these disciplines come together to form the information landscape that the library provides the university. The subject liaisons have a forum among the groups to negotiate for their areas within a broader context, educating each other about what's going on in related disciplines. This is also a good forum for interdisciplinary databases. Each group negotiates within itself its prioritization, broadening its perspective again, and the ERRC put together the big picture by fitting all those priorities into the landscape of the university's needs. The librarians believe this structure worked well for us, and we hope to use something similar for future evaluation projects.

Next Steps

What are the next steps in database evaluation? East Carolina University's evaluation project has taught its librarians the importance of maintaining lines of communication, both within the library and with the other departments on campus. The next step is to extend this process through the coming cycle of both academic and fiscal years and consider ways to establish a cycle balancing acquisitions work, cataloging, and the subject liaisons' input. Librarians at ECU don't consider the recent database evaluation a now-finished project, but rather the beginning of continuing collection analysis.

Appendix One: Evaluation Criteria

Evaluation criteria are arranged by four topics: usability, content, curriculum needs, and vendor. The committee will also seek out reviews of the databases to complement the members' own evaluations. The criteria currently in use by the committee include, but are not limited to:

I. Usability:

1) Ease of navigating interface

2) Search options (limits, combining results, truncation, proximity, sorting, browsing, SDI availability)

3) Linking ability (includes open-URL compliance)

4) Email options

5) Print options

6) Save options

7) Usage statistics (by month, database and year), including:

   a) Number of logins (or sessions)

   b) Number of turn-aways

   c) Number of searches

   d) Time periods for reporting: monthly, and length of access to statistics (prefer at least two calendar years at a time—all of previous and current year data available)

   e) Availability of viewing and downloading statistics: via CSV, Excel file, available on password protected server,

8) Depth of indexing

9) Data accuracy

10) Auto-logoff availability

11) Email alerts

12) Special software required for data manipulation?

13) Ease of off-campus, remote use

14) Availability and ease of use for database "help" and FAQ documents

II. Content:

1) Uniqueness of content, including indexed titles and

2) Overlap/fit with other databases

3) Core database/index for subject area?

4) Interdisciplinarity

5) Full text availability

a) File format (PDF, PostScript)

b) Full text value (includes core journals)

c) Embargo?

d) Cover to cover full text?

e) Duplication of print titles held by Joyner or Laupus (most important for a proprietary database)

f) If duplication is evident, what is the preferred format for subject area?

6) Backfiles/archive (including full text issues above)

7) Competing electronic resources for consideration?

8) Buffet versus big-deal buying? That is, can the library consider just part of a database, and will the part considered meet the library's needs?

III. Curriculum Needs:

1) Teaching faculty input

2) Growth of programs (recent and planned)

3) Distance education needs of programs

4) Library service point input

a) Reference Department

b) Interlibrary Loan request history

IV. Vendor Criteria:

1) Cost, including the following aspects:

a) Recent years' increases

b) Number of simultaneous users

c) Competing vendors for same product

d) Can sub files be purchased as separate units

2) ADA compliancy

3) Provision of statistics (preferably COUNTER compliant; see www. projectcounter.org)

4) Training

5) Truth in advertising regarding content

6) Licensing issues:

a) Provision for off-campus and distance education use

b) Inter-library loan

c) Coursepacks

d) Electronic reserves

7) Database response time

8) Stability of vendor; reputation

9) Timeliness of updates

10) MARC records availability, cost

11) Web-browser compatibility

12) Support, including:

a) Resolution of problems

b) Response time

V. Reviews:

Choice:

Charleston Advisor:

Other source (name: _____):

DATABASE EVALUATION: POLICY AND PROCEDURE

Audrey Powers, Information Technology Librarian, University of Montevallo, Alabama

Evaluating Databases for Acquisitions and Collection Development

This evaluation process was initially developed to *guide librarians through a collaborative process with objective results*. It enables librarians to evaluate databases for acquisitions, retention, and withdrawal purposes. The advantages of using this evaluation process are that it is customizable, it is based on library objectives, it is adaptable for a variety of user populations and it can be administered manually or electronically. It can be used to evaluate existing database collections, either an entire collection or discipline-specific databases; to evaluate trial databases, either single or multiple; and to conduct database comparisons such as comparing a trial database to an existing database. It is customizable for use with multiple user populations such as librarians, library staff, faculty, students, the public, and administrators. The first time we did the evaluation, we evaluated the entire database collection. As we proceeded, the process was refined.

The database evaluation process is broken down into three phases:

Phase I: Prepare

Phase II: Gather data

Phase III: Results

During Phase I, determine your criteria, develop the evaluation form, aggregate the databases, assign team leaders, and develop a project timeline.

During Phase II, obtain *known data,* distribute the evaluation forms, conduct the *evaluations*, and collect the completed evaluation forms. During Phase III, collate, analyze, and interpret the data, present the data, discuss the results, and recommend an action plan.

This database evaluation project is customizable based on the objective, audience, and type of library. The first time we did the project it was a manual process. The evaluation forms were distributed on paper, one form for each database (see figure 1). A copy was given to each librarian; it was completed and returned to the team leader.

The evaluation form included general information, *known data, evaluations,* need, and comments.

In the *known data* portion of the form the cost, use and cost/use data were gathered from database statistics provided by the database publisher. "Duplication" is the reported number of journal titles duplicated in other databases. Generally, if duplication was 50% or more, this was noted for further scrutiny. Since we are a member of several consortia, we wanted to compare the databases in our database collection to colleges and universities with the same mission, or those institutions we considered our peers.

Content, unique content, ease of use, instruction, and overall quality were defined and agreed upon prior to beginning the evaluation process.

Need is based on the user population, curricula, and accreditation, and of course everyone likes to comment on particular nuances and make observations about each database.

DATABASE EVALUATION FORM

Database _____

URL _____

Evaluator _____

Known Data

Cost:

Use:

Cost/use:

Duplication:

Peer comparisons:

Evaluations

Content:	0	1	2	3	4
Unique Content:	0	1	2	3	4
Ease of use: 0	0	1	2	3	4
Instruction: 0	0	1	2	3	4
Overall quality:	0	1	2	3	4

0 = Inappropriate 1 = Very Unsatisfactory 2 = Unsatisfactory 3 = Satisfactory
4 = Very Satisfactory

Need: _____ Inappropriate _____ Useful ____ Essential

Comments:

Figure 1. Sample Database Evaluation Form.

Initially, the 100+ databases were equitably distributed among the librarians, and like subjects were kept together. In order to keep the process moving, each database grouping was assigned a team leader and a due date. Each team leader was responsible for completing the database information and *known data* and distributing the forms to the other librarians. Each librarian was responsible for evaluating the databases, completing the form, and returning it to the team leader. (See table 1.)

Table 1. Database Grouping.

Team Leader 1 Due Date Subject	Team Leader 2 Due Date Subject	Team Leader 3 Due Date Subject	Team Leader 4 Due Date Subject	Team Leader 5 Due Date Subject
Database 1	Database 1	Database 1	Database 1	Database 1
Database 2	Database 2	Database 2	Database 2	Database 2
Database 3	Database 3	Database 3	Database 3	Database 3
Database 4	Database 4	Database 4	Database 4	Database 4

If the primary reason for conducting the database evaluation project is cost, use, or both, a cost per use analysis can be done. By calculating the cost per use of a database, it can be determined whether the database costs too much or is used too little. Often low use can lead to other probing questions such as whether the database has been publicized appropriately, is easily accessible, or is taught enough. Once the cost/use analysis is complete, the information can be compiled into a chart that details low cost (LC), high cost (HC), low use (LU), and high use (HU). In this particular situation, if funding is an issue, high cost/low use (HC/LU) databases can be identified for further analysis. (See table 2.)

Table 2. Cost per Use Analysis.

Database Name	Cost	Use	Cost/Use	Comments
Database 1	LC	LU	LC/LU	
Database 2	HC	HU	HC/HU	
Database 3	LC	HU	LC/HU	
Database 4	**HC**	**LU**	**HC/LU**	

When the librarians completed their evaluations and returned the forms, the results were compiled for further analysis and discussion. (See table 3.)

Table 3. Data Summary.

Database Name	Cost	Use	Cost/Use	Duplication (≥50%)	Peer Comparisons	Evaluations (0-4)	Need

Some of the compiled results from the team leader for the science databases are shown in table 4.

Table 4. Results.

Science Databases	Cost	Use	Cost/Use	Duplication (≥50%)	Peer Comparisons	Evaluations (0–4)	Need
ASTI	.62	1	.62	OK	5 of 17	2.6	1
BasicBIOSIS	22.32	36	.62	69.8%	11 of 17	3.2	3
BioAgIndex	22.32	36	.62	50%	7 of 17	2.6	2
EventLine	0	0	.62	NCD	0 of 17	2.3	1
General Science	25.42	41	.62	52%	15 of 17	3.2	3

After the initial database evaluation project, faculty and students were asked to evaluate trial databases, and we converted the process from manual to electronic. Figures 2 and 3 are database evaluation forms customized for faculty and students. The biggest difference between the two evaluation forms is that *known data* were not provided to students. Since the process became electronic, access to the database is from an embedded URL in the database name at the top of the evaluation form.

FACULTY EVALUATION FORM

Please complete and submit this form. Access the database by clicking on the name of the database.

Database Name

Known Data

Cost:

Use:

Cost/use:

Peer comparisons:

Evaluations

Content:	0	1	2	3	4
Unique Content	0	1	2	3	4
Ease of use: 0	0	1	2	3	4
Instruction: 0	0	1	2	3	4
Overall quality:	0	1	2	3	4

0 = Inappropriate 1 = Very Unsatisfactory 2 = Unsatisfactory 3 = Satisfactory 4 = Very Satisfactory

Need: _____ Inappropriate _____ Useful _____ Essential

Comments:

Figure 2. Sample Faculty Evaluation Form.

STUDENT EVALUATION FORM

Please complete and submit this form. Access the database by clicking on the name of the database.

Database Name

Content: 0   1   2   3   4

Unique Content: 0   1   2   3   4

Ease of use: 0   1   2   3   4

Instruction: 0   1   2   3   4

Overall quality: 0   1   2   3   4

0 = Inappropriate 1 = Very Unsatisfactory 2 = Unsatisfactory 3 = Satisfactory 4 = Very Satisfactory

Need: _____ Inappropriate _____ Useful _____ Essential

Comments:

Figure 3. Sample Student Evaluation Form.

After using the database, the evaluator completes the database evaluation form and clicks on Submit. The results are dumped into an Access database and then further manipulated in Excel. (See tables 5 and 6.)

Table 5. Results—Access Database.

Database	Content	Unique Content	Ease of Use	Instruction	Overall Quality	Need
Westlaw	2	3	2	1	2	Inappropriate
Accessible Archives	1	2	0	0	0	Inappropriate
Cambridge Scientific	3	1	1	1	1	Inappropriate
Facts on File	1	1	2	2	1	Inappropriate
Facts on File	3	2	2	3	2	Useful
Accessible Archives	3	4	3	3	3	Useful
Westlaw	3	3	2	2	3	Useful
Accessible Archives	3	4	3	3	3	Useful
Cambridge Scientific	4	3	2	2	3	Useful

Table 6. Results—Excel Database.

Database	Content	Unique Content	Ease of Use	Instruction	Overall Quality	Need
Facts on File	1	1	2	2	1	Inappropriate
	3	2	2	3	2	Useful
	4	4	4	4	4	Essential
	3	4	3	3	3	Useful
	0	0	0	0	0	Inappropriate
Results	2.20	2.20	2.20	2.40	2.00	

DEVELOPMENT OF ELECTRONIC RESOURCES AMONG ACADEMIC LIBRARIES IN CHINA

Yurong Y. Atwill, Asian Studies Librarian, The Pennsylvania State University Libraries, University Park

Introduction

This study provides an overview of China's major e-resources, domestically produced and imported for use in China's major academic libraries. A primary aim of this chapter is to offer insight into the importation of e-resources by consortia and the government's involvement through systems such as China Academic Library & Information System (CALIS), a government-supported center for academic libraries.[1] The successful development of electronic databases among China's academic libraries occurs primarily because of the cooperation of academic libraries and government support, as well as the rapid growth of China's information technology (IT) industry.

Overview of Chinese-Produced E-Resources

As a result of the thriving IT industry in the early 1990s, widespread reorganization and reconstruction of information sciences and library management took place. As market demands for information resources from academic libraries increased, IT companies began to create bibliographic and full text databases. Six companies have emerged as the industry leaders, creating and marketing their e-products as the industry standard. Three of these—Superstar, Apabi Digital Library, and Scholar's Home—specialize as e-book/e-library providers,[2] while the remaining three—Tsinghua Tongfang Optical Disc Co. (TTOD), Chongqing VIP Information Consulting Company (VIP), and Wanfang Data Company—focus more on e-periodicals.

Chinese E-Books

By October 2004, the three major e-library companies had, within a relatively short period of time, established topically broad but academically solid products. Superstar claims it has digitized 1.2 million items, with 800,000 available online. Similarly, Apabi has published over 100,000 titles, of which 70% have been published since 2002.[3] Scholar's Home also offers over 100,000 titles, the bulk of which have been published since 1999.[4] A large number of Chinese libraries has purchased the above three products. For example, "out of 1400 Chinese universities or colleges, 50% use Apabi."[5] The success of these three companies among China's academic libraries is largely due to their relatively low prices, the large number of available titles, and the ease in navigating the databases. All three companies also offer very flexible payment methods for individual users to purchase a reader's card online. Detailed information about three e-book products can be found at http://www.ssreader.com/, http://www.apabi.com/, and http://www.shusheng.net/.

Chinese E-Journals

The three most popular full text e-journals are TTOD's China Academic Journals, VIP's Chinese Scientific Journal Database, and Wanfang's China Online Journal. Detailed information about these products and services are available at the Web sites of these companies: http://www.global.cnki.net/, http://www.cqvip.com, and http://www.wanfangdata.com.

Overview of Imported E-Resources

Tables 1 and 2 are select lists of e-resources commonly acquired by Chinese universities. They are not inclusive and represent only a handful of the most prestigious universities; thus they may not include the majority of academic libraries in China. Nevertheless, the data offer a picture of foreign products that have successfully entered into Chinese libraries and institutions.

The data in both tables were obtained in December 2004 from the following Web sites:

Beijing University, http://www.lib.pku.edu.cn/

Tsinghua University library, http://www.lib.tsinghua.edu.cn/

Fudan University, http://www.library.fudan.edu.cn/

Zhejiang University, http://libweb.zju.edu.cn:8080/

Wuhan University, http://www.lib.whu.edu.cn/

Table 1. Imported E-Periodicals.

	Beijing University	Tsinghua University	Fudan University	Zhejiang University	Wuhan University
Academic Press	X	X	X	X	
ACM Digital Library	X	X	X	X	X
AGRICOLA		X		X	
American Chemical Society	X	X	X	X	
American Institute of Physics	X	X	X	X	
American Mathematics Society	X		X		
American Physical Society	X	X	X	X	X
American Society of Civil Engineers		X		X	X
American Society of Mechanical Engineers		X		X	X
Beilstein/Gmelin	X				X
BIOSIS Previews	X	X	X	X	X
BMA					X
CAB	X			X	
Cambridge Science Abstracts	X				X
Cell (Press)	X	X	X	X	X
EBSCO Academic Search Premier	X	X	X	X	X
EBSCO Business Source Premier	X	X	X	X	
Ei	X	X	X	X	X
Electronic Journals from Chicago	X	X			
Elsevier ScienceDirect	X	X	X	X	X
EMBO					X

(Continued)

Table 1 (Cont.)

	Beijing University	Tsinghua University	Fudan University	Zhejiang University	Wuhan University
EMERALD	X				X
ERIC	X			X	
FSTA				X	
Gale Biography Resource Center				X	X
Genome Database	X				X
High Wire Press (free)	X	X	X	X	
IEEE/IEE	X	X	X	X	X
IEICE Transactions Online		X	X		
Ingenta	X			X	X
ISI	X		X	X	X
Institute of Physics	X	X	X	X	X
ISTP/ISSHP	X			X	X
Journal Citation Report (JCR)	X		X	X	X
John Wiley	X	X	X	X	
JSTOR	X	X	X		
Kluwer online	X	X	X	X	X
LexisNexis	X	X		X	X
Maney	X	X			X
Medline	X	X		X	
MicroMedex					X
Nature Online	X	X	X	X	X

	Beijing University	Tsinghua University	Fudan University	Zhejiang University	Wuhan University
OCLC FirstSearch	X	X	X	X	X
OVID Inspec	X			X	X
OVID LWW	X		X		
Oxford University Press	X	X	X		
ProQuest ABI/Inform Global	X	X		X	X
ProQuest Academic Research Library	X	X		X	X
ProQuest Asian Business	X	X		X	
ProQuest Digital Dissertation	X	X	X		X
ProQuest European Business	X			X	
ProQuest Medical Library		X	X	X	
ProQuest Science Journals		X			
PsycINFO	X			X	
PubMed				X	
Royal Society of Chemistry	X	X	X	X	X
SCI Expanded					X
Science Online	X	X	X	X	X
SIAM Journals Online		X	X		
SPIE International Society for Optical Engineering			X	X	
Springer LINK	X	X	X	X	X
Taylor and Francis Journals	X		X		
Web of Science	X			X	
WorldSciNet	X	X		X	X

Table 2. Imported E-Books and E-Libraries.

	Beijing University	Tsinghua University	Fudan University	Zhejiang University	Wuhan University
AMS Books Online (Free)	X				
Cancer Handbook	X				
Ebrary		X			
Encyclopedia of Astronomy & Astrophysics	X				
Encyclopedia of Life Science	X				
Gale				X	
Knovel (Free)		X			
NAP (Free)	X				
NetLibrary	X	X	X	X	X
Pest-Bank				X	
Safari		X		X	
SpringerLink	X	X	X	X	X
World Bank e-library					X

In general, Chinese libraries and users are very eager to obtain e-resources that offer full text materials. The government has been very supportive and initiated various projects to improve resource sharing and resource building by establishing systems such as CALIS, which is actively involved with the selecting and purchasing of foreign databases. For additional information about what foreign e-resources Chinese libraries own, see the library Web sites of major CALIS centers listed in appendix 1 or check major provincial universities' library sites.

Consortia and Role of CALIS

In many cases, e-resources from foreign countries are purchased through various forms of consortia, instead of by individual libraries negotiating and licensing directly with foreign vendors. Very often the initial contact may come from one specific institution, through which a consortium deal may eventually be established. Although "the library consortia are not centralized power structures but an alliance," CALIS plays a key role in facilitating and organizing consortia.[6] Participating institutions (CALIS or non-CALIS members) "have full autonomy in deciding which college library consortium to join" and for which projects.[7] The consortia can be roughly categorized as central, regional, and local.

Central

CALIS often plays a central role in forming and implementing consortia for the purchase of various products. Its Web site (http://www.calis.edu.cn/calis_index1.asp?fid=5%20&class =3&sub=GD0005#) lists up-to-date information on current projects and provides guidance and procedures on how to join a specific consortium. CALIS's routine process for selecting and purchasing a foreign e-resource includes the following:

- initial evaluation of products,

- organizing trials,

- second evaluation,

- price and service negotiation (between CALIS and the e-vendor),

- organizing consortia,

- reports on forming of consortia,

- signing contracts (CALIS signs the contracts for consortia, while participating libraries sign membership contracts.),

- payment (Member libraries send payment to agents designated by e-vendors.), and

- ongoing renewal, new membership, and training.[8]

E-vendors like EBSCO and ProQuest often designate Chinese companies, such as Zhongke Co. (China Science) and Yaxin Co. (AsiaInfo), as their agents. Contracts often involve three parties. Agents representing foreign companies provide services and handle the payments. For such projects, libraries neither sign contracts nor make direct payment to foreign e-vendors. Through such consortia deals, lower and affordable prices are provided to a larger number of libraries throughout China, making imported e-resources available to many more users.

An example of such a setup is the content of 23,000 journals purchased from EBSCO and packaged as CALIS Current Contents of Western Journals (CCC), which became a database in CALIS. CALIS tries to motivate and encourage libraries at all levels to participate. The CCC database provides links to full text articles if the institute subscribes to the e-journal through other e-resources. CCC database is also linked to the print holdings of three major library online systems in China. Because government subsidies are provided, all CCC participating libraries are required to provide their holdings data. Thus ILL service can be quickly conducted, and usage of the journals will be improved. Prices are offered at three levels, with the biggest discounts provided to small and lower level institutions. The pricing model demonstrates the mission of CALIS to support cobuilding, corecognizing, and cosharing of resources among academic institutions.[9]

Regional

As powerful as it is, CALIS is not the only system that organizes consortia for acquisition of Chinese or foreign e-products. Regional consortia may be formed to lead or colead with CALIS in the purchase and selection of a specific database. In 2003, CALIS and Shanghai Library Consortium (SLC) joined together to purchase Netlibrary e-books. In an effort to increase the participating institutions, CALIS worked with libraries of higher education, while

SLC focused on the non-academic libraries. The collaboration provided many public libraries and their users with full access to those e-resources.

Local

The formation of local consortia, often organized within a province, is designed to obtain better deals for purchasing Chinese-produced e-resources and to lower costs of imported e-resources. Funding, or the lack of it, is a constant issue for libraries at this level. The available e-resources in local libraries are very limited compared to the largest and most well-funded institutions. However, they strive to provide their users with much-needed foreign e-resources by having their local consortia represent the group, joining CALIS or other regional projects. Fully aware of the situation, CALIS often offers substantial discount to such consortia. For example, if half of the libraries of all four-year colleges within a province agree to join the local consortium and participate in group purchase of CCC, CALIS offers a further price reduction of 20%.[10]

Other Comments

Forming a consortium is a common practice among China's academic libraries, but importation of e-resources is not limited to this method alone. Some libraries, especially the better funded ones, still purchase products directly with foreign e-companies or agents due to difficulties in forming a consortium and the hassles that may be involved in such cooperative ventures. There are various approaches foreign vendors can take to initiate a deal. A successful start will be establishing personal contact within specific libraries. Winning the trust of top administrators or librarians in-charge pays far greater dividends in China than in most American libraries. The vendor may also approach one of the CALIS subject or regional centers directly if no specific library or librarian contact can be established. Identifying and selecting a successful Chinese company as your agent to represent and market your interests sometimes can be a faster and more lucrative course of action, as the agent knows bureaucratic shortcuts and can open the door for your product with other interested parties.

Conclusion

Not only are e-resources in Chinese libraries rapidly changing, but more choices and access to a variety of resources virtually guarantee that more changes are in store in the near future. From a Chinese perspective, the timing of e-resource expansion could not be better. Since joining the World Trade Organization in 2001, the "Chinese government has implemented various procedures to eliminate illegal reproduction of publications."[11] As a result, libraries have to pay a much higher price for continuing purchase of foreign publications. In a very short period of time the number of subscriptions to foreign periodicals and acquisitions of foreign monographs has dropped dramatically. To solve this problem libraries have been actively searching for alternatives and have quickly turned their attention to developing e-resources. Through various consortia projects, many libraries have not only made up their previous losses due to actual price changes, but have increased acquisition of foreign resources by turning to e-publications. In addition, many small academic libraries that have had very limited budgets to purchase foreign publications in the past now can join the local consortia and take advantage of much-discounted prices offered through CALIS.

Overall, Chinese libraries and scholars have been interested in and have demanded foreign publications. Academic institutions and the Chinese market are hungry for more e-resources, both domestically produced and foreign imported. Many of them have the means to pay for and get what they desire. They welcome and watch for the arrival of more high-quality products from various fields and countries to satisfy the large number of users. As long as the services and products are of high quality, there is always a way to find mutual ground between the libraries and e-vendors.

Notes

1. "CALIS is one of the two public service systems planned by the Chinese Higher Education Shema '211 Program' authorized by the State Council of China." Aiguo Li, "Calis: Acquiring Electronic Resources," *Library Collections, Acquisitions & Technical Services* 27, no. 2 (2003): 261.

2. Anthony W. Ferguson and Angela Ko, "eBooks in China," *Against the Grain* 42, no.6 (2004): 42–50.

3. http://www.apabi.com/ebookdown/index.htm (accessed October 31, 2004).

4. http://www.lib.pku.edu.cn/is/webbase/shusheng.htm (accessed October 31, 2004).

5. http://www.apabi.com/project/pro_1/pro_a3.htm (accessed October 31, 2004).

6. Li, "Calis," 261–67.

7. Ibid., 264.

8. http://162.105.138.185/database/liucheng.htm (accessed October 31, 2004).

9. http://www.calis.edu.cn/calis_index1.asp?fid=5%20&class=3&sub=GD0005# (accessed October 31, 2004).

10. http://www.calis.edu.cn/calis_index1.asp?fid = 5%20&class = 3&sub = GD0005# (accessed October 31, 2004).

11. Yurong Atwill, "Changes and Adjustments: Collection Development in a Chinese Academic Library," in *Charleston Conference Proceedings 2002,* edited by Rosann Bazirjian and Vicky Speck (Westport, Conn.: Libraries Unlimited, 2003), 97–101.

Appendix 1: CALIS Subject and Regional Centers

Sciences & social sciences/humanities	Beijing University (http://www.lib.pku.edu.cn/)
Engineering	Tsinghua University (http://www.lib.tsinghua.edu.cn/)
Medicine	Beijing University Medical School (http://library.bjmu.edu.cn/)
Agriculture	China Agricultural University (http://www.lib.cau.edu.cn/)
South China	Zhongshan University(http://www.lib.cau.edu.cn/)
East China	Nanjing University (http://lib.nju.edu.cn/)
Central China	Wuhan University (http://www.lib.whu.edu.cn/)
Southeast China	Shanghai Jiaotong University (http://www.lib.sjtu.edu.cn/)
Northeast China	Jilin University (http://www.jlu.edu.cn/libary/)
Southwest China	Sichuan University (URL unavailable)
Northwest China	Xi'an Jiaotong University (http://www.xjtu.edu.cn/tsda/tsda.htm)

COLLECTION DEVELOPMENT ISSUES IN HEALTH SCIENCES LIBRARIES: SERIALS AND OTHER MATTERS

Ramune Kubilius, Collection Development/Special Projects Librarian, Galter Health Sciences Library, Northwestern University, Chicago, Illinois (Moderator)
Jo Anne Boorkman, Head, Carlson Health Sciences Library, University of California, Davis
Anne Prussing, Associate Director for Collections and Access Services, Biomedical Library, University of California, San Diego
Barbara Schader, Science, Mathematics and Engineering Librarian, California Polytechnic State University, San Luis Obispo
Dan Doody, President, Doody Enterprises, Chicago, Illinois

About four dozen librarians, publishers, and vendors attended this fourth annual gathering. The 2004 Charleston Conference theme contended that "All the World's a Serial," and the fourth annual Lively Lunch, on health sciences collection development issues, focused on challenges and opportunities in both the serials and non-serials arenas of collection development.

Moderator Ramune Kubilius distributed a selected list of trends (since the 2003 Charleston Conference) that she and Elizabeth Lorbeer of Rush University compiled. (The list was also posted on the Charleston Conference Web site). Highlights included health sciences developments in the open access movement,; changes in commercial publisher ownership and licensing, U.S. National Library of Medicine projects, content and management updates in nonprint audiovisual resources, e-supplements, and PDAs.

Jo Anne Boorkman and her colleagues, Anne Prussing and Barabara Schader, discussed some successful collaborative and cooperative collection development ventures that have taken place since 1998 among librarians in the University of California Health and Life Sciences Selectors Group (see http://gml.lib.uci.edu/uchls/index.html). All three of the speakers had served as conveners of the group, formally established in 2000, which attempts to complement the cooperative collection activities already in place among the university system consortia. The speakers each highlighted a different aspect of the selectors group, its history, and its current activities. The selectors' group focuses on smaller or health sciences niche collection issues, including providing a resource liaison to manage and monitor licenses for individual products that may not be that relevant to the larger collective. Some of the accomplishments of the group include cooperatively compiling recommended wish lists (including e-books), deselecting print resources, and negotiating smaller second-tier publisher e-package licenses not covered by the California Digital Library. Challenges included identifying a shared list of priorities (life sciences, medical, etc.) as well as working around institutional cultures and bureaucracies. The group, initially temporary, is sanctioned to continue collaborating for the foreseeable future.

Dan Doody (Doody Enterprises, http://www.doodyenterprises.com/) shared his 12-year experience developing the editorial properties of his company and the resulting products and services. He discussed the opportunities for reinvention and evolution of existing review services that presented themselves in early 2004 after the demise of the venerable Brandon/Hill core lists. Book vendors and librarians approached him about developing a product to fill the resulting gap. His company already had a book review system in place for the health sciences—identified reviewers, a review system, and an archived database of the reviews existed. The philosophy of the resulting new list and its construction differs from B/H lists; books are received from 250 English-language publishers, not sought out in core list developers' institutional libraries. Doody-identified and recruited content expert reviewers were joined by librarian reviewers to select core titles in 120 specialties in the health sciences. The librarian reviewers were recruited in late spring/summer 2004 through a variety of health sciences information professional channels in a relatively short period of time. A new procedure was developed for selecting the core titles, and a scoring system was devised to provide a quantitative assessment of the core lists. Unlike the cyclical B/H lists published in issues of *Journal of the Medical Library Association* (and its predecessor title) that were available in the print journals and later in the free open access journal and on a producers' Web site, *DCT* will be available for a nominal annual license fee. Serials will not be covered in *DCT,* and questions remain about how serials core lists could/should be developed. The *Doody Core Titles in the Health Sciences* (www.doody.com/dct) covers book and software titles only and was released in 2004.

Discussion followed presentation of each portion of this Lively Lunch. Although limited time and a cramped venue presented some restrictions, speakers and participants exchanged some remarks and questions about the topics under discussion. The varied interests and backgrounds of attendees was illustrated by the fact that some participants had not yet heard the news that the Brandon/Hill core lists had ceased being updated. Other participants indicated that their collection responsibilities covered a broad spectrum of subjects, more than health sciences, so core lists of well-respected health sciences book titles were very useful. (Interestingly, by a show of hands, few attendees at the session had attended the preceding session that had focused specifically on core lists.) One attendee indicated that he was a librarian reviewer for the *Doody Core Titles in the Health Sciences*. A printout of the California selector group's Web site was circulated, and a number of participants indicated they planned to visit the site's public documents for ideas and inspiration. From questions and comments people made, it seemed that the collection development collaboration model of the California health and life sciences librarians can be envied, observed, and emulated.

SOMETHING VENTURED, SOMETHING GAINED: ACQUIRING RESOURCES FOR A NEW DOCTORAL PROGRAM

Charles S. L. Marlor, Acquisitions and Serials Librarian, Central Connecticut State University, New Britain

Lynn Johnson-Corcoran, Collection Development Librarian, Central Connecticut State University, New Britain

As Central Connecticut State University (CCSU) embarks on offering its first doctoral degree, the Library is charged with increasing and enhancing its collections to meet the needs of the new doctoral degree candidates. This chapter describes the trials, tribulations, and successes of our first foray into securing resources to support a doctoral program.

CCSU is the oldest public institution of higher education in Connecticut and one of four regional universities that comprise the Connecticut State University system. CCSU was established in 1849 as the New Britain Normal School, with its mission being the preparation of school teachers. In 1933 the Normal School became Teachers College of Connecticut. In 1955 a graduate school was established, and in 1959 the name changed again, this time to Central Connecticut State College. CCSC became CCSU in 1983. CCSU's current enrollment is 9,000 FTE.

Because CCSU was originally founded as a school of education, it has always been strong in providing programs for aspiring and practicing teachers. The Department of Educational Leadership has been offering a variety of master's programs, including an M.S. in educational technology and educational leadership, as well as a sixth-year certificate for administrators and supervisors. The doctorate in educational leadership was licensed in December 2001, after much ado because the University of Connecticut, , until that point, was the only public institution of higher education in the state authorized to award a doctorate. The Ed.D. program at CCSU is designed for educators who are working full time and can attend classes evenings, weekends, and summers. The program is designed to prepare professionals in the field of education to become principals, superintendents, and curriculum and assessment specialists. Twenty-five students per year are currently accepted into the program, and our first cohort graduated in May 2005.

Year 1: The Reactive/Chaotic Year

Special funds were allocated for library materials for the first three years of the new program. Beginning with FY 2002–2003, $70,000 was earmarked for both print and electronic resources. We were informed of this special funding in a rather informal manner in the summer of 2002. There was also talk of hiring a librarian who would be dedicated exclusively to the Ed.D. cohort. This position never materialized, but the anticipation of the position helped contribute a certain sense of limbo to the project. Being good librarians, we awaited further instructions and direction from the faculty in the educational leadership program. Unfortunately, we gradually learned that silence and confusion were the only rewards for expecting others to begin spending the allocation. As a result, after seven months of merciless and futile hounding of the faculty by the acquisitions librarian, the money was redirected to payment of large university utility bills. A portion of the money was returned to the Library after much wringing of hands and justification of need, by providing lists of material to the university's CFO. As a result of this intervention, we were able to purchase about $5,000 worth of monographs, upgrade Academic Search Elite to Premier, and subscribe to PsychArticles. We learned that it was a mistake to not take immediate charge of the situation. In the second year we took a totally different approach to the issue.

Year 2: The Proactive/Productive Year

The Ed.D. program named a director, Karen Beyard. In addition to being a senior member of the faculty from the department, she also has an MLS. At this point the proposed "education librarian" was clearly not forthcoming, so the Library put together a team of librarians composed of the heads of acquisitions and collection development, the digital resources librarian, the systems librarian, and a member of the Reference Department to fill the void. This team worked closely with the program director. We developed a plan of action that would allow us to intelligently spend the second year's entire allotment, and to spend it in a timely fashion!

First, we identified collection strengths in three areas:

- *Serials:* A comprehensive review of serials resulted in the determination that the current collection of education and interdisciplinary journals was excellent and would support research at the doctoral level.

- *Monographs:* A check of our holdings against the list of relevant materials listed in *Books for College Libraries,* 3d ed., confirmed our solid base of core materials in the education field. An additional review of the monograph collection revealed the need to weed some antiquated material and replace it with current publications. In addition, the monograph collection was found to be severely lacking in titles that addressed research methodology as well as some works from core publishers of scholarly treatises in the field.

- *Online resources:* Already knowing that our online journal collection supported research at the doctoral level, we reviewed specialty database holdings at peer institutions that offer the Ed.D. There were two conspicuous omissions in our holdings that we needed to acquire.

Second, the collection development librarian worked closely with the program director to fine tune the BNA profile for the Ed.D. program. (CCSU uses Blackwell as its primary vendor and uses its subject profiling and new title online notification system, Collection Manager). Additional subject areas were added to the profile, and certain categories of publications were removed from the profile during this process. In addition, the program director was given access to online use of Collection Manager so that she could directly request titles for purchase. To date, she is the only non-librarian on campus who is accorded this privilege.

We identified the databases that peer institutions had that we did not. Before purchasing them, we set up trials and asked for input from the entire university. The content of the databases was compared with the content of those to which we already subscribed to ensure that we would not be duplicating, to any significant degree, content that we currently owned. An enormous amount of "comparison shopping" was done to obtain best pricing for the databases, including consortia, publisher direct, and vendor, and in every combination and permutation of simultaneous user. We subscribed to the databases that we identified as being essential to the program. By the end of year 2, the Ed.D. program had funded the purchase of more than 700 scholarly monographs and three very expensive databases.

Year 3: Clear Sailing/Pragmatic

The profile is working well. A new liaison from the Library was assigned to the program director. Databases are meeting needs, and a schedule of trials for potential database additions has already been established. There is a streamlined and efficient working relationship between acquisitions and the program director. A July 2004 report to the Connecticut Department of Higher Education and the Board of Governors for Higher Education touts significant improvements to the Library's support of the new Ed.D. program.

The thrust of our efforts during this last year of supplemental funding is to develop a plan for maintaining our progress and continue to add essential resources as needed. The current state of our regular acquisitions budget precludes any hope of being able to absorb the ongoing costs of the already existing Ed.D. materials, not to mention further development. We need to develop a plan that will ensure continued funding for resources now considered essential or core. We plan to produce a detailed, comprehensive, well-documented report that will explain what each new database is, what it does, its usage figures, and pricing. The report will go to the Connecticut State University central office, the CCSU administration, and the CCSU Council of Deans. We will also communicate with the faculty in the Ed.D. department and across campus who have benefited directly by having access to the new online resources and urge them to lobby for renewed funding for the Library. We plan a no-holds-barred approach to this endeavor. Should no new funding result from this plan, it will not be because those with the power to allocate funds did not have all the information needed to make a well-informed decision.

For year 4, hope springs eternal . . .

DO SCIENCE RESEARCHERS USE BOOKS?

Nisa Bakkalbasi, Science/Electronic Resources Librarian, Purchase College, New York
David Goodman, Associate Professor, Palmer School of Library and Information Science, Long Island University, New York

Abstract

Books, as well as journals, are cited in scientists' journal articles. We examined the books cited in the journal articles that were published by authors at a large university during 1981–2001. We found that (1) the citation data conform to Zipf's Law, (2) most citations are to recent titles, and (3) there are differences between different disciplines that appear to conform to traditional assumptions about user practices in different scientific disciplines.

Introduction

Librarians make collection management decisions such as what books to buy, relegate to storage, or withdraw using circulation statistics, inter-library loan data, and local citation data. Most recent investigations have examined the use of journal articles, not books. In this study, we examine available citation data for books from the journal articles published by authors at a large research university during 1981–2001. A careful literature review suggests that there is no standard assessment tool to measure book use, and that even the use of citation data in collection management is still a point of debate.[1] However, if we accept the premise that local citation analysis measures one aspect of book use, collection management decisions will benefit from the analysis presented in this chapter.

Methodology

The term *book,* in this chapter, refers to any material not classified as a journal or dissertation. We focused primarily on the science titles because the data source most heavily represents the literature of science, although it is not limited to it.

Data Source

The data for this study were extracted from the Web of Science database. The dataset comprised an abbreviated title and the frequency of citations for each year. Table 1 is a sample record from the original dataset.

Table 1. Sample Record from the Raw Dataset.

ABBREVIATED TITLE	'01	'00	'99	'98	'97	'96	'95	'94	'93	'92	'91	'90	'89	'88	'87	'86	'85	'84	'83	'82	'81
MOL CLONING LABORATO	5	14	23	15	12	9	20	9	13	10	8	3	1	12	11	5	5	2	0	0	

For the purpose of this particular study, the raw data set has undergone detailed processing and cleaning. First, we excluded all records with fewer than eight citations, as the primary purpose of this study would be served by identifying highly cited books. Then, we removed all ambiguous titles, nearly 15% of the records, which cannot be accurately identified. That left a total of 1,132 book titles and 17,657 citations for those book titles. The records are completed by entering the full title, author, Library of Congress classification number, publisher, publication date, and total number of citations. Table 2 is a sample record from the processed dataset.

Table 2. Sample Record from the Processed Dataset.

FULL TITLE	AUTHOR	PUBLISHER	PUB. DATE	LC CODE	CITATIONS	0	1	2	3	4	5	6	7
Molecular cloning : a laboratory ...	Maniatis, EF	CSH P	1982	QH442 ...	177	0	0	2	5	5	11	12	1

Frequency Distribution of Citations

In table 3 we show the descriptive statistics for the number of citations across all disciplines.

Table 3. Descriptive Statistics for Number of Citations.

Number of Titles	No. of Citations						
	Minimum	Maximum	Mean	Median	Mode	Standard Deviation	Coefficient of Variation
1132	8	180	15.6	11	8	13.11	0.84

The number of times a book is cited ranges from a minimum of 8 to a maximum of 180, with an arithmetic mean of 15.6 and a median of 11. The measures of central tendency and dispersion suggest a highly skewed distribution, which tends to be prevalent in library and information science.[2] The frequency distribution of the citations in figure 1 provides a better visual insight. Figure 1 shows that the frequency distribution of citations is highly skewed, with a single peak where 219 titles were cited eight times. The shape of the distribution suggests that a few books are cited very often, while many others are cited rarely.

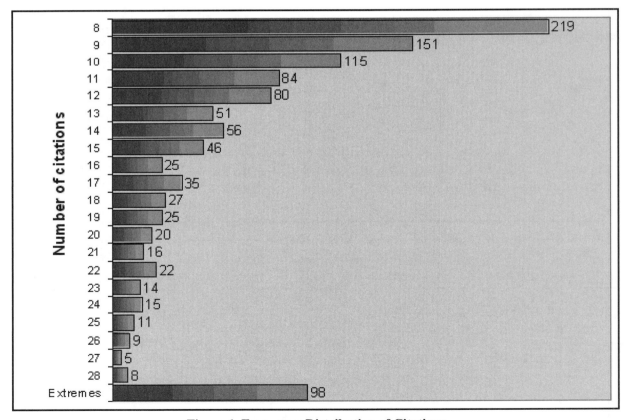

Figure 1. Frequency Distribution of Citations.

Figure 2 shows the cumulative distribution of citation frequencies of books cited by journal articles. The graph suggests that Zipf's Law[3] applies to citation data in this study. For example, 80% of the books are cited 19 times or fewer, while 2% of the books are cited 50 times or more.

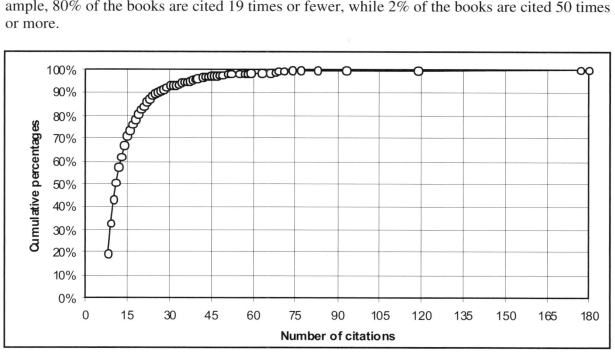

Figure 2. Number of Books Cited by Journal Articles.

General Characteristics of Books Cited

Table 4 shows the number of titles cited and the total number of citations for selected disciplines.

Table 4. Number of Citations by Discipline.

Discipline	Number of titles	Total number of citations	Average number of citations	Percent of citations
Physics	171	2604	15.2	14.7
Mathematics	131	2282	17.4	12.9
Social Sciences	146	1851	12.7	10.5
Biology	85	1832	21.6	10.4
Astronomy	68	1086	16.0	6.2

The number of citations varied across the major disciplines. Five disciplines—physics, mathematics, social sciences, biology, and astronomy—made up more than 50% of the citations. In this dataset, physics yielded the highest number of titles and citations. Biology titles had the highest average number of citations—not surprising, since 4 of the top 10 cited titles come from this discipline (see table 5).

Table 5. Top 10 Titles Across All Disciplines.

Full Title	Author	Published Date	Discipline
Numerical recipes: the art of scientific computing	Press, WH et al	1986	Mathematics
Molecular cloning : a laboratory manual	Maniatis, EF	1982	Biology
Escherichia coli and Salmonella typhimurium : cellular and molecula	Neidhardt, FC	1987	Biology
Methods in yeast genetics : a Cold Spring Harbor Laboratory course		1985	Zoology & Botany
Computers and intractability : a guide to the theory of NP-completen	Garey, MR et al	1979	Mathematics
Quantum Hall effect, the	Prange, RE et al	1987	Physics
Combustion theory : the fundamental theory of chemically reacting fl	Williams, FA	1985	Chemistry
Drosophila : a practical approach	Roberts, DB	1986	Biology
Numerical recipes in C : the art of scientific computing	Press, WH et al	1988	Mathematics
Experiments with gene fusions	Silhavy, TJ et al	1984	Biology

Figure 3 shows the top 10 publishers of the books cited in the dataset.

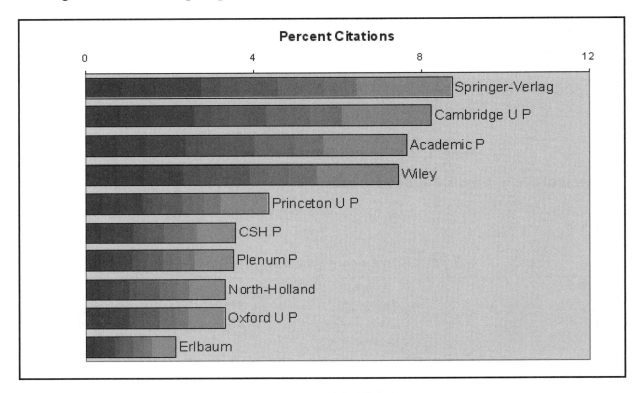

Figure 3. Top 10 Publishers.

Analysis of the Age of Cited Books

In this section, the citation age for each book was calculated by subtracting the year of publication of the cited book from the year of publication of the citing article. Table 6 shows the age distribution of 17,657 citations using five-year intervals. The largest number of citations was 5,786, to those titles in age group 5–9, accounting for approximately 33% of the citations. Citations to older books, 15 years and older, made up a smaller percentage of the total. As we expect in the sciences, most citations are to recently published books.

Table 6. Age Distribution of Citations Across All Disciplines.

Age (in years)	Total No. of Citations	Percent of Citations
0-4	5,034	28.5
5-9	5,786	32.8
10-14	3,990	22.6
15-19	1,957	11.1
20-24	422	2.4
25-29	32	0.2
>29	436	2.5
	17,657	100.0

Table 7 shows the total number of citations in different age groups for each discipline. Note that the most frequently cited publications for many of the selected disciplines are in the same age group: 5–9 years old. When we compare disciplines, we observe that biology and physics appear to be representative of all disciplines. For astronomy, however, it appears that newer books, 0–4 years old, are cited most frequently. For mathematics, books remain citable for relatively longer periods.

Table 7. Age Distribution of Citations by Selected Disciplines.

Age (in years)	Percent of Citations				
	All Disciplines	Biology	Mathematics	Physics	Astronomy
0-4	28.5	28.9	18.3	27.0	43.3
5-9	32.8	32.6	34.7	31.0	32.0
10-14	22.6	24.3	28.7	22.7	16.9
15-19	11.1	11.8	13.7	12.4	4.8
20-24	2.4	2.0	3.5	3.6	1.8
25-29	0.2	0.3	0.0	0.3	0.0
>29	2.5	0.0	1.1	2.9	1.3

Life Span of a Book

In this section, we examined the life span of a book in terms of the number of references to them. We examined a subset of the data that had a full 15-year citation history regardless of when the book was first published. That subset includes 533 books and 7,521 citations.

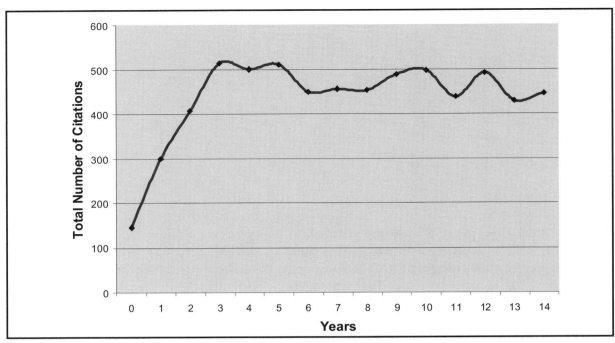

Figure 4. The First 15 Years in the Life Span of a Book.

In this dataset, the number of citations increases rapidly within the first four years of a book's life and remains reasonably steady or perhaps decreases very gradually in subsequent years.

Conclusions

This study reports on a single large research university. There is no reason to think that it is not representative of similar universities for the subjects covered. (Note that we did not study the use of books by researchers in medicine or the preclinical sciences.) Although the extensive study of this dataset gave us several insights into how researchers in different fields use books, for the present we remain descriptive. In that light, we conclude the following:

- **The citation data conform to Zipf's Law**. From a statistical point of view, the frequency distribution of book citation data in this analysis conforms to Zipf's Law. In other words, a few books are cited very often while many others are cited rarely. Although the observation may be obvious, we believe that confirmation of a common insight with statistical data analysis is useful. The implication of this observation in terms of collection management is that the libraries might justify acquiring multiple copies of heavily used books even in very tight budget years, while relying on cooperative collection for rarely used titles.

- **Most citations are to recent titles, with observable similarities and differences across different scientific disciplines**. The citation patterns in this study show that more than 60% of the citations are to recent titles, younger than nine years old. In his study, Koenig raised the question, "how much this pattern is due to the fact that most material available for citing is recent, and how much is due to the fact that older material loses its 'citability'."[4] Based on the fact that the university's library has the resources to provide easy access to materials of any format and age, we can comfortably conclude that references to recent titles imply that recent publications remain more relevant to scientific research and older books lose "citability" with age. There are also notable similarities and differences across different scientific disciplines in terms of citation ages. The data suggest, for example, that during the early years, the citation patterns for biology and physics appear to be representative of all disciplines, whereas mathematics and astronomy appear to behave differently from other disciplines. For example, newer astronomy books are cited more frequently (less than 8% of the citations were from books 15 years older or older), whereas we observed a significant number of older mathematics books being cited (more than 8% of the citations were from books 15 years old or older). Please note that we have used a "trained eyeball test" to reach this conclusion, not a formal discriminate analysis technique. We leave the formal statistical assessment to a future study.

- **Book citations increase rapidly within the first four years after the publication date.** In general book citations increase rapidly within the first four years after the publication date and remain steady for many years before they decline rather gradually.

- **Researchers cite books**. Researchers are citing books, which leads us to believe they are using books at this university. The most relevant statistic to support a definitive statement of this type is the average number of book citations in a journal article as well as the relative ratio of book citations to the total number of citations. Unfortunately, the data source does not allow us to relate a specific reference to its source. However, our findings allow us to make a reasonable assertion, if not a definite conclusion, that scientists still rely on books as a source of information while performing research. It is interesting to point here to the results of the McDonald study on Caltech's humanities and social sciences faculty publications, which also shows that "they are still citing books in their research,"[5] and therefore our findings are consistent with other research libraries.

This study sets the stage for further analysis of book citation patterns, an area that appears to be understudied. It also demonstrates the usefulness of local citation analysis as a tool for collection management, if used with caution. That our conclusion by and large amounts to common sense can be seen as the validation of the empirical rules of thumb that constitute common sense, or alternatively as validation of the bibliometric approach.

Notes

1. M. B. Line, "The Use of Citation and Other Statistics in Stock Management," *IFLA Journal* 27, no. 4 (2001): 247–52.

2. S. J. Bensman, "Probability Distributions in Library and Information Science: A Historical and Practitioner Viewpoint," *Journal of the American Society for Information Science* 51, no. 9 (2000):816–33.

3. G. K. Zipf, *Human Behavior and the Principle of Least Effort: An Introduction to Human Ecology* (Cambridge, Mass.: Addison-Wesley, 1949).

4. M. E. D. Koenig, "Citation Analysis for the Arts and Humanities as a Collection Management Tool." *Collection Management* 2, no. 3 (1978): 247–61

5. John McDonald, "The Book Is Dead: Citation Rates in the Humanities and Social Sciences," in *Charleston Convention Proceedings 2001* (Westport, Conn.: Libraries Unlimited, 2002), 143–50.

Bibliography

Bensman, S. J. "Urquhart's and Garfield's Laws: The British Controversy over Their Validity." *Journal of the American Society for Information Science* 52, no. 9 (2001): 714–24.

Blecic, D. D. "Monograph Use at an Academic Health Science Library: The First Three Years of Shelf Life." *Bulletin of the Medical Library Association* 88, no. 2 (2000): 145–51.

Bowman, M. "Format Citation Patterns and Their Implications for Collection Development in Research Libraries." *Collection Building* 11, no. 1 (1991): 2–8.

Brooks, B. C. "Theory of the Bradford Law." *Journal of Documentation* 33, no. 3 (1977): 180–209.

Budd, J. "A Citation Study of American Literature: Implications for Collection Management." *Collection Management* 8, no. 2 (1986): 49–62.

Fussler, H. H., and J. L. Simon. *Patterns in the Use of Books in Large Research Libraries.* Chicago: University of Chicago Press, 1969.

Wehmeyer, S., and J. M. Wehmeyer. "The Comparative Importance of Books: Clinical Psychology in the Health Sciences Library." *Bulletin of the Medical Library Association.* 87, no. 2 (1999): 187–91.

Nisa Bakkalbasi is the science/electronic resources librarian at Purchase College Library at the State University of New York at Purchase. Her responsibilities include information literacy instruction, collection development for the sciences, and faculty liaison to the Natural Sciences Division. In addition, she manages activities related to the evaluation, acquisition, and accessibility of the library's electronic resources. She received a B.A. in mathematics and an M.S. in applied statistics from the University of Alabama, and an M.S. in library and information science from Long Island University. She collaborates in various research projects with Dr. Thomas Krichel to examine NEP (New Economic Papers), a current awareness service for RePEc digital library.

David Goodman is an associate professor at the Palmer School of Library and Information Science, where he teaches courses in academic libraries, scientific and technical library resources, and acquisition and selection of electronic resources. He was formerly chemistry librarian, biology librarian, and research librarian (in succession) at Princeton University Library and is a founding member of the executive committee of COUNTER.

The 2004 conference theme, "All the World's a Serial," reiterated the attention that serials are receiving in collection development. Open access journals and their influence on the publishing industry were addressed during several key presentations. Other serial issues included topics on serials review processes, pay-per-view journal articles, and the need to provide access to older journal material.

Journals

THE JOURNAL OF OPINION: RELIC OR COUNTERFORCE?

Victor Navasky, Publisher & Editorial Director, The Nation Magazine, *New York City*

I want to make the case that the journal of opinion, which many consider to be a relic of the eighteenth century, a print artifact shortly to disappear into cyberspace, is a counterforce to some of the worst and most dangerous trends in the culture. I am talking about commercialization, commoditization, bureaucratization, and tabloidization—the oversimplification of complex materials.

But we at *The Nation,* along with most librarians and some publishers (and the ALA), are a critical force for promoting the free flow and unimpeded distribution of news, knowable information, and opinion for individuals, institutions, and communities, and against the use of governmental power to suppress the free exchange of ideas and the surveillance and invasion of privacy of library and bookstore users and customers.

Like the average library, the independent journal is not run to make a profit. Its mission cannot be measured in financial returns. But as must librarians everyday, we must be certain that we and our customers get value for their money.

Undoubtedly before we get back to New York there will be a new technological development and everything I have said will be outmoded, but for now I'm honored to be here fighting alongside you to preserve the values of privacy and the freest possible inquiry that we together hold to be essential if we are to enable our citizens to help close the deliberations gap in our deliberative democracy.

When I speak of the journal of opinion , forgive me if I make my case mostly in terms of *The Nation*—that's where I hang my hat. I think I could easily make it in terms of Bill Buckley's *National Review*. Well, almost as easily. Its current editor, Rich Lowry, has said that *The National Review*, like *The Nation*, exists to make a point, not a profit. Someone once asked Buckley how he, America's avatar of the free market, could justify his dedication to an institution that had done nothing but lose money. His reply: "You don't expect the church to make a profit, do you?"

Like a library, we need to run an independent magazine like a business or else we will be out of business. But if business is all we are, we deserve to be out of business. As *The Texas Observer*'s founding editor, Ronnie Dugger, wrote in the fiurst issue back in 1952: "We have to survive as a business before we can survive as a morality; but we would rather perish as a business than survive as an immorality."

Actually, the economics of most journals of opinion are beyond the comprehension of most people in traditional publishing. Let me say a brief word about it from the bottom up. When I arrived at *The Nation* in 1978 we had 20,000 subscribers. These days the big thing in magazines is to have youthful demographics. When a friend of mine, the advocacy journalist Jack Newfield, heard I had been hired as editor of *The Nation*, he asked how many paid subscribers we had. I said 20,000 but 8,000 were libraries. This seemed impressive to me because libraries have more readers per copy than individual subscribers, but Jack's response was "oh, 8,000 libraries and 12,000 nursing homes." Our joke was that when our subscribers expire they really expire. But the truth is we now have more than 180,000 subscribers, and 21,000 of them belong to a group we call *The Nation* Associates, who send in an annual gift over and above their subscription price. And our joke turned out to be no joke. So many people remembered us in their wills that we literally started a little club called "the legacy group" inviting people to do just that.

When a reporter from *The New York Times* got hold of our brochure describing the legacy group, she was astonished and asked whether we knew of any other magazine that had asked subscribers to remember them in their wills? We didn't. When you think about it, even though *The Nation* is technically for-profit—if we were non-profit we wouldn't be able to endorse candidates for public office—we are an educational institution, so why shouldn't we behave like other educational institutions? When Ronald Reagan was elected we received a call from the White House informing us that the administration had cut back on its magazine budget and asked if we would donate a complimentary subscription to the White House library. We discussed the matter and decided to offer Reagan a subscription at our special student rate on the theory that as a proponent of supply side economics he could use the information we could supply.

Like most libraries, the journal of opinion may be small in size yet large in influence. The impact of these journals, like the impact of your library, is not to be underestimated. Dwight Macdonald wrote in 1957 that when he was editing his small journal, *Politics*, he often felt isolated, comparing his few thousand readers with the millions and millions of non-readers—such is the power of the modern obsession with quantity. But many years after his journal went under he ran across so many nostalgic old readers in unexpected quarters that he had the impression he was better known for *Politics* than for his articles in *The New Yorker*, whose circulation is roughly 70 times greater. As he said, a "little magazine" is often more intensively read (and circulated) than big commercial magazines, because it is a more individual expression and appeals with special force to individuals of like minds.

In the run-up to the 2004 election, books by former Secretary of the Treasury Paul O'Neill, , Richard Clark, formerly with the National Security Council, and *The Washington Post*'s Bob Woodward all suggested that the Bush administration had it in mind to invade Iraq before 9/11. But readers of *The Weekly Standard* and *The National Interest*, conservative and neoconservative journals, would have read the case for invading Iraq in the late 1990s, before George W. Bush was elected, even as readers of *The Liberator* magazine read about abolition decades before it happened.

The journals of opinion examine, in a critical spirit, what *The Nation*'s long-time editor, Carey McWilliams, likes to call the idols of the tribe. That's "idol" as in *American Idol*—the dogmas of the week. They question the official line. And Carey added re: *The Nation* "it has been influential to the degree that it has held to this basic policy—one does not need to have a large circulation in order to destroy an idol of the tribe; one pinprick will collapse a balloon. The influence of the journal of opinion extends far beyond the range of its readership."

These journals then are influential because of the quality rather than the quantity of their audience, even as libraries are influential less because of the number of their visitors than because they almost always leave a library knowing more than when they entered.

One of the criticisms leveled at these journals is that they are written for the elite, the privileged few. Not only that, in the case of the journal of opinion it is further said that we preach to the choir. In fact judging from *The Nation* I can tell you these magazines are read by diverse publics. In our case we perform a knitting function, bringing together groups with very different ideas—the peace movement, feminists, trade unionists, civil libertarians, environmentalists, and human rights activists. It is easy, especially in the aftermath of the presidential campaign, to lump these groups under the label of liberal elitists. But each of these groups has its own belief system, and their agendas are frequently at cross-purposes. Thus a reader who agrees with *The Nation*'s pro-choice stand on abortion may disagree with its First amendment defense of pornography. And even if it were true that we always told all of our readers what they wanted to hear, there would still be some value in that many readers need and want facts, figures, and a vocabulary to document and articulate their intuitions.

There is nothing wrong, by the way, with preaching to the choir. They need it as much as anyone else. And there is nothing wrong with catering to readers in an age of television. Even though they are ideological, it's a mistake to think of independent journals as predictable.

As proof I am going to quote the first sentence in the first paragraph of the first story on the first page of the first issue of *The Nation* magazine, which was founded and paid for by a group of malcontents in and around the abolitionist movement. The date was July 6, 1895. And in my opinion the sentence is one of the most extraordinary first sentences in the history of American magazine launches. "The week was singularly barren of exciting events." Would Tina Brown or Graydon Carter have had the courage to launch a magazine with such a sentence?

When I am not publishing *The Nation* I teach at Columbia University's graduate school of journalism, and I can assure you that such a workload violates every single convention of journalism as it is routinely practiced at all of the country's best papers.

If I were writing this story for *The New York Times*, the first thing my editor would ask me to do is find a responsible authority figure to quote, as in: "President Andrew Johnson said today that 'the week has been singularly barren of exciting events'."

E. L. Godkin, *The Nation*'s founding editor, was able to lead with that unique sentence because *The Nation* was independent. It was, like most—not all, but most—journals of opinion, what today is called a stand-alone publication. These small circulation periodicals are not beholden to corporate bureaucrats or big advertisers. This in itself can be liberating. You can sit around at the end of an editorial meeting and nobody is going to ask "but what are our advertisers going to say?" What advertisers? (Most big magazines strive for at least a 50–50 ad to edit ratio; at a journal of opinion like *The Nation* advertising is only a 10% factor.)

Remember, *The Nation* first appeared the year the Civil War ended. Now contrast *The Nation*'s opening line with the immortal opening statement of William Lloyd Garrison's abolitionist paper, *The Liberator*, whose subscription list *The Nation* inherited: "I will not equivocate—I will not excuse—I will not retreat a single inch."

I like to think that at its best the independent journal of opinion draws on the two traditions exemplified by these two lines: 1) the tradition of untrendy truth-telling, of critical reasoning, and 2) the passionate commitment to change society for the better, to crusade against injustice.

Even the impassioned Garrison, who believed in truth (what he called "the incendiary spirit of truth that burns up error"), also believed in free discussion and untrammeled inquiry (because slavery "could not stand up to free discussion"). The independent magazine is dedicated to the art of open inquiry, of discussion, of debate.

Garrison believed that *The Liberator*'s independence was the guarantee of its role as an open forum. He would accept advice on any subject but one: how to run the paper. In his valedictory he referred to *The Liberator* not as a propaganda sheet for his various causes but as "a weekly method of communicating with each other."

Garrison blessed *The Nation* as heir to *The Liberator*, but this dual legacy of emancipation for the slaves and an independent free press as a means of agitation and discussion was not without its complications.

The Nation's original 1865 prospectus promised that the new weekly was not going to serve any sect, party, or movement. It was going to be a conscience, a gadfly to "wage war upon the vices of exaggeration and misrepresentation." The editorial formula was to have the best thinkers of the day apply reason, logic, criticism, moral criticism to the key problems of the day. E. L. Godkin, the Anglo-Irish journalist who came to this country in 1856 and invented *The Nation* a decade later, worked it all out. He raised $100,000 in capital and signed on the elite. They were the most thoughtful of the then literary establishment, including Henry Wadsworth Longfellow, James Russell Lowell, William James, Henry Adams, and William Dean Howells. Their books, I suspect, may still be found on your shelves.

Despite *The Nation*'s buzz-less lead, subscriptions started coming in at the rate of 40 a day. There seemed to be no stopping *The Nation*.

And then it almost stopped. The money men had a problem. The largest single contributor to Godkin's $100,000 capital was the Boston abolitionist George Luther Stearns, a lead-pipe manufacturer who had supplied John Brown with the weapons that were used at Harper's Ferry.

Godkin, whose *Nation* did endorse the early Reconstruction program, balked at proselytizing for the radical Reconstructionist program favored by Stearns and other shareholders. Not only that, but from the perspective of Stearns *The Nation* was wasting space by running frivolous pieces like "a day at the races in Saratoga."

At traditional journals, when the literary men fall out with the money men (and at traditional journals it used to be mainly men), the money men find new literary men. Not so at *The Nation*.

Godkin, the editor, found new backers, or rather he organized a new company, which guaranteed him editorial independence.

By the way, the author of that piece on "a day at the races" was a young, relatively unknown writer named Henry James, who went on to write more than 250 essays and reviews for the magazine.

Today, journals of opinion have a virtual monopoly on independent journalism. An exception is *The Weekly Standard*, owned by Rupert Murdoch. To me, it's an open question whether a conglomerated journal of opinion is a contradiction in terms.

In the early 1980s Ben Baddikian, dean of the graduate school of journalism at Berkeley, wrote a book called *Media Monopoly* (Beacon Press, 1983; 6th ed. 2000). He documented an alarming statistic: that 50 corporations dominated more than half of all the information and entertainment companies in this country. He called them our own ministry of information and culture. When he republished the book a few years later the number was down to 27. Then *The Nation* asked him to take another look, and the number he projected for the end of the century was six; depending on how you count them, he was right. No public issue is more urgent than how to make these transnational communications corporations accountable to readers, listeners, and viewers unless it is how schools can keep corporations from controlling their educational materials.

Independence means being beholden to no one. It's difficult for those who are beholden to the market to understand. Perhaps the best way to make that point is to tell you what happened on the occasion of *The Nation*'s 120th anniversary when we put together a special issue on how perceptions of the United States had changed over the previous generation. We invited observers from countries around the world to give us their impressions of the shift. Carlos Fuentes from Mexico wrote that "we are left this final image of the U.S.: a democracy inside but an empire outside; Dr. Jekyll at home, Mr. Hyde in Latin America." Margaret Atwood from Canada talked about pressing her nose against the windowpane of the United States, and we asked Gore Vidal, who splits his time between LA and Ravello, Italy, to give us the view from Ravello, which he proceeded to do in a brilliant essay on the United States as an empire.

Anyway, shortly thereafter I received a written invitation to have lunch with Bob Guccione, the proprietor of *Penthouse* magazine. After being given a tour of the magnificent statuary in his eastside mansion we were joined by his circulation, marketing, and advertising executives. Fine wines were served, and he asked me how much it cost to get Gore Vidal to write his essay. When I told him we paid each of the contributors to that issue $25, he almost choked on his $100 bottle of wine and told me what he had offered Vidal; I think it was $50,000 for an article, and Vidal declined. Guccione then proceeded to pass out Cuban cigars and brandy and to muse about how perhaps he might be interested in buying *The Nation*. Indeed, he said, he had been thinking about it for some time. The irony is that people like Vidal write for *The Nation* because of its noncommercial values and would never write for someone like *Penthouse*'s publisher at *Nation* prices.

Like libraries, which are in the business of providing their visitors with the information they need to function as citizens in a deliberative democracy, of equipping and inspiring them to carry on the national conversation, the independent journal of opinion has a special relationship to the production and consumption of serious public discourse.

By creating a press that incessantly appropriates, consumes, and recycles ideas, the much celebrated market economy has turned over to these stapled artifacts of the print culture something of a monopoly in the business of serious political discourse, rigorous policy debate, the power of reason, and the importance of moral argument in the journalistic culture.

Neither journals nor libraries believe in letting other institutions set their standards. In your world I know it's partly a question of not letting the would-be censors set the standards for what books and materials you may order.

Let me tell you now this business of standards works in the world of the journal of opinion.

A few years ago I embarked on a book project. With my unerring instinct for the bestseller list I persuaded my publisher that the world was waiting for the definitive book on the role of the journal of opinion. One of the reasons I claimed it was worth doing was that as far as I knew, nobody had ever done it before. Of course that alone might have suggested to a more canny business head that the market prospects for such a project were dim. I preferred to take it as a good sign.

I soon discovered that I was wrong, that these magazines indeed had a Boswell, although he was an unlucky one—the German philosopher Jürgen Habermas, whom I had previously regarded as indecipherable—both because of his jargon-ridden translated-from-the-German-prose and his historic connection to the Frankfurt school, the bastion of something called critical theory, which I found indecipherable in its own right.

But Habermas had also invented the notion of the public sphere (which I put halfway between the political or governmental sphere and the private and personal sphere), and it turned out that he identified the journal of opinion as a sort of house organ to the public sphere. In 1962 he elaborated his theory in a study that he jauntily titled *The Structural Transformation of the Public Sphere: An Inquiry into a Category of Bourgeoisie Society* (various editions and publishers). It was not translated into English or published in this country until 1989, but its first half turned out to include an ambitious analytic history of the organic connection between these journals and opinion formation in a democratic society.

Stripped bare, Habermas's theory, in the enlightenment tradition, includes the idea that to flourish, democracy demands continuous conversation, open argument, and debate. He traces the development to the coffeehouses and taverns that grew out of the salons of court, but also to the periodical press, which set the agenda of coffeehouse debate—especially in England, where censorship was minimal. By the beginning of the eighteenth century there were an estimated 3,000 coffeehouses in London alone. (I wonder if Habermas inspired Starbucks?) Unlike the earlier newsletters, which had reported on the journeys of princes and foreign dignitaries, on balls and other news of and from the court, these new periodicals, like Addison and Steele's *Tatler*, Defoe's *Review,* and Swift's *Examiner,* included essays and satires that criticized the Parliament and crown. Because this criticism was carried out in public, it had something of a transforming effect on parliament and helped to usher in an era of parliamentary democracy.

And so when I was invited to address a symposium in Copenhagen I said yes, provided my ticket included a stopover in Frankfurt, Germany.

Habermas had all sorts of wise things to say. But when I got to the 64 dollar question and asked, what would you say is the role of the journal of opinion in this era of electronic media and the Internet? he looked at me with what I took to be pity as if to say, any fool would know the answer to that. And indeed he said that the answer was simple and obvious, and as soon as he said it, it was. To you it may sound like a platitude, a cliché, but to me his pronouncement had all the clarity of the Liberty Bell. What he said was that the role of these little journals was nothing less than to set the standard. To set the standard for public discourse. Not bad. We set the standards, not others.

We are both in the business of helping to overcome what I just the other day heard Amy Gutman, the new president of the University of Pennsylvania, call "the deliberation deficit."

Even though libraries are notoriously quiet, they paradoxically make possible our deliberation democracy. They are literally the opposite of the shout shows that now dominate cable television and talk radio.

If the public opinion polls are to be believed, more and more people get their news from television. To understand what television is doing to us, I recommend to you the work of the late Neil Postman, who happened to be on *The Nation*'s editorial board (conflict-of-interest alert). But he pointed out that television, which is in the business of moving rather than preserving information, is constantly devaluing the news it ostensibly serves up. The viewer knows that no matter how bad the famine in Somalia, it will shortly be followed by a commercial for Burger King or perhaps McDonald's. What would you say about the possibility for serious discourse if I were to pause here to tell you that I will return to my discussion in a moment and then proceed to say a few words on behalf of Calvin Klein jeans? You might be justified in thinking that I had no respect for you and certainly no respect for the subject. And if I did this not once but several times in the course of this afternoon, you'd think the whole enterprise unworthy of your time. But we don't think a typical television news show equally unworthy because we no longer expect continuity from our journalism. I can hardly overestimate the damage that juxtaposing the ravages of AIDS with a word from Burger King does to the possibility of serious discourse. By the time you are 40 years old, you will have seen more than a million commercials. Postman pointed out that the message implicit in these commercials is in the private rather than the public interest.

As the late Kit Lasch said, what democracy requires is a public debate, not information. Of course it needs information, too, but the kind of information it needs can be generated only by vigorous debate. We do not know what we need to know until we ask the right questions, and we can identify the right questions only by subjecting our ideas about the world to the test of public controversy. Information, usually seen as the precondition of debate, is better understood as its by-product.

The ideal of a deliberative democracy is as old as our republic. The declaration of independence was written to present reasons that impelled the colonies to separate themselves from Great Britain.

The ultimate test is not whether the views of the participants carry the day, but whether, unlike today's shout shows on cable TV or radio where nobody listens, nobody hears, nobody really engages, they are taken into account.

We are also partners in our implicit joint effort to restore the great traditions of debate that began around the end of the nineteenth century, the era of the Lincoln/Douglas debates.

Libraries provide the information, the knowledge; journals of opinion like *The Nation* take it to its next step.

Finally, John Kenneth Galbraith once told me that you should say finally when you still have 10 minutes to go; it puts the audience at their ease.

Here is my proposal: that we partner with each other. We are already political partners in our opposition to such things as the U.S. Patriot Act.

But I have something more specific in mind.

The Nation Digital Archive: At first we were told that what we needed to do was put our archives on a CD ROM. No sooner had we arranged that than we were told we had to put our archives on DVD. Then, voilà, we were told to do none of those things. We found a partner in the Kanda Software Company of Cambridge, Massachusetts, and now The Nation Digital Archive has been available to libraries and the general public on a subscription basis since early in 2001. It contains the full text of every word published by *The Nation* since 1865 as well as scanned images of every page—over 200,000 pages of material in all. Representing an unmatched collection of primary source material, the archive, because it starts the year the Civil War ended, seems to us nothing less than an alternative history of the United States. It is available in about 150 institutions, ranging from high schools to premium academic research libraries.

But surprise, we have somewhat belatedly discovered that the world of electronic database publishing isn't the same as it was in the late 1990s when—believe it or not—we weren't even sure that every public library would necessarily have access to the Internet. Many librarians tell us that they prefer to work with a consortium. What this means for this old stand-alone isn't always clear.

We've worked hard to make our archive fully searchable via Google and the other search engines and to make it easy to retrieve an article found in this way by adding abstracts and support for OpenURL links.

We've even contemplated the possibility of licensing our content to a major aggregator if, and it's a big "if," we can negotiate a fair return that takes into account the intrinsic value of the intellectual asset as well as the investment we've made in undertaking such a large-scale conversion of print to digital (and incidentally, we did it without resort to Third World outsourcing).

So tell us where we go from here. And, as we have done ever since 1865, we will undoubtedly go our own way, but it will be nice to hear from you.

A NON-US, NON-UK PERSPECTIVE ON OA (OPEN ACCESS)

Heather Grace Morrison, Project Coordinator, BC Electronic Library Network, Burnaby, British Columbia

Open access (OA) is being talked about, and implemented, around the globe, by everyone from the United Nations to individual authors, editors, and publishers, as well as collaborative groups. As of October 2004, requests for a government mandate for OA had gone forward not only in the United States and the United Kingdom, but also Croatia. The Scielo (Scientific Electronic Library Online) collections of Latin America are very substantial, full OA journal collections. In the developing world, OA is seen not only as the best means to access the research results of others, but as an opportunity to contribute their own scholarly research findings.

The purpose of this session at the conference was to present a few OA projects and perspectives on open access from around the world, from my viewpoint as an enthusiastic advocate. For more information about OA, see Peter Suber's excellent Open Access Overview, at http://www.earlham.edu/~peters/fos/overview.htm.

For the purposes of this chapter, a simple definition of open access is used: making scholarly journal articles freely available to anyone, anywhere, over the World Wide Web. There are two basic types of open access. The "gold" road is OA publishing, that is, journals that are published as fully open access in the first place. The "green" road is OA self-archiving, where authors make a copy of their articles openly accessible, whether in an institutional repository (IR) or on a departmental or personal Web site.

People talk about the OA movements as based on faith and vision, not down to earth. So let's start here—with vision. How is this for a vision statement?

We . . . the peoples of the world . . . declare our common desire and commitment to build a people centred, inclusive and development-oriented Information Society, where everyone can create, access, utilize and share information and knowledge

Beautiful, isn't it? This statement was developed by representatives of the world's governments, at the first United Nations Summit, with invited participation from the corporate community. That is, the World Summit on the Information Society (WSIS), first phase, Geneva, December 2003.[1]

For anyone who cares about scholarly communications and/or libraries, the WSIS documents are well worth reading. For example, the Declaration of Principles talks about the importance of sharing research results. Being able to both access and contribute information, ideas, and knowledge is stressed, as is a rich public domain with easily accessible information. The Principles discuss institutions such as libraries being strengthened to promote the preservation of documentary records, and free and equitable access to information. Librarians are portrayed as playing an active role in promoting the information society.

Open access is specifically mentioned in both the WSIS Principles and the Plan of Action. Principle A28 states "We strive to promote universal access with equal opportunities for all to scientific knowledge and the creation and dissemination of scientific and technical information, including open access initiatives for scientific publishing."[2]

The WSIS Plan of Action supports a number of approaches to facilitate access: affordable access (the HINARI/AGORA type approach), open access, or open archives. For example,

"Encourage initiatives to facilitate access, including free and affordable access to open access journals and books, and open archives for scientific information."[3] For e-science the goal is to promote electronic publishing, differential pricing, and open access initiatives to make scientific information affordable and accessible in all countries on an equitable basis.[4]

The WSIS hopes to use information and communication technologies (ICTs) to achieve the Millennium Declaration goals, such as eradication of extreme poverty and hunger; universal primary education; gender equality; maternal health; combating HIV/AIDs, malaria, and other diseases; ensuring environmental sustainability; and developing global partnerships for the attainment of a more peaceful, just, and prosperous world.

There are some real challenges here—broadband in every village, primary education for everyone around the world. There are people working hard to figure out how to achieve these goals!

Open access is much easier to achieve than the main goals of the WSIS. We are already doing most of the work on a voluntary basis, and paying more than what would be needed for a fully open access scholarly communications system, in my author's opinion. There are transitional issues, of course, but the resources are already there.

One of the most substantial OA collections around the world is Scielo (Scientific Electronic Library Online).[5] Scielo includes more than 200 AO journals online from Brazil, Chile, Cuba, and Spain. It features an English/Spanish/Portuguese search portal. Subjects covered include health sciences, social sciences, agriculture, psychology/psychiatry, animal science, veterinary medicine, and engineering.

Outside the United States and United Kingdom, government subsidy is a common means of supporting academic publishing. In places where profit is unlikely, this is necessary, as this is often the only means of ensuring that academic work is published. Where this is the case, the difference between OA and non-OA in economic terms is simply that OA costs less—there is no need to spend money to develop and support authentication mechanisms to prevent people from accessing the information.

Scielo Cuba lists 15 OA journals, all medical titles. Looking at this list in conjunction with the National Instistutes of Health proposal in the United States, it looks like we have two world leaders in making their medical information accessible, in different ways. Considering the historical and political differences of the two countries, it seems unlikely that this was planned! According to the Scielo Cuba Web site, Cuba has plans to eventually make all its scholarly knowledge openly accessible.

The Scielo collection is substantial; libraries should be helping users to find and use this resource. If a tiny communist country like Cuba, with a GDP of $32 billion, can figure out how to make its scholarly knowledge fully openly accessible, while our largest commercial STM publishers, for example Reed Elsevier with a gross revenue of $8.8 billion, seem to be having trouble with this, maybe these for-profit commercial, capitalist publisher types could learn something from communist Cuba!

Bioline International,[6] a non-profit initiative managed by scientists and librarians, assists publishers and authors in developing countries with making their journals and articles openly accessible. One of the goals of Bioline is to reduce the "South to North" knowledge gap, so that scholars in developing countries have the opportunity to contribute to the world's collective knowledge. There are more than 30 OA journals hosted on the Bioline Web site. Publishing on this Web site is not required, nor is making journals openly accessible, although this is encouraged.

Initiated in 1993, Bioline International's goal is to assist publishers in developing countries. Open access was not part of BI's original mandate, but rather a conclusion reached based on experience. Bioline International is coordinated by the University of Toronto Library, the Reference Centre on Environmental Information, Brazil, and Bioline/UK.

One of the journals produced with Bioline International's assistance is the *Journal of Postgraduate Medicine* (*JPGM*), one of the oldest medical journals from India, continuously published since 1911. *JPGM*[7] illustrates the high quality and careful attention to detail of Bioline's work. The site is visually pleasing and highly functional. The *JPGM* prominently displays a lengthy list of leading literature databases where the journal is indexed, ranging from Index Medicus to CAB Health, Cancerlit, and Toxline, to name a few.

Indexing is a real concern to publishers and authors outside the United States and United Kingdom—even if you give your articles away for free, if people are using indexes that don't include your journals, your articles will not be found.

The "green" approach to OA, or authors' self-archiving, is very much in evidence outside the United States and United Kingdom as well. We'll look at three "green" projects: the Bioline International e-prints archive, the Indian Institute of Science and E-Print Archive, and CARL Institutional Repositories. To date, collection growth has been slow but steady. My prediction is that the "green" approach will show a dramatic growth increase within the foreseeable future.

Bioline International provides a free e-prints archive for authors from developing countries. There are more than 1,640 records in the archive.[8] A search by date in October 2004 illustrated the slow growth in use of the archive, from 148 articles published in 2001 to 622 for 2004.

The E-Prints Archive of the prestigious Indian Institute of Science contains more than 1,000 items.[9] Like Bioline International, there is a gradual increase in the number of items submitted over the years. The earliest publication date in this e-prints archive is 1975. This illustrates one of the advantages of the "green" approach—it provides a means to open up access to previously published articles.

The Canadian Association of Research Libraries (CARL) members are committed to the development of institutional repositories. As a glance at the CARL Institutional Repository site in October 2004 illustrates,[10] this program is very much in the early developmental stages. At this time, of the 27 university library members of CARL, only 7 have operational institutional repositories. Many repositories are still in the early planning stages. Simon Fraser University Library acts as coordinator of the CARL metadata harvester. So far, SFU's own Institutional Repository, with only 17 items, is still in the project stage—in the process of perfecting the software and policies.

Let's look at the SFU Library D-Space Institutional Repository Project,[11] to see why I believe that the slow growth of IRs will be replaced with very dramatic growth in the very near future. Even though SFU is not one of the larger repositories at this time, it's the one I am most familiar with.

According to the SFU Library Web site, advantages of the SFU D-Space are:

- for the user, easy remote access through the World Wide Web;

- for the contributor, digital access, long-term preservation, and a variety of formats; and

- for the institution, access to selected research of the university through one interface.

In addition to peer-reviewed journal articles by SFU faculty, the SFU Library IR will host other kinds of information, such as the papers from the Digital Games Research Association Conference held in Vancouver June 16–20, 2005.[12] The conference could add up to 100 papers to the IR. This illustrates one of the reasons why I believe that IRs will show dramatic growth—because the growth, in some cases, will come from the addition of entire collections (whether conference proceedings, departmental, or individual author collections), not always just one article at a time.

The SFU Library Institutional Repository is where you will find my own works. This is where you will find the PowerPoint slides for this presentation—converted to pdf so as to be accessible to anyone. As an author, I appreciate having the IR, which both looks after my work (makes sure it is archived) and makes it accessible. (I can cite my own work, and know that anyone who sees the citation can click through to the article.) This demonstrates a second reason why I anticipate rapid growth in the IRs in the near future: Once authors experience directly the benefits of self-archiving, in terms of both impact and convenience, they will likely be very interested in ensuring that their works are added to the IR.

An additional advantage of the institutional repository is that it makes available to the university community the work of its own faculty. Three of the first five titles (60%) are articles published in journals not purchased by SFU Library: *Collection Building, Library Hi Tech News,* and *Letter of the LAA.* These are not expensive journals; it's just that no library can afford to subscribe to all the journals.

A brief look at a few of the many recent and upcoming conferences around the world devoted to OA illustrates the third reason why I expect rapid growth in the development of institutional repositories: the many OA conferences being held around the world. Some examples from 2004 follow:

- Pretoria, July (http://isis.sabinet.co.za/dspace/handle/123456789/38)

- India, September (Journal of Postgraduate Medicine Gold Con, http://www.jpgmonline.com/gc_pdetails4.asp)

- Halifax, Nova Scotia, October 2004 (Canada October Institutional Repositories: The Future is Now!, http://www.carl-abrc.ca/frames_index.htm)

- Kiev, Ukraine, December (http://www.irf.kiev.ua/en/anns?doc:int=1234)

Watch for the OA self-archiving approach to grow dramatically in India, for instance, where their conference emphasized e-prints and author self-archiving.

The Public Knowledge Project (PKP) of the University of British Columbia[13] has created free, open source software for creating and managing journals (Open Journal Systems) and conferences (Open Conference Systems). Like Bioline, open access is optional—but encouraged.

Let's look at some projects and journals that use the PKP software and talk about the evolution of business models for online journals. We'll see why OA just makes sense!

African Journals Online (AJOL),[14] a collection of over 200 African journals online, uses Open Journals Systems software. Abstracts are freely available online, but not full text—yet. *The Sahara Journal: Social Aspects of HIV/AIDs* is the first of these journals to become freely available online.

A search for an article in *The Nigerian Journal of Health and Biomedical Sciences,* like most of the AJOL journals, yields a freely available abstract. Users are invited to click a link that says "Request article."

Ordering the article involves a requesting process. For some requestors, there is a charge involved.

Note that anyone who has Internet access who can get to this point can access many materials for free, such as Scielo journals and *JPGM.* Many will also have access to significant subscription resources, whether they are connected with a library that can pay the subscription fees or access has been provided for free through HINARI, AGORA, etc.

Articles from *The Nigerian Journal of Health and Biomedical Sciences* are more difficult to access than these other resources, even for the users who are entitled to free copies of the articles. Is it obvious yet why people are more likely to read and cite an article from this journal once it becomes freely available online?

We've looked at why *not* making an article OA can discourage use. Now let's look at some reasons why giving away knowledge benefits us. We get more value from giving away our information than we possibly could get from cost recovery.

If the article were OA, it would be more likely to be read and cited by some people the author would probably like to be reading and citing the article—other researchers, or commercial entities like pharmaceutical companies that just might want to invest in the author's research.

The knowledge we give away just might result in an epidemic being discovered early and contained in another country, and never affecting us at all. Similarly, what our neighbor learns about food handling improves our own food safety, whenever we import our food. What our neighboring country learns to protect or repair in its environment affects our own air, water, etc.

One interesting example of an OA journal that uses PKP software is the *Asia-Pacific Forum on Science Learning and Teaching.*[15] This appears to be an ad hoc collaboration, involving Canadian software, a Hong Kong publisher, and sponsors from several different geographic regions and of several different types, from government to non-profit to commercial publishers. This is also a partially bilingual journal, with articles and abstracts in English and/or Chinese.

The United Nations sponsored a forum on open access September 20–October 4, 2004, entitled "Open Access to Scholarly Publications: A Model for Enhanced Knowledge Management?" (Forum messages are available at http://groups.undp.org/read/?forum=gpnet-oa.) Following are some comments based on this discussion, which illustrate that OA is a worldwide phenomenon.

An open access journal from Poland, *e-polymers*[16] is seen as the answer to the paradoxical situation that scientists in universities cannot (or hardly can) afford to subscribe to journals which—at the same time—they strongly support by submission of high-quality papers, refereeing, etc. Its creation is an act of self-defense of the scientific community. *e-polymers* appears to be experimenting with OA funding models. The Web site includes advertising, mentions a membership model, and states that it is free to libraries worldwide on request (while all articles are readily accessible from the Web). The total cost of publication is calculated at about the price of 10 subscriptions to a leading journal in this field.[17]

H. G Rucinque, of Bogota, Columbia, edits the OA journal *GeoTropico*,[18] Rucinque states that "in Latin America, Africa and large parts of Asia and Oceania, inaccessibility to scholarly publications is the common fact. Open access is the alternative to stay updated in the Third World, as well as the least costly outlet for publication."[19] Rucinque has been publishing *GeoTropico* as an OA journal using personal funds. While this is not recommended as a sustainable model for OA publishing, it does show just how important open access is for some.

For a German doctor working in the field of leukemia research in the field in Chernobyl and Siberia, "access—or rather the lack of access to current research results was always a crucial factor." Rolf Neth welcomes ever-increasing OA to scientific results as a human right to information issue and is convinced that not only is OA the best possible model for philosophical reasons, it is the only sustainable economic model at some point in the future for scholarly communication.[20] Neth and his colleagues developed the Wilsede Portal for free science information transfer.[21]

In Croatia a proposal for government-mandated OA has gone forward: "For instance, in Croatia, majority of scientific journals is subsidized by the government. They are mostly non-profit journals whose publishers are learned societies. A number of them cannot even afford an online edition. If the government has offered a tool for easy online publishing (preferably with OAI compliance), asking for OA to online edition in return, such an arrangement would probably be beneficial and acceptable to all."[22]

In summary, there are many OA initiatives, of both the "gold" or open access publishing and "green" or self-archiving varieties, springing up around the world. Outside the United States and United Kingdom, profits are unlikely for journal publishers, and a subsidy-based funding model is common. With a subsidy model, the difference between open access and subscription is that OA costs less (no subscription tracking, authentication, and associated support). The Scielo collections offer substantial content. Bioline International and the Public Knowledge Project provide support and technology to assist Third World publishers. The "green" or self-archiving approach is being pursued around the world, from India to the Ukraine to Canada. The author predicts that the present slow but steady growth in institutional repositories will be replaced in the near future by dramatic growth.

Desire for OA has been expressed by many individuals and groups around the world, ranging from official government representatives along with representatives from the corporate community at the World Summit on the Information Society to individual authors, editors, and publishers around the globe.

Looking back from the future, what will historians see as the truly new events of our times? Terrorism? There is nothing new about people trying to control each other through fear and terror—it's a recurrent theme throughout human history. From my viewpoint, what is truly new and exciting about our times is the kind of global cooperation we have seen with the mapping of the human genome. This illustrates that when we work together there is great potential to solve common problems and advance all our knowledge together . . . this is the potential of OA.

Notes

1. *Declaration of Principles*, Principle A1, [Online], available: http://www.itu.int/wsis/.
2. World Summit on the Information Society (WSIS), first phase, Geneva, December 2003, *Declaration of Principles,* Principle 28A.
3. World Summit on the Information Society (WSIS), *Plan of Action,* C.3 10.1.
4. Ibid., C.7.22.b.
5. http://www.scielo.org
6. http://www.bioline.org.br/
7. http://www.jpgmonline.com/
8. http://bioline.utsc.utoronto.ca/
9. http://eprints.iisc.ernet.in/
10. http://www.carl-abrc.ca/frames_index.htm
11. http://www.lib.sfu.ca/about/projects/institutional_repository/about/mission.htm
12. http://www.digra.org/
13. http://www.pkp.ubc.ca/
14. http://www.ajol.info/
15. http://www.ied.edu.hk/apfslt/
16. http://www.e-polymers.org/
17. Gpgnet, http://groups.undp.org/read/messages = ?id = 97695#97695
18. http://www.geotropico.org/
19. Gpgnet, http://groups.undp.org/read/messages?id = 98810#98810
20. Gpgnet http://groups.undp.org/read/messages?id = 98584#98584
21. http://www.internet-portal-wilsede.com/
22. Tibor Toth and Iva Melinschak Zlodi, Gpgnet, http://groups.undp.org/read/messages?id = 98579#98579

IS FREE TOO EXPENSIVE? OPEN ACCESS AND LIBRARIES

Walt Crawford, Senior Analyst, Research Libraries Group, Mountain View, California

When this topic was chosen in July 2004, here's what I was seeing and expected to find: From what I'm seeing in continued testing of OpenURL resolvers and some other informal investigation, libraries are being relatively slow to actually treat open access (OA) journals and OAI (archived) articles as seriously as they treat wildly expensive journals, or even the hundreds of bundled journals they claimed not to want. Does OA make a difference if it's not reflected in the online catalogs and the resolvers—if libraries aren't actively promoting access?

As of early September 2004, the Directory of Open Access Journals listed 1,250 refereed OA journals. Hundreds of other freely available journals and magazines are available through other resources, either as true OA journals or with free availability after an initial embargo.

As of September 2, 2004, University of Michigan's OAIster includes just under 3.5 million articles and other OA documents, as harvested from institutional and other repositories following the OAI protocol for harvestable metadata.

More than a thousand refereed journals. More than three million articles (and other scholarly documents), including—presumably—hundreds of thousands of articles that would otherwise be trapped behind toll-access walls. That's a lot of value for libraries, particularly academic libraries, and it's all free for the taking.

So what are libraries doing about it? My sense as of early summer was fairly negative. The reality is somewhat better. Since there are really two different kinds of access—OpenURL access to full text articles from indexes, and OPAC inclusion of freely available journals—I'll describe the landscape and the tests separately for each kind.

OA and OpenURL

When new users of Eureka OpenURL are interested, I prepare a sample profile of how their resolver works against up to 16 Eureka citation and bibliographic databases, testing up to 700 records in the process. I became aware that a number of the records in the sample search results used for OpenURL testing are available free of charge—but only because of links in a handful of resolvers.

Roughly a year ago, I encountered a new and intriguing form of OpenURL link. The Universite du Quebec au Chicoutimi, a relatively small and remote campus, offered article searches in OAIster as a way to enhance their full text resources. The searches worked on some of my results. This, I thought, was wonderful: A way to make OAI repositories *meaningful* additions to the scholarly landscape as provided through libraries and indexes. I did a piece on the OAIster link in *Cites & Insights* in November 2003—and devoted the February 2004 "Crawford Files" in *American Libraries* to this powerful addition to OpenURL. Naturally, I expected to see some take up the idea—after all, *American Libraries* reaches 64,000 librarians.

I also knew that some OAI articles were available through Google and other Web indexes—although, when I've tried searching for such articles in the past, I usually find many more snarky comments about the articles than I do articles themselves. Still, it's a plausible OpenURL path, if nowhere near as direct as OAIster.[1]

I needed to do some QA work with Eureka OpenURL in late summer 2004. I took the opportunity to do an informal test of the extent to which these two methodologies were showing up in OpenURL—and the extent to which freely available full text was being made, well, freely available.

In addition to OAIster and Google access, I checked six journals with free full text access—selecting these six because all six are indexed in Anthropology Plus, Eureka's combined world-class anthropology indexes. That inclusion meant two things: One, that the journals were significant enough to be indexed by selective professional indexers;and two, that I could put together a saved result of six records, one from each journal, which made testing much easier. I'll name the journals—or, really, five journals and one magazine—when I get to that part of the results.

I wound up testing a fair cross-section of ARL libraries and modest samples of other college and university libraries. I checked 47 ARL libraries, including 17 of the top 25, 16 of the next 35, and 14 of the remaining 50-odd institutions. I also checked 16 other institutions calling themselves colleges or institutes, 25 other institutions calling themselves universities, and three libraries outside North America, for a total of 91 libraries. So what did I find?

OAIster: Not Yet

Not one of the 91 OpenURL resolvers offered the possibility of searching article titles in OAIster or any similar index. Not one. Chicoutimi wasn't one of the 91 sample cases. So much for the 64,000 librarians reading "Crawford Files" and acting on what they read!

I hope this picture will change in the future. OAI repositories may be a great way to provide open access to the In Crowd—those who know where to look and what to look for—but without access from citation indexes and the like, it's a fairly minimal form of open access. Sure, the dozen scientists who would otherwise receive offprints can be pointed to the author's repository—but what about the rest of us?

The Google Alternative

Google title searches, either alone or as one of several Web index choices, turned up a little more often, but "little" is the appropriate word. Maybe that's the way it should be, given that my results in following such searches were usually pretty abysmal.

Eighteen percent of all tested resolvers offered Google title searches—but only 11% of ARL libraries tested. That breaks down to 18% of the top 25, *none* of the middle 35, and 14% of the bottom 50+. Meanwhile, 25% of the colleges offered such links, as did 28% of the non-ARL universities—and *all three* of the overseas institutions.

Six OA Periodicals: Good Results

When it comes to refereed OA journals, the news is better, at least for the five journals sampled here (the sixth periodical turned out to be a magazine). In all of these tests, I counted *any* OpenURL link, including those to paid full text resources, but I noted which ones included free access.

Current Anthropology—recent issues of which are freely available—was offered by 90 of the 91 libraries, including 46 of 47 ARL libraries and all of those tested in the top 60; let's call it a clean sweep. (The one OpenURL resolver that did *not* link to *Current Anthropology*, either as a free or paid resource, did link to four of the other five journals.) This was also the journal with the most instances in which paid (aggregated) links were included but *not* free ones: 23 of the 90 failed to include the free link, and only four included *only* the free link.

American Journal of Archaeology was a somewhat distant second: 69 total or 76%, including 81% of ARL institutions tested. That's the only other tested journal available as a paid resource, and two of the 69 institutions linked only to a paid version.

The next two are tied. *Revista de antropologia* and *Mana* (the *Mana* from Rio, since there's more than one) were both offered as free OpenURL links at 56 of 91 institutions (62%) and at 71% of the top 25 ARL institutions, but at only 50% of the middle 35 and 64% of the bottom 50+. Some 68% of non-ARL universities offered both links.

Just a tad behind was *Chungara*, linked from 52 of 91 institutions (57%). That includes 53% of ARL institutions, (65% of the top 25), and 68% of non-ARL universities tested.

Trailing—more so outside of ARL—is *Himal*, now *Himal South Asia*, an English-language magazine from Nepal with enough significant material to justify selective indexing in Anthropology Plus. It's not in the Directory of Open Access Journals because it's not a refereed journal. It is freely available, however. Thirty-seven of 91 (41%) linked to *Himal*—but that included 21 of the ARL sample (45%) and 59% of the top 25. If you spot a trend here, "the rich get richer," with top ARL libraries doing a more effective job of using free resources, you're not mistaken.

Including Google access for a total of seven possibilities, the 91 libraries averaged 4.2 of the seven links—but only 4.1 of those were free. For the 47 sampled ARL libraries, the average was 4.1, with 3.9 free—but for the top 25, it was 4.7, with 4.2 free.

Looking at distribution, 12 of the largest ARL libraries (71% of those tested) had links to at least five of the seven resources, as did seven of the next 35 (44%) and eight of the bottom half (57%). Nine of 16 college libraries (56%) had at least five resources, as did a mere 10 of 25 non-ARL universities, or 40%.

To sum up: The biggest universities are doing a good job of providing links to free full text through OA journals, but not through OAIster. Elsewhere, it's sketchy, but promising—after all, five of the six periodicals were linked to by at least 57% of all institutions sampled, which included some fairly small and specialized universities and colleges.

OA Journals and Online Catalogs

What about open access journals and library catalogs? In some cases, free may be too expensive—even with copy cataloging or mass loading of purchased records, some cost is associated with adding any journal to a catalog. Still, everything in the Directory of Open Access Journals is supposedly refereed, and 1,250 journals represent a significant increase in the holdings of any small library and most larger ones.

While I could only do the OpenURL test because I was doing QA work against resolvers, or with advance cooperation from all the libraries involved, anyone can do the tests I did for OPAC inclusion of OA journals. I reached all catalogs through the open Web. During the research, I dropped the three overseas libraries (response took too long). I also dropped one non-ARL university that uses a metasearch engine to front-end its online catalog and, as a result, took too much time and too many steps for the simple searches I was doing. Finally, one college shared a union catalog with another college in the sample and, as a result, represented effectively redundant information. As a result, this set of tests involved 86 libraries in all: the same 47 ARL libraries, 15 college libraries, and 24 non-ARL university libraries.

The 20—Why and What

I kept the six freely available periodicals from the OpenURL tests and added fourteen more journals, all from the Directory of Open Access Journals. I took no more than two or three journals from a subject area—three from medicine, since biomedicine is such a large portion of journal publishing and specifically OA publishing, and one or two from a range of other disciplines.

I limited selections to journals that began in 2000 or earlier, assuming that some libraries might take a while to add journals or be wary of journals with short track records. I'll list the journals a little later, from the most widely held to the least widely held. I also checked holdings in the RLG Union Catalog.

Eight of these 20 periodicals are available in print form as well as online. I only counted periodicals for which *electronic* access—with a link to the free journal or a paid full text version—was reported. I did note cases where a catalog included both and where a library included the print but not the electronic version, and calculated an overall holdings figure for each library.

I searched journals by title or, if provided as a separate index, by journal title. If the catalog home page included a separate tab for *all* journals, I used that tab. But if the catalog home page included a separate tab just for e-journals, or if the "journals" page explicitly said it lacked substantial portions of the journal collection, I used the primary title index.

The decision not to search entirely separate e-journal lists was a factor in one ARL library—the one with the worst results, three e-journals out of 20. Notably, re-searching the 20 in the e-journal catalog only added six more. Two colleges and three non-ARL universities also had separate e-journal lists that I didn't search, and these were also among those with the lowest e-journal results in their primary catalogs.

Overall Results

Nobody had all 20 journals in electronic form—but quite a few came close. Five (6%) had 19 of 20; seven more (8%) had 18 of 20, and two of those had 19 including print holdings. Five more had 17 e-journals. Since none had 16 and only one had 15, there's an obvious breakpoint: 20% of the catalogs included at least 85% of the journals.

It's worth naming the top 12—those with at least 90% of the e-journals in their catalogs. Among sampled ARL institutions, that list includes Indiana, Vanderbilt, Kansas, Illinois at Chicago, and Ohio. Colleges include the Claremont Colleges, Bowdoin, and Lafayette College. Non-ARL universities include Calgary, Georgia State, New Hampshire, St. Lawrence, and, unsurprisingly, Drexel.

The next big clump is at 13, with nine catalogs. Adding a few others, there were 18 additional catalogs with more than half of the journals (11 or more), for a total of 41%.

Another 17 catalogs (20%) had 8, 9, or 10 of the 20. Nineteen more (22%) had 5, 6, or 7. Finally, 14 catalogs (16%) had fewer than one-quarter of the e-journals, including one that had none at all (although it had four of the 8 print titles).

Maybe I should include the six libraries with 10 e-journals in the "half or better" category. That makes a total of 41 (48%) of the catalogs.

On average, each catalog included 9.9 e-journal titles—and 10.9 of the 20 titles including print-only holdings. (The RLG Union Catalog had all 20, but you'd expect that.) In that "rich get richer" vein, note that ARL institutions averaged 10.5 e-journal titles and 11.9 total titles —and that institutions among the top 25 averaged 10.9 and 12.8 respectively, as compared to 8.1 and 9.0 for non-ARL universities. (Colleges did well: 11.0 e-journals, 11.1 including print.) On the other hand, only one of the 90%+ institutions was among the top 25 ARL institutions.

Ten of the catalogs clearly referenced DOAJ, providing links through that interface. Of those, half had full cataloging (including subjects) for the DOAJ records. I didn't check cataloging level in each case, although it's clear that at least one library used a minimal entry system to include DOAJ journals, and at least one other library included purchased records with complete serials information but little or no subject cataloging.

Detailed Results

Following are the 20 titles as most frequently represented in the total set of 86 online catalogs, noting also their representation among the 47 ARL libraries and those among the top 25, and the holdings count in the RLG Union Catalog. The overall picture is a fairly even distribution. Four show up as e-journals in 80% to 99% of the catalogs. Five show up in 55% to 70%. Five more show up in roughly half—47% to 50%. Four show up in 22% to 36% of catalogs—and the last two are in only 7% and 10%, respectively.

- *Current Anthropology* turned up most often—as an e-journal in 85 of 86 catalogs (99%) and in all 47 of the ARL catalogs. It's not the most reported in the RLG Union Catalog, with 69 holdings, but it is second.

- *American Journal of Archaeology* was second, reported in e-journal form in 88% of catalogs, 91% of ARL catalogs, and 94% among top 25 samples. There were 66 holdings in the RLG Union Catalog.

- The most widely cataloged *pure* e-journal is the *New Journal of Physics*: 81% overall, 91% in ARL, 94% in top 25 institutions—but there were only 19 holdings in the RLG Union Catalog.

- Fourth is *Law and Contemporary Policy*, which has the most holdings in the RLG Union Catalog (99), possibly because it's held as an e-journal, as a print journal, or as a series of separate print monographs. 80% included it in e-journal form, including 85% of ARL catalogs and—again—94% among the top 25.

- Fifth is *BMC Biomedical Ethics:* 70% overall, 81% ARL, 76% among top 25 institutions—and 11 holdings reported in the RLG Union Catalog.

- Sixth is *Postgraduate Medicine*, a print-and-electronic journal: 63% overall, 70% ARL, and 82% among the top 25; 31 holdings in the RLG Union Catalog.

- Seventh is *Psycoloquy*, another pure play: 58% overall, 68% ARL, 71% in the top 25; 11 holdings in the RLG Union Catalog.

- Eighth is *Documenta mathematica*: 57% overall, 70% ARL, 76% in the top 25, 13 holdings in the RLG Union Catalog.

- Ninth, and the last to be included in more than half of the catalogs: *Journal of World-Systems Research*: 55% overall, 62% ARL, 59% in the top 25, 12 holdings in the RLG Union Catalog.

- Tenth, in exactly half of the catalogs: *Stanford Technology Law Review*, in 51% of the ARL sample but 76% of the top 25, 14 in the RLG Union Catalog.

- Tied for eleventh in 49% of the catalogs: *CLCWeb* and the *Electronic Journal of Sociology*. They're not tied in the ARL sample, where *CLCWeb* gets 55% of the ARL sample and 59% of the top 25 (12 in the RLG Union Catalog), while *EJS* shows up in 47% of the ARL sample, 41% of the top 25 (10 in the RLG Union Catalog).

- Twelfth, and at the bottom of the "middle group": *IEEE Distributed Systems*: 47% overall, 55% ARL, 47% top 25, 9 in the RLG Union Catalog.

- Thirteenth and highest of the lower group—significantly ahead of number14—is *InterJournal*: 36% overall, 34% ARL, a mere 24% of the top 25—and 4 in the RLG Union Catalog

- Fifteenth: *Revista de antropologia*. 26% overall and ARL, 35% top 25, 14 holdings in the RLG Union Catalog.

- Sixteenth: *Chungara*. 23% overall, 15% ARL, 18% top 25, 18 in the RLG Union Catalog.

- Tied for seventeenth, the bottom of the lower group: *Mana* and *Sociologias*, each with 22% showings—but *Mana* in 19% of ARL, 24% of the top 25, and 12 RLG Union Catalog, while *Sociologias* shows up in only 13% of ARL, 12% of the top 25, and three RLG Union Catalog.

- Next to last: *Acta medica*, 10% overall, 6% ARL, and *none* of the top 25; two RLG Union Catalog. This is the Czech *Acta medica*.

- Finally, there's the magazine: *Himal South Asian*, in 7% of the 86 catalogs and 9% ARL—but 12% of the top 25, and 22 RLG Union Catalog holdings. That final figure is probably wrong, as it covers three variant titles.

Explanations and Suppositions

I can think of various explanations for the relatively poor showings here. It *does* cost money to add records to catalogs, particularly for institutions that want subject access. Six of the journals may be non-English, and only one of those six is in the top half—but that also says something about the power of OA to broaden the international coverage of institutions. I don't know much about the prestige of these journals (other than the first two, where I assume high prestige), but it's noteworthy that the journal in twelfth place is published by a prestigious international organization, IEEE.

Some institutions have apparently decided to treat e-journals separately. That's a defensible decision, particularly if the alternative is catalog entries with no subject access—but it's less than ideal. Keyword access won't yield material that's not in the catalog. A few of these titles would show up in keyword searches.

Closing

Overall, the news is better than I expected. Free e-journals are being treated as OpenURL resources by most OpenURL users sampled, albeit selectively (which may be appropriate), with DOAJ emerging as an important aggregator of OA pointers. On average, these institutions included almost exactly half of the tested OA journals in their online catalogs—and quite a few show near-universal inclusion.

The catalog tests are easy to replicate. Taking another list of, say, 20 to 50 DOAJ titles—perhaps chosen on a different basis or as a structured sample—I'd guess you could test a typical OPAC in five to ten minutes, maybe 15 minutes for a run of 50 titles. A library school class could probably test all of the ARL libraries against a 50-title list—or at least all but a few that might limit OPAC access—as a relatively small class project. Such a project would be interesting.

Now, about linking to OAI articles . . .

Note

1. This chapter was written, and then presented at the Conference, before Google Scholar came along. That service changes the picture somewhat.

THE NEW AND IMPROVED SERIALS REVIEW PROCESS IN THE AGE OF THE ELECTRONIC JOURNAL

Jill Emery, Director of the Electronic Resources Program, University of Houston Libraries, Texas
Mary Beth Thomson, Head of Acquisitions, University of Houston Libraries, Texas

Introduction and History

The University of Houston Libraries has been conducting an annual serials review project for more than 15 years. The process began as a method of dealing with double digit increases in journal costs and a steady decline in the University of Houston Libraries' materials budget. Each year faculty members and subject librarians identified journal titles to add or cancel. This annual serials review process has been maintained in most subject areas out of budgetary necessity and because it was discovered that many faculty want to be involved in the ongoing development of the journals collection. Over the course of the last several years, the project has become a mixture of cancellations within the sciences, an opportunity to review the journal collections within the social sciences and the humanities, and a time for requesting electronic access to current print subscriptions.

During the last few years, the serials review/cancellation process began to increase in complexity as the number of serials available in electronic form continued to grow. Due to the differences in identifying, reviewing, evaluating, and managing print and electronic journals, the annual journal review process had to begin incorporating the expansion of print journals to include electronic access and the selection and evaluation of electronic-only journal subscriptions.

The University of Houston Libraries embarked on a multi-year process to streamline and integrate the evaluation, selection, and processing of electronic journals into a serials review process that had previously been established for print subscriptions. The first phase of the process was the formation of a task force in the summer of 2002 whose charge was to begin to develop a strategic plan to manage the development of both print and electronic journal collections. Then in December 2003 a follow-up task force was formed to implement the recommendations for migrating to electronic journals made by the first task force and approved by the Libraries' administration. Through these efforts some of the groundwork was laid for the continual process of identifying and evaluating electronic access to print subscriptions or of adding electronic-only journals. Documentation developed by the task force was used as a part of the new serials review process conducted during the spring of 2004.

The Libraries were already participants in several publisher-based electronic plus print contracts, as well as some electronic access only licenses. But what about those journals not a part of a current contract such as BioOne or Project Muse or published by, say, Oxford or Elsevier? We wanted to document whether electronic access was available, how it was being made available, and the current cost of adding electronic access. Who was keeping track of the addition of electronic access to existing current journal subscriptions? Faculty members at the University of Houston, especially in the sciences, are involved in journal selection, want to continue to have input into both title and format selection, and had expressed concern with big package contracts. Based on past collection evaluation projects, we know faculty in some departments are ready to go to electronic access only across the board, whereas in other departments faculty want to have the opportunity to evaluate their portion of the Libraries' journal collection title-by-title.

As an organization we were past the question of whether or not to migrate to electronic-only access, as I imagine are most of you. In fact, one of the first task force recommendations was that all new journal subscriptions would be for electronic-only access whenever available, appropriate, and affordable. We were and still are attempting to address the questions of when we should go to electronic-only access; what processes, guidelines, and criteria we should follow; how will this happen in an organized manner; and who will be involved. How do we account for the title-by-title selection and evaluation process as well as for the broad-based journal package deals often available through consortia memberships? How do we as an organization stop thinking in terms of electronic journals being in some way special and begin to consider them as the norm?

Purpose and Process

The purpose of the spring 2004 serials review project was to identify current print journal subscriptions for which electronic access was available but for which the Libraries had yet to establish connectivity. How far along were we really in migrating to print plus electronic access or to electronic-only access? Were there subject areas or publishers that could be identified as possible priorities for migration?

The Libraries' materials budget for fiscal year 2004/2005 was increased by $310,000 for books and journals and by $55,000 for electronic databases. The total materials budget was just under $6 million. The Libraries have over 17,000 current journal subscriptions, 3,000 individual electronic journals subscriptions, and approximately 23,000 aggregator electronic journals in the online catalog. Due to the increased materials budget, subject librarians were not required to cancel journal subscriptions as a part of the spring 2004 serials review project. Instead, the serials review was an internal research project focused on evaluating and documenting the availability of electronic journals in all subject areas. No new for-fee subscriptions were to be added to the budget except for engineering, and then only due to an ongoing journal collection development/cancellation project by the faculty of that college. Only electronic journals identified as open access (OA) journals or those free with our current print subscriptions were considered for addition to the journals collection.

Documentation and Schedule

So how did we proceed? First a packet of information was developed for each subject librarian. Then in late February 2004 a subject librarians' meeting was held during which the project was explained and the informational packets distributed and reviewed. The distributed documents were also made available from the Acquisitions and Collection Development Department's intranet site. We included some of the same information as in previous years, such as

- the projected materials budget,
- the projected serials budget allocation for each subject fund,
- a spreadsheet of current journal subscriptions,
- a serials list explanation document, and
- various journal request and ordering forms.

I should point out that the serials titles spreadsheet was populated with data indicating whether or not a current print subscription included electronic access. This information was exported from the Libraries Innovative Interfaces system into the serials titles spreadsheet. For those titles, no further research or action was required. Subject librarians were requested to perform a title-by-title search of all other journal titles. Although the inclusion of a serials list spreadsheet was not new, there were several additional columns added to the spreadsheet, including

- pricing of electronic access with print;

- whether or not electronic-only access was available, and if so the cost;

- how the journal was being accessed (e.g., Ingenta, Metafind); and

- a column to include any special notes such as "current year only available."

There were several new documents added to the informational packet, including

- a publisher informational spreadsheet and overview,

- an electronic journal pricing offers overview,

- a list of resources for locating OA journals,

- an electronic journal selection criteria list,

- a licensing overview document, and

- an electronic journal archiving statement.

The publisher informational spreadsheet and the electronic journal pricing offers overview were developed as a method of distributing known information. Up until then, this information was not easily available and not necessarily known by the subject librarians. So for some publishers, the subject librarians could simply cut and paste information from one document to the serials spreadsheet.

After the initial subject librarians' meeting, several training sessions were held. The training sessions' purpose was to demonstrate how to begin the research process. Several sample searches were performed using the Ulrichs database, with the results then explained. Several publisher Web sites were used as examples of how to find and then to interpret access and pricing information. We reviewed the spreadsheet columns to be completed and discussed the difference between accessing a journal via an aggregator's database and adding electronic access to a current print subscription. Subject librarians were encouraged to ask questions and to request help in completing the spreadsheet. We also encouraged them to skip titles for which information was clearly not available, or in cases where the publisher had to be contacted for pricing and then responses were not received.

In mid-April I held a box-lunch discussion meeting for all subject librarians. The group discussed what was and wasn't working in their research efforts, what we could have done differently, and what were the perceived benefits. Toward the end of the spring semester forms were to be submitted requesting electronic access to the "free with print" journals or those identified as "open access" and appropriate for our collections. We also requested that the serials titles spreadsheet, completed to date, be submitted. Subject librarians, however, had until the end of June to complete the title-by-title research and to submit a completed spreadsheet for each of their subject areas. In previous years the serials review projects were completed by the end of May, soon after the end of the semester, with the results being submitted to the Serials Department by the first of June. Since we were not adding or canceling any for-fee journals the timeline was extended.

Documentation Explained

The publisher information spreadsheet and overview identified major publishers/providers and the platform where their content was hosted. This document also outlined the pricing scheme used by the publisher at the time of the serials review if it was known. Finally, it was noted if we already had a signed license with the publisher/provider or if there was any other condition or note. Table 1 is an example of what this document looked like.

Table 1. Publisher Information Spreadsheet.

Publishers with Various Imprints Noted	Pricing with Print Subscriptions	E-Access Only	How Available	Conditions/Notes
Carfax Publishing	Free	Not available	MetaPress	Part of Taylor & Francis Group
Cell Press	Additional costs	90% of print subscription	Cell Press/ ScienceDirect	Licensed
Cold Spring Harbor Laboratory Press	Free	Not available	Publisher site/highwire	Click-thru license/must register for access
Company of Biologist	Additional costs	About 10% cheaper than print subscription	Company of Biologists Web site	Licensed

The publisher overview document just explained the five columns to the subject librarians.

In an attempt to explain to the subject librarians the various pricing models that could be encountered, an overview of various publisher/provider pricing models was provided. The models explained were freely available on the Web, OA, free with print, for-fee with the subscription, flip pricing, for-fee archival subscriptions, for-fee archival one-time purchases, electronic-only pricing schemes, and big deals. Following is an example from this document:

For-Fee with Print Subscriptions: These are scholarly journals where the electronic access is an additional fee on top of the print subscription. These fees are usually percentages of the print costs such as a 5%, 10%, 25% surcharge for electronic access. Often this type of electronic access is also limited to a specific time period; usually a rolling window of 4-5 years worth of access and a separate charge is instituted on a subscription basis for archival rights. These titles do have to be licensed by us and require specific access set-up.

Open access journals were just beginning to make a presence when we began this serials review, so we included information for subject librarians to identify and choose OA titles to be added to their subject areas. The document they were given for identifying and choosing OA titles was a spreadsheet that looked table 2.

Table 2. Open Access Journals Spreadsheet.

Access Site Name	Title List Available	Site URL	Title List URL	Notes/Comments
BioMedCentral	Yes	http://www.biomedcentral.com/	http://www.biomedcentral.com/browse/journals/	Not all titles freely available; some titles have subscription costs
Directory of Open Access Journals	Yes	http://www.doaj.org/	http://www.doaj.org/alpha	All of titles listed are freely available as open access titles in multiple disciplines
Electronic Library of Mathematics	Yes	http://www.emis.ams.org	http://www.emis.ams.org/journals/.	Freely available mathematics titles form around the world in full PDF & PostScript supported by the European Mathematical Information Service; mirrored around the world

In addition to these informational documents, an electronic journal selection criteria document was drafted by the electronic journals task force. This document outlined the conditions that were necessary and preferred along with content considerations as well as added features that subject librarians might want to consider when choosing electronic versions of titles. The necessary conditions basically insured that the content would work within our computing environment, license terms were in agreement with our acceptable licensing language, and we could purchase access to these titles through our subscription agents. For the preferred terms, we asked subject librarians to identify publishers and titles that provided perpetual rights to electronic access and that allowed access to all constituents of the UH Libraries community. When looking at the content, the subject librarians were to ensure that the content was relevant to coursework in their subject area and indicate whether duplicate coverage would be maintained with another format such as print or microfilm versions; if graphical displays were satisfactory; if the content represented a stable number of years of coverage, what the archival rights may or may not be; which content display mechanism was being used, PDF, HTML, or PostScript; and finally, whether printing quality met the needs of their faculty and students. Added-value or added-feature considerations were linking to either A&I resources or other content platforms; searchability across an entire content platform; what type of bibliographic software content could be downloaded into; and any other capabilities not found with print resources such as sound components, video-streaming, or animation.

The University of Houston Libraries do not have a standard license agreement that we send to publishers and providers, but we do have a set of criteria that we use when negotiating licensing agreements that we compare against each license we receive to help in our negotiations. This document was also provided to the subject librarians to inform them of various points that may hinder purchase of and access to electronic journals. Most of the necessary terms are those that every academic library abides by, such as governing domain, authorized user definition, access setup, not taking responsibility for third-party actions, not accepting major content changes, not allowing to be indemnified, dispute resolution, etc. We also insist on the purchase of electronic journals through a third-party agent and typically do not enter into multi-year agreements at this point except in special situations. An electronic journal archiving statement was also drafted by the electronic journals task force to clarify the UH Libraries role in trying to provide consistent and perpetual electronic access to content. This statement outlines our commitment to specific providers such as JSTOR and an indication to investigate alternative electronic provision via services such as LOCKSS and the development of an institutional repository.

Proposed Outcomes

So what were we hoping to accomplish with this research-intensive project? Seven desired outcomes were stated in the project's overview. Not all of the outcomes were realized, but overall, almost everyone involved agreed the process was very beneficial. The first outcome listed was to document whether current print subscriptions included electronic access. As mentioned previously, the serials list spreadsheet now includes both print and electronic journal subscription information. Subject librarians are able to go to one document and determine whether electronic access was available at the time of the last review and know whether or not electronic access was requested as a result of the recent review.

The second outcome was to gain knowledge about, and skill in, evaluating and identifying journals available electronically but currently only subscribed to in print; the third was to document publisher specifications for access to the electronic format for those journals currently only available in print. All but a few of the subject librarians were able to complete their portions of the journal title research, and we are continuing to work toward 100% participation. More than 300 journals were identified as providing electronic access free with print that had not previously been identified or were OA journals selected to be added to the collections. Of course since the summer several of those journal publishers have begun charging for the addition of electronic access. Subject librarians were also able to document publisher price and access specifications for many other journals.

The next three outcomes were to evaluate the electronic version of journals based on stated criteria, to gain knowledge about the current state of and changes in scholarly communication, and to increase our skill base in conducting research into the availability of journals being published in specific subject areas. Everyone involved in the process has become much more aware of the different methods by which publishers are making journals available, and our knowledge of the changes taking placing in journal publishing and pricing has increased tremendously. Hundreds of electronic journals were evaluated as part of this process. The selection and evaluation criteria were tested and will likely be updated and revised. A subject librarian's ability to answer faculty questions about the availability of electronic access has increased immensely, and as a group we have had more in-depth discussions about archiving and licensing issues.

The final outcome was to prioritize journal titles for migration to electronic access. For most of the subject librarians this was the one outcome they were not able to realize.

What's next? The last outcome, prioritizing journals for migration to electronic access, will continue as a priority for us during the next serials review cycle spring 2005. Subject librarians, in consultation with faculty, will focus on those journals for which migration to electronic-only access is possible. The number of journals subscribed to in print format will continue to decrease. We will continue to streamline and integrate the evaluation, selection, and processing of electronic journals into the serials review process. Subject librarians will perform periodic reviews of those titles still showing as available in print format only in order to document when and if electronic access becomes available, and we will continue to identify and add appropriate open access journals to the journals collections.

PURCHASING NEW JOURNAL SUBSCRIPTIONS?: WHY? BECAUSE WE HAVE PAY-PER-VIEW USAGE STATISTICS THAT PROVE WE NEED TO OWN THEM!

Beth R. Bernhardt, Electronic Journals/Document Delivery Librarian, University of North Carolina at Greensboro

Abstract

During 2002, the University of North Carolina at Greensboro (UNCG) set up several different types of pay-per-view options that have provided its users with access to more than 3,500 unsubscribed electronic journals. Now with over two years of usage statistics available, the collection management team has identified and acquired subscriptions to over 20 new journal titles. This chapter addresses the decision-making criteria (such as frequency of purchase versus cost of a subscription) used by the collection management team. Information on the various types of pay-per-view options that are available is given.

Overview

The University of North Carolina at Greensboro is classified by Carnegie as a Doctoral Intensive University I, with an FTE of approximately 15,000. The Jackson Library collection consists of 2.8 million items, 22,485 electronic journals, and 205 databases. The university is committed to increasing enrollment to 18,000 by the year 2007. The university is also changing the focus of its curriculum from music and education to fields such as genetic counseling, exercise physiology, technology, and biological studies. With the growth in several different subject areas, the library needs to add resources to the expected collection. By providing pay-per-view titles to its users, Jackson Library can monitor usage to see what journals patrons are using and in what subject areas.

Pay-Per-View Options

There are several different options for pay-per-view available to libraries. UNCG chose the following:

> FirstSearch—83 titles (added in 2002)
>
> EBSCO—1,644 titles (added in 2002)
>
> Wiley InterScience—340 titles (added 1/2004)
>
> OVID LWW—187 titles (added 7/2004)
>
> Ingenta—318 titles (added in 2003)
>
> ScienceDirect—1,426 titles (added in 2003)
>
> TOTAL—3,998 titles

Options for access and payments for these different choices are addressed later in the chapter.

Reasons for Pay-Per-View

There are several reasons why Jackson Library decided to provide unmediated pay-per-view access to journals for their users. The first was to provide more titles and more back issues to our users. Another important reason was to allow users to be able to retrieve articles faster than using inter-library loan. The users were given instant access to most journal articles that they required. Based on our experience to date, Jackson Library strongly believes offering unmediated access to pay-per-view titles gives the library a creative tool for ongoing, focused collection development.

Criteria for Selection and Creating Access

Jackson Library uses several criteria when deciding which pay-per-view journals to add. A typical journal would have to meet one of the following requirements: 1) The library does not have a current subscription to the journal; 2) the library has the print version but there is an extra charge for online access; or 3) the library has electronic access through an aggregator, but there is an embargo on the title. Once the journal has been identified, the title is added through our electronic journal management system, Journal Finder.[1] In order to view a pay-per-view article, all users on and off campus must go through an authentication page. Once at the authentication page, the patron is alerted that the library will subsidize payment of the article and to use this service responsibly. The staff at Jackson Library works with the various vendors to provide the most user-friendly and seamless access to these titles.

Implementing the Options

The first option that Jackson set up was FirstSearch Direct Article Access.[2] FirstSearch allows the library to activate selected titles through the administration module for pay-per-view. Libraries can set up deposit accounts to pay for the articles ordered through membership organizations such as SOLINET. The most important feature of FirstSearch is that access to the journal article is easy for the user and has no barriers (such as having to register with the site) to deter users from ordering an article. FirstSearch provides monthly usage statistics from the administration module. The statistics include the title of the journal, the number of abstracts viewed for a given title, the number of articles ordered, and the cost associated with each title.

EBSCOHost Electronic Journal Service Pay-Per-View[3] is the second option Jackson Library used to add titles to our collection. One of the best features that EBSCO Pay-Per-View provides is that the user can view the article he or she has chosen for seven days. EBSCO will set up deposit accounts for libraries and provide a monthly invoice of the articles ordered. The monthly invoice provides the title of the article, date that the article was ordered, the journal title, publisher of the title, cost of the article, and patron's e-mail address. In order to use the EBSCO pay-per-view service, a library must have a subscription to the enhanced version of EBSCO's Electronic Journals Service. When ordering an article from EBSCO, the user must register a name and e-mail address with the company.

The next option that Jackson Library added was Wiley's Article Select.[4] Wiley allows patrons to access the selected journal article for 24 hours. Instead of a deposit account, Wiley has a token system to purchase articles. Libraries can purchase tokens at a certain cost; the more tokens a library purchases, the lower the cost is per article. When ordering tokens from

Wiley, libraries need to know that in order to receive usage statistics on the articles purchased, they must be a Wiley's Enhanced Access License Customer. Tokens are only good for two years. Wiley has different access options for libraries that range from no barriers to the user to a username password that only the library can use.

The most recent addition to Jackson Library's pay-per-view options comes from OVID. OVID is providing pay-per-view access to institutions for the Lippincott Williams & Wilkins journal titles. OVID allows libraries to set up a deposit account to purchase articles. The user can access an article without any barrier. OVID provides monthly usage statistics that include the journal title, the number of times articles were ordered from a particular journal, and the cost of each article.

The next option for pay-per-view that Jackson Library subscribes to is from IngentaConnect.[5] Libraries using IngentaConnect can set up payment accounts to provide users access to articles from non-subscribed publications. IngentaConnect allows the user to view an article for 24 hours. Libraries are e-mailed monthly usage statistics that include the date of order, the patron's name, the journal title, as well as the author, volume, date, and cost of each article. In order for users to receive an article through IngentaConnect, they must register with the site. Once registered, they have to sign in and then retrieve the article they need.

The last option Jackson Library has to offer is from ScienceDirect.[6] ScienceDirect has several ways of setting up pay-per-view. Jackson Library chose the document delivery option. When a user asks for an article, he or she fills out a form and the order is sent to the library via e-mail. The article is then retrieved by a staff member using the library's username and password to ScienceDirect, and then the article is e-mailed to the requestor. If a library has an account with ScienceDirect, it can set up a deposit account for billing. If a library doesn't have an account with ScienceDirect, it can use a credit card to obtain the article.

Usage Statistics

In 2002, Jackson Library started collecting usage statistics for pay-per-view titles. Jackson Library tracked the dates of orders, total titles available, articles ordered, cost associated, and how often titles were accessed through our electronic journals management system (Journal Finder). Table 1 summarizes the statistics from the different pay-per-view options, including dates of coverage, total titles available, total articles ordered from unique titles, articles accessed through Journal Finder, average cost of an article, and the percentage of users who ordered an article after they were forwarded to the pay-per-view Web site. The percentage of users who ordered articles from the pay-per-view sites that did not require a username, password, or registration was significantly higher than those pay-per-view options that had some type of registration. For example, when a user selects a title and goes to the FirstSearch site, following authentication no additional information is required. This explains why the percentage of articles ordered is 47–50%. On the other hand, if a user goes to EBSCOhost for an article, he or she is asked to register a username and password, and this creates a barrier. Because of this, the percentage of articles ordered is only around 16%. These statistics were cited to other publishers like OVID and Wiley in order to help create pay-per-view options that offer seamless and friendly access.

Table 1. Pay-Per-View Usage Statistics.

Options	Dates Ordered	Total Titles Available	Articles Ordered	Accesses to Titles Through Journal Finder	Average Cost of an Article	Percentage of Users Who Ordered an Article after They Visited the Web site
FirstSearch	1/1/2002–12/31/2002	83	84 articles ordered from 28 unique titles	186	$22.75	45%
FirstSearch	1/1/2003–12/31/2003	83	106 articles ordered from 20 unique titles	204	$24.97	52%
EBSCOhost	1/1/2002–12/31/2002	1,644	1169 articles ordered from 360 unique titles	7,296	$19.48	16%
EBSCOhost	1/1/2003–12/31/2003	1,403	829 articles ordered from 320 unique titles	7,630	$22.21	11%
Wiley	1/1/2004	340	463 articles ordered from 127 unique titles	887	$15.00	38%
OVID	7/1/2004 –9/30/2004	187	197 articles ordered from 61 unique titles	423	$22.75	47%
Ingenta	1/1/2003–12/31/2003	318	202 articles ordered from 105 unique titles	1,700	$24.14	12%
ScienceDirect	1/1/2003–12/31/2003	882	149 articles ordered from 72 unique titles	1,825	$22.00	8%

Cost for Pay-Per-View

The total cost for pay-per-view in 2002 was $24,677.00. When tracking statistics, the library also noted how much it would cost to subscribe to these journals. That cost in 2002 came out to be approximately $203,000. Since the pay-per-view program in 2002 had been so successful, we pursued more pay-per-view opportunities with other publishers. In 2003, the cost for pay-per-view increased to $44,189, with journal subscriptions costing approximately $349,000. Jackson Library has identified journals we need to own, and with the new consortia plans for 2005–2007, the library will budget around $35,000 a year for pay-per-view.

Impact on Inter-library Loan

Inter-library loan requests for ordering journal articles have decreased by 18% from fiscal year 2001–2001 to 2003–2004. In 2000–2001, there were 6,371 articles ordered. In 2003–2004, the number of journal article orders dropped to 5,234. With less pressure to order as many journal articles, inter-library loan has been able to keep pace with the new university programs and increasing population without having to add new staff.

Impact on Collection Development

Jackson Library reviewed the titles ordered from January 1, 2002, to December 12, 2003. The staff created spreadsheets that tracked information such as date of order, titles, costs of article, if we owned the journal title in print, and if there was electronic access available through a database aggregator. Figure 1 shows the percentage of articles ordered from unique journal titles. The percentage of titles that had four or fewer articles purchased was 84%, five to nine articles purchased was 9%, and ten articles or more was 7%. The 84% is where we wanted our pay-per-view program titles to fall. Jackson Library focused its attention on the 9% and 7% titles. These statistics were studied to look for ordering patterns for the two-year period. If a journal title had been ordered more than 10 times, the cost for the subscription was less than pay-per-view, and the pattern of orders was scattered over 12 months or more, then the journal title was ordered.

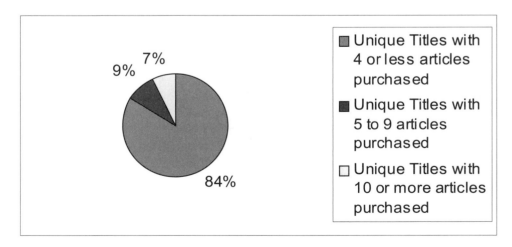

Figure 1. Articles Ordered from Unique Journal Titles.

By the end of 2003, we had recommended 20 titles for new or added electronic access to the subscription. *Current Directions in Psychological Science* is a good example of a new title ordered. The statistics showed that we had ordered 19 articles from this journal at a cost of $21.00 per article. The purchasing pattern for this title was one to two articles a month over a year. The electronic subscription price for that journal was $280.00. *Social Indicators Research* is a title that Jackson Library subscribed to in print, but electronic access cost extra. The statistics showed that 11 articles had been ordered from this journal at a cost of $20.50 per article. Again, the purchasing pattern was one to two articles a month. The added cost for electronic access to this journal is $200.00.

Conclusion

Jackson Library has determined that having pay-per-view options allows us to take a first-hand look at what users need. Since UNCG is growing in several different subject areas, the library needs to add resources to the collection. By providing pay-per-view titles to the users, Jackson Library can monitor usage to see which journals patrons are using and in what subject areas. For the first time, we can offer titles and determine whether or not these titles are being used. In the coming years, Jackson Library will continue to work with publishers to provide pay-per-view content to its users. The library will continue to ask for seamless and friendly user interfaces for pay-per-view titles and continue to monitor usage statistics for collection development.

Notes

1. Journal Finder, http://journalfinder.uncg.edu/uncg/.
2. FirstSearch Direct Article Access, http://www.oclc.org/firstsearch/documentation/daa.htm.
3. EBSCOHost Electronic Journal Service Pay-Per-View, http://www.ebsco.com/home/ejournals/ejsfacts.asp.
4. Wiley InterScience, http://www3.interscience.wiley.com/aboutus/ppv-articleselect.html.
5. IngentaConnect, http://www.ingentaconnect.com (Librarians section).
6. ScienceDirect, http://www.info.sciencedirect.com/accessing_content/pay_per_view/index.shtml.

THE AGONY AND THE ECSTASY: MAKING ELECTRONIC COLLECTION DEVELOPMENT DECISIONS BY COMMITTEE

Eleanor Cook, Professor and Serials Coordinator, Appalachian State University, Boone, North Carolina

The characters and voices (in order of appearance):

> Silky Searyals, Serials Librarian
> C. D. Velmento, Collections Librarian
> Randy Reference, Reference Librarian
> Ernestine Persono, Redundant Publishing
> Elsie Shock, Moredock Publishing
> Mrs. MyTee Big Donor
> Helen, fellow Librarian
> Geeky Gagline, Systems Librarian
> Madame Director

The Players:

> Eleanor Cook, Appalachian State University (Silky)
> Paul Orkiszewski, Appalachian State University (C. D.)
> Allan Scherlen, Appalachian State University (Randy)
> Stefanie Dubose, East Carolina University (Ernestine, Elsie, Helen)
> Lauren Corbett, Emory University (Mrs. Donor, Geeky, Madame Director)

With special thanks to John Abbott, Appalachian State University, Script Consultant.

The "shtick" is *another* day-in-the-life—the "Electronic Resource Committee" is meeting today.

Set:

> Office with table and chairs Laptop computer

Props:

> Fake phone
> Spinner
> Projector showing the players and their names in real life, etc.

Cast on stage:

> Silky Searyals, serials librarian extraordinaire [Eleanor Cook]
> C.D. Velmento, collections librarian [Paul Orkiszewski]
> Randy Reference, reference librarian [Allan Scherlen]
> The Voices (in order of appearance)
>> Voice I: Ernestine Persona, Redundant Publishing (AnsMa)
>> [Stefanie Dubose]
>> Voice II: Elsie Shock, Moredock Publishing (AM) [Stefanie Dubose]

Voice III: Mrs. MyTee Big Donor (phone) [Lauren Corbett]
Voice IV: Helen, fellow librarian (off-stage) [Stefanie Dubose]
Voice V: Geeky Gagline, systems librarian (phone) [Lauren Corbett]
Voice VI: Madame Director (AM) [Lauren Corbett]

Silky Searyals walks into her office, drops her overflowing bookbag. Sits down, musing. C. D. Velmento and Randy Reference enter.

SS: Good morning, Randy. Hi, C. D. Have a seat and we'll get this Electronic Resources Committee meeting started.

The phone rings just as C. D. and Randy are seated and begin whispering to each other.

SS: Guys, I'm going to let the answering machine get it so we can get started. *(waving her hand in that direction)*

Answering machine, Ernestine Persono: "Hi, This is Ernestine Persono from Redundant Publishing and we have just come out with a new 60-volume set covering the salient aspects of Richard Nixon's gardening habits. I am ready to put it in the mail to you on approval, I just need your okay. Please call me back at 884-457-7891 *(so swiftly that it is unintelligible)*. We also have it available on 100 floppy disks that you can load locally for up to one simultaneous user. See ya. Beep.

SS: Sorry 'bout that. Geeky Gagline, in Systems, said she wasn't going to make the meeting this morning, but that she might call. Now—what do we have on the agenda? Let's see, the last time the Electronic Resources Committee met, we reviewed . . .

C. D.: Excuse me, Silky. Randy and I were just talking and we need the committee to discuss Reference's feelings about S.E.X.

SS: What do you mean?

C. D.: The Reference people don't know what to call it and we are loading it into the system.

SS: Say what? SEX? Why are they talking about that?

C. D.: I didn't say S.E.X., I said S.I.X. *(turning to Randy)* Didn't I? Oh well, whatever the hell it is called. I have gotten three e-mails today from Reference and they are totally confused about S.E.X . . . I mean S.I.X. Do we need a task force to rename it?

Randy: Hey, the students might just go for S.E.X.—just look at what they download on the public terminals. But personally, I'd like to propose some twists on the idea of "special effects."

C. D.: Hey, he's got something there . . .

SS: I don't think so. There was something else we were going to deal with today. I had it here somewhere. *(She shuffles through her papers.)*

C. D.: Was it about those publisher changes? I heard that Klinger bought out Skewer, but I just read in *Serials Times* that Confederate Book Dealers, Inc. may acquire them both . . .

Randy: That can't be right because Tailor & Chef bought CBD, or was it bought by Own-it-All, Inc.?

C. D.: Own-it-All, Inc., believe it or not, was interested, but you're right, it was Tailor & Chef. . . . Anyway, so where do we send our payments now?

SS: Look, guys, these kinds of changes are nothing new, and there has always been a sure-fire way of handling them. Allow the master to demonstrate: My random payment generator has a number of choices. Today's choices are: Own-it-All, Inc., Halibut-Ton Info. Co., Cut 'n Run Subscription Agency, or Sweet 'n Sour Limited. *(Silky pulls out her game spinner thing and flicks it with a finger.)* Let's see . . . the winner is . . . *(They wait anxiously for the spinner to stop.)*

Randy: *(Eager)* What DOES it say?

SS: *(wherever the pointer stops)* It's . . . . !!!!!

C. D.: Excellent. I'll get right on it with accounts payable. *(Starts to exit stage hurriedly as SS signals him to stop. C. D. returns to his seat.)*

SS: Wait—you can do that later—the Electronic Resources Committee still has a lot to cover. We're not done yet.

C. D.: Oh yes. I knew there was a reason I had blocked out two hours on my calendar for this meeting. *(turning to Randy)* They always seem to go on forever.

Randy: Tell me about it. Hey have you gotten tickets yet to the concert? I hear it's nearly sold out.

SS: *(to herself)* I better check my messages from the weekend. Geeky may have left a message for the committee *(presses button. C. D. and Randy continue talking among themselves, oblivious to SS.)*

BEEP! Answering machine, Elsie Shock: Good morning Missus Searles. This is Elsie Shock representing Moredock Publishing of the UK. This call is to let you know that Moredock has acquired 400 of your titles previously owned by StratosVier Publishing. We are prepared to offer you a nine-year contract with the inflation rate pegged to your choice of either the number of Elvis impersonators attending the Super Bowl or something equally as ridiculous. Please call me at your earliest convenience. By the way, until I hear from you, we have turned off e-access to all 400 titles. Cheerio.

> *SS leans back and shakes her head again. Randy and C. D. are still talking, oblivious to SS.*

SS: Ok let's get back to the meeting. Excuse me, guys. Can we get back . . . ? *(The phone then rings and after hesitation and resignation she picks up it up.)*

SS: Hello, this is Silky. How can I help you?

Phone, Mrs. MyTee Big Donor: Miz Silky? Miz Silky? Well hello my dear. How arrrrrrre yoooou? This is Miz Mytee Big Donor, and the head of your university suggested I call you about my donation . . . we have been very good friends for many years . . . .

SS: I haven't heard about this yet.

Phone, Mrs. MyTee Big Donor: . . . from my late husband's priceless collection of fine books and recordings. These items, of course, are near and dear to us and I am sure they are very valuable and my husband, who attended your school for almost a full semester, has remained attached to The University for all these years, rest his soul.

SS: This is really not my area, but tell me what you have . . . .

Phone, Mrs. MyTee Big Donor: Oh Silky! May I call you Silky?

SS: Sure Mrs. Donor (*rolls her eyes and says loud enough for C. D. and Randy to hear*) (*C.D. and Randy take notice.*)

Phone, Mrs. MyTee Big Donor: Let me tell you. We have many years of Reader's Digest Condensed Books in perfect condition. Can you come over to the house today or tomorrow to write down all the titles before you take them . . . in case I need to borrow them back from you sometime?

SS: I am not sure . . . you really need to talk to . . .

Phone, Mrs. MyTee Big Donor: And the records, Silky, the phonograph records . . . they are jewels.

SS: Really, what do you have?

Phone, Mrs. MyTee Big Donor: Let me tell you. You can't find records like this anymore. My husband just adored Burt Bacharach, the Jackie Gleason Orchestra, and Mitch Miller. Best of all, he collected all the Time-Life and K-Tel sets. Of course you'll keep these in my husband's memory in a separate, locked collection, you understand? (*yippy dog barking in the background.*). Silky Dahlin', I have to get back to you. FiFi is demanding my attention. I'll call you back! Bye.

> *SS takes phone from her ear, looks at the handset, and shakes her head again, setting it down. Looks at C. D. and points.*

C. D.: Thanks for taking that one. She'll be on my case soon enough.

SS: Oh yeah—that one is YOURS for sure!

Voice from off-stage, Helen: Silky! There is a campus forum about to start in a few minutes. There's gonna be coffee and cookies. Let's go.

SS: Helen, I'm in a meeting right now, sorry . . .

Helen: Hey, it should be fun. And I think you want to go to this one. The university president is about to announce support for total open access.

SS: Oh, really??? (*C. D. and Randy also look visibly interested.*)

Helen: Yeah, but here's the kicker—he just read an article on open access after C. D. lectured him the other day in Faculty Assembly about the importance of supporting OA. I warned C. D. this could backfire. Looks like the Pres thinks we don't need any more money for serials.

> *SS looks curiously at C. D. He shrugs and holds up his hands, surprised.*

SS: *(after hesitating.)* Sorry Helen, I'm going to have to pass. C. D. and Randy and I are having an Electronic Resources Committee meeting right now. Tell us all about it when you get back.

Voice, Helen: OK—I'll bring you some cookies. . . . Bye.

C. D.: *(yelling to Helen)* Don't forget Randy and me!

Phone rings. Silky answers.

SS: This is Silky. Can I help you?

Voice, Geeky: Silky? This is Geeky down in Systems.

SS: *(To C. D. & Randy)* It's Geeky. *(to the phone)* Hello Geeky. Are you coming to the meeting?

Geeky: You may have gotten my message that I can't make the meeting today. You've probably heard that Sid is off to the Greek Islands on sabbatical for six months and so I'm handling all of Systems for a while, until I can get the adjunct I was promised and my students are trained on the system. Do I need to be at this meeting?

SS: Well, there are those 20 Hungarian math journals with totally different URLs that I need you to link up in the Proxy Server—nothing important though. Will you have time to handle that? *(Rolls her eyes)*

Geeky: Oh heavens! Sid was supposed to do those! I'll try to get hold of Sid by e-mail. He's the only person who can get into that part of the system. But don't worry, I'll take care of it.

Silky: Well, Geeky, I'm so glad to know you are here for us. *(Hangs up and shakes her head)* *(Turning to C. D. & Randy)* Ok, where were we?

Randy: Silky, have you had a chance to check on getting the Mega Resource Database Center. You know, from Storm Publishers?

SS: Randy, I haven't gotten to it. Recently all my time has been taken up with the Hungarian math journals and the S.E.X. project.

Randy: Silky, we're adults here. You don't have to use euphemisms with me, I came to talk business. . . . When do you think we'll be getting the Mega Center Database?

SS: Randy, It costs $90,000 up front and another $30k a year.

C. D.: I suggest we get the Universal Collective Archive Database (otherwise know as U-CAD) instead. If we cancel 50% of our print subscriptions and don't buy anymore electronic resources this fiscal cycle, we can make the first payment now before the discount deadline, and only be committed for two more years.

Randy: But MRDC has a deep discount of 5% if we meet the 48-hour deadline, and the popular culture program needs it for the archives of Spiderman, Batman, and Wonder Woman comics for the past 45 years. Someone promised them it would be up and running this month.

SS: That was the trial. The trial was over last month. Don't you read your e-mails?

Randy: Look, I have been pretty busy too, and not just with S.E.X.!

SS: And anyway, the popular culture program only has 10 students in it, not exactly our largest program.

C. D.: Look—if we subscribe to either U-CAD or MRDC we'll have to kiss Psychopathic Behavior Full text goodbye. After all, the Psychopathic faculty and students are all distance learning . . .

SS: And aren't we glad they're not actually on campus!

C. D. continues: It's the second largest graduate program on campus and our psychopathic resources are pretty skimpy, as Randy pointed out in our last meeting. The pricing has come down from $20,000 to $19,995 per year for this important full text core collection. Well, mostly full text; it doesn't include book reviews, letters, errata . . .

SS: Really, we're at the breaking point with our budget. We can't add much more without canceling current subscriptions. We absolutely have to talk about what subscriptions we need to keep, and what to cancel . . .

Randy: One last thing, Silky. We found out that the University's Poison Dart Frog Research Extension Institute has thousands of free Internet resources that they keep asking about getting into the catalog. Oh my gosh—I have to get going. I have another meeting and I thought this meeting would only last twenty minutes! Gotta go! (Rushes out.)

C. D.: *(to Silky)* Actually, I have to be at that same meeting too. So much for the two-hour time slot! We'll talk more next week See you, Silky. *(to Randy)* Wait up, I have to ask you about that concert.

> *SS shrugs her shoulders in resignation and shakes her head again. Grabs her coat.*

SS: *(to herself)* This meeting is obviously jinxed. *(to Helen, offstage)* Hey Helen, have you left yet? I think I COULD use a break after all . . .

> *Exits hurriedly as phone rings in background.*

Answering machine, Madame Director: Silky, this is Madame Director. I am calling about Mrs. MyTee Big Donor. I meant to call you before. She should be calling you . . . *(unintelligible)*

END.

WHAT ACADEMIC AUTHORS WANT AND FEAR

Anthony Watkinson, Independent Information Consultant, Oxon, United Kingdom

Abstract

This contribution is the write-up by the convenor (a publisher) of a panel session that also included two academic information scientists, a librarian, and the head of an organization representing authors. Our concerns were with what scholars want from their publishing vehicles in the digital environment and what worries them about how their publications may be used or not used. We were mainly interested in journal articles. Publishers tend to interact with academics, and librarians meet them primarily as users, but this schizophrenia can be overemphasized. We tried to set out what evidence there is from our own research and that of others.

Authorship

I am preparing this chapter as the sole author. However, three of the following sections are records of the presentations of my three collaborators in the panel session. With the exception of short introductions prepared by me (indicated in the script by italics), the text of these sections is prepared from material produced by my collaborators, with some editing and splicing by me—as indicated in these introductions. I feel it is reasonable for me to add that I certainly do not agree with everything written by my collaborators, but it was the purpose of the session to provide differing views. They will not agree with me, either.

Introductory Remarks

Most of us who attended the conference are intermediaries, many in scholarly communication. Most of us, although print still plays either a central or at least a large part in our lives, concentrate on the digital environment. We attempt to work out the impact the change in standard format will have on our lives and on the lives of those we serve. Because journals have been online for some time, at least in science and medicine, most academics interact with their formal literature in its digital mode and, to an increasing extent, submit their "manuscripts" in electronic form also. Here we emphasize journals. In the humanities and social sciences and in some applied areas the online journal is not yet occupying a central position. This may be because books or conference proceedings are the main vehicles for scholarly communication, or because many journals are still print only, or for both reasons. Nevertheless, one can generalize that scholarly communication is in general moving in the direction pioneered by STM journals, and this applies to books as well as journals in the humanities and social sciences.

It is often pointed out that academics have a split personality.[1] Publishers meet them primarily as authors or editors. Librarians meet them primarily as users. Publishers tend to feel (with some justice) that they know what their authors want from the vehicles that publishers provide for their formal communications. Librarians lament the fact that what academics learn as users does not seem to have much impact on how they act as authors or editors—or at least not sufficiently.

Yet in a sense it is nonsense to talk about such a dichotomy as if it was much more than a metaphor. Academics are of course rounded personalities, or at least as rounded as most of us—in spite of what we intermediaries sometimes feel. Publishers are always concerned about the way in which academics use their publications, what they want from them as users, and librarians do increasingly take note of how academics understand their role as authors, especially now that many librarians are actively trying to get them to change their habits.

The convenor of this panel is rather hostile to panels that reflect a common purpose and a common framework of ideas. Such panels can often result in advocacy sessions rather than illumination based on dialogue. This panel was not like that for the following reason: It was politely adversarial.

The idea for the panel came to the convenor in the spring. As he will explain in the last section of this contribution, he had been thinking about evidence for supposed attitudes/views of the academic community. The open access (OA) agreement was the stimulus to this interest, but the content was and is wider. He was struck during the spring by one occasion attended and one discussion. During the hearings of the Select Committee of the British House of Commons the evidence given by Jane Carr[2] was challenging. She spoke about academic author concerns resulting in an investigation by the Authors Licensing and Collecting Society (ALCS), over which she presides. Bodies representative of author communities (learned and professional societies) have spoken and written about what authors want (and they will be quoted), but Jane Carr provided another perspective. At the preconference to the Fiesole Retreat in March,[3] a conversation with Dr. Carol Ann Hughes (an academic librarian) suggested to the convenor that interaction with academics as authors was throwing up concerns about publishing that were not coming his way as a publisher. It even suggested that the sort of response to the education sessions mentioned by Dan Greenstein in his Nature article,[4] have some basis in fact, at least in California—rather a surprise to a publisher. We, all of us, rely a lot on our own experience when we make assertions about the wishes of the scholarly body or indeed the national view.

Both Jane Carr and Carol A. Hughes gave presentations as part of this panel.

The first presentation was by Professor David Nicholas of University College London and Dr. Ian Rowlands of City University London. These full-time academic researchers are colleagues in the CIBER Institute. They were academics looking at academic authors. (Their survey is available at http://ciber.soi.city.ac.uk/ciber-pa-report.pdf.) Theirs is by far the biggest and most rigorous survey that has so far addressed the topic of what academic authors want. The presentation by Nicholas and Rowlands summarized this work.

Because the convenor is also a director of the CIBER Institute, he feels that he should explain with some care his relationship to this project, especially as he is also a consultant to the main sponsor, the (UK) Publishers Association. He scoped the project in its original form before the research started. However, he had nothing to do either with the scope or form of the questionnaire or the methodology or the report that was produced when the results came in. For the convenor this last paragraph is important and he will return to it, by implication, in the last section.

In his instructions to the panel, the convenor asked for evidence-based presentations. He was thinking of evidence being equated to surveys in discussions of this type. He now realized that he used the word naively. As will be seen below, Jane Carr kindly took him to task. An example from another field altogether has occurred to the convenor. This is a description of the complex issues involved in evidence-based medicine, now a decade old and maturing, which can be found in an article by Gabbay and Le May.[5] to be found at http://bmj.bmjjournals.com/cgi/content/full/329/7473/1013. In spite of the topic explored here, readers of this contribution interested in "evidence" may find it of interest.

One final word on this point. Most of us select evidence that fits in with what we believe to be the case. In that sense most of us are advocates. We are selling something. We are not dispassionate. However, there is advocacy grounded on evidence, and advocacy that depends on suppression of facts one knows of. I hope all of us are in the former category.

Views from Two Academic Information Scientists

David Nicholas and Ian Rowlands

Professor Nicholas and Dr. Rowlands prepared the text, but Dr. Rowlands gave the presentation. Their heading was "The Author Speaks Out." In the introduction mention has been made of the survey on which the presentation was based and where to find it. I have also explained my own relationship to the work described. The text here is based very closely on the slides and not expanded except to increase clarity in a few instances, because the survey is rapidly being mined for articles and other presentations, some of which have become available since the conference. A list of CIBER publications can be found at http://www.ucl.ac.uk/ciber/virschpub.php. Further surveys are being planned.

The background to this work is an international opinion survey, designed and piloted by CIBER, managed by National Opinion Polls (NOP), and funded by the Publishers' Association and CIBER (January 2004). The Web-enabled questionnaire was based on a critical incident approach. This standard technique involves asking the respondents what happened last time they were published. The mailing lists were licensed from Thomson ISI. The lists were 91,500 senior authors who had published a peer-reviewed journal article in the previous 18 months. The sample was worldwide and covered all the STM disciplines plus social sciences and the humanities. It also covered all sectors, universities, medical schools, government, and industry. The research team received 3,787 fully completed responses from 97 countries. These were checked to make sure that the balance in the original list was retained; it was.

The key finding was that the authors wanted to retain the traditional virtues of the classical print journal. Authors told us that they placed the greatest value on journal titles that were well-targeted, were of high quality and standing, and provided an efficient service. These values probably have not changed much since the birth of the scholarly journal in the mid-seventeenth century. They also wished to have the ability to exploit new publishing opportunities.

Authors are opportunists (as has been shown by other CIBER work presented at previous Charleston conferences) and will adapt their publishing behavior to the available dissemination outlets. The CIBER survey revealed three types of author behavior—"traditionalists," "easy riders," and "speed merchants."

There is no doubt, as is made clear particularly from the free-form comments by those surveyed, that authors want a more liberal and easier to comprehend copyright system. Authors publish for prestige, not for money. Their views are a mixture of indifference, ignorance, and principled resentment. They feel very strongly that they should be able to make freer use of their materials, especially in teaching and within the peer group, than they think they are able to do under current arrangements.

They also say that they want a more electronic mode of scholarly communication. This is probably in line with what publishers are already doing, but nevertheless the wish was expressed.

Although only a small minority of authors have experience of alternative publishing media, more than half say that they MIGHT try self-publishing, institutional repositories, or open access (OA) journals in the future.

What authors do not want is to throw the paper out with the bath water. While many senior authors are aware of the problems facing the journals sector, and many are very unhappy about the behavior of some publishers, CIBER's survey suggests that many aspects of the current system are working reasonably well. Authors' basic needs for journal access, quality markers, registration, and archiving are largely being met.

"Author pays" OA models are deeply unpopular with many scholars, who are resistant both in principle and in practice ("can't pay, won't pay"). The patchiness and complexity of the research funding landscape are major and under-recognized barriers.

Views from an Authors' Representative

Jane Carr, Chief Executive of Authors' Licensing and Collecting Society (ALCS)

ALCS is the UK rights management society for all writers. What this organization does is described at http://www.alcs.co.uk/pages/main_fs.asp?hub=about.

The following is based on a script provided by Jane Carr. Information from the PowerPoint slides presented at the session is integrated where possible and appropriate.

Anthony asked us as panelists to use an evidence-based approach. As I looked for, and at, different surveys of authors' views and different kinds of publishing models and contracts, I realized that the apparent conflicts and inconsistencies stem as much from the questioning as from the responses. To state the obvious, surveys are designed to answer a particular question or group of questions, which must therefore, of necessity, limit the answer. (How many times have you been frustrated by multiple choice responses on a questionnaire, which prevent you from responding as you wish?) Focus groups may produce a more open and wide-ranging debate but can also be subject to the influence of the dominant personality present or a particular group of issues, however well-moderated. One-to-one interviews may draw out detail, but as supplementary case studies to illustrate a particular view or standpoint.

This is in no way intended to denigrate surveying, the value of which has been richly illustrated by David Nicholas and Ian Rowlands. It is rather to remind you of the reasons why we all respond differently, at different times, to different questions or questions posed in a different context, for a different reason, by a different person or group. Authors are no different in this respect. I have therefore found myself looking at surveys and other literature, not so much because of the questions asked but for the clues and common threads in the responses, and for the ways in which the questioning body or the type of questions may have influenced the responses.

For example, when at ALCS we survey our academic authors—of whom there are some 19,000 (all UK) on our membership lists—there is both an implicit and an explicit understanding that we as an organization are concerned with the collective management of what we have historically called secondary rights. We are highly unlikely to influence an academic author's career opportunities or professional reputation (as a university or publisher can), and we cannot play a direct role in extending access (as a library or learned society can). What we offer is public promotion of authors' rights—copyright, moral rights, and the right to remuneration —and payment of royalties on international secondary rights managed collectively on behalf of authors.

To illustrate how this often implicit rather than explicit understanding can influence the response, let me show you responses from different surveys:

First, there is a 1999 international survey for the Association of Learned and Professional Society Publishers conducted by Key Perspectives Ltd (referenced in the concluding section). It is five years old now, but one of the closest to the subject of this session and therefore a good benchmark. There were over 3,218 author responses from a total of 10,970 questionnaires distributed, a response rate of 20.3%. Sally Morris (the executive director of ALPSP) described the aim of the survey in her introduction to the published report. It was that "given all the pressures on the traditional journals model, that learned society publishers should understand what motivated their authors, what worried them about the present system, and how they expected and would like things to evolve in the future."

This, I thought when I joined the ALCS in January this year, was almost exactly what I wanted to know. The four main areas on which opinions had been sought confirmed this—what are the main motivations for publishing, how do authors decide where to publish, what concerns do authors have about the publishing process, and what are their hopes and aspirations for future publishing?

The survey revealed that authors' publishing objectives were communication with one's peers, career advancement, personal prestige, and funding. The last objective was more important in science than it was for the arts. Financial reward was a low priority for more than half the respondents.

Key factors in achieving publishing objectives were communication to the widest possible audience, publication in journals with high impact, quality of peer review, and retrievability through abstracting and indexing. Speed of publication was also highly rated by authors in the sciences. Enhancement of one's personal publications list was more highly rated for authors in the arts.

Authors' rankings of where to publish were as follows:

1. The perceived reputation of the journal (41.4%)

2. Impact factor (16.8%)

3. Subject coverage (6.4%)

4. International reach (5.1%)

5. Inclusion in abstracting and indexing services (4.5%)

Thereafter sciences and arts begin to differ. Arts academics are concerned with page charges and the retention of copyright, and scientists are concerned with speed to publication.

There were concerns about the publishing process. For example, in the section on copyright,

• 27.1% did not know whether copyright policies limited their ability to disseminate their work;

- 61.4% did not know whether copyright policies are regularly flouted by authors;

- 61.4% also thought that copyright should remain with the author (86% in social sciences/education); and

- only 11.1% were prepared to hand over copyright to their employer or funding body.

Other concerns were about the publishing process, in particular publishing delays, where there were fears that someone else might publish similar work first, that the work would be out of date upon publication, and that career progress might be impeded. There were also concerns about peer review. Some felt that there should be a more public, open, and faster system of appraisal, that it blocks innovation and opens the way to plagiarism and bias. It was suggested that payment for reviewing could well be a requirement in the future.

Future developments projected included

- a continuation of the system more or less in the present form (69.7%);

- more open peer review post-publication;

- an increase in electronic publishing and rapid peer review system (50.8%), with concerns about the future of the hard copy journal;

- peer review continuing as essential to the quality of the published work;

- the danger of plagiarism;

- the potential for mixed media; and

- scholarly publishing changing from knowledge dissemination to the building of a CV/reputation (52.9%).

The results of the survey are still valuable today, but what began to interest me was 1) the methodology and 2) the clues to current and future thinking implicit rather than explicit in the responses. In terms of the methodology, the questionnaire was dispatched with a covering letter by participating publishers; responses were to be sent electronically or by post to ALPSP. To what extent would these clear signals that the questionnaire originated from publishers influence the responses? To what extent did the publishers unconsciously "select" their respondents, given that the response rate (of 29.3%) was so high?

Within the responses, the importance of pre-publication dissemination to peers of drafts by e-mail or other means—with all the benefit of hindsight—clearly signals the burgeoning of OA and self-archiving models. Likewise, the somewhat alarming percentage of "don't knows" on key issues in relation to copyright and dissemination (again with the benefit of hindsight) points to alternative copyright models—copyright retention by the author, author pays, Creative Commons—and CopyLeft or anti-copyright movements.

In April and May 2004 ALCS undertook a survey of academic authors, specifically to ascertain what concerns they had about scanning of their works and their subsequent storage and availability for downloading and copying. In this survey the questions on the editing and reformatting of works generated the greatest response rate, with 97% of respondents commenting, particularly on the dangers of editing or the replacement of original words and phrases. A large proportion of writers supported the options of a "print-out once only" facility and a "view on screen only" facility but rejected any downloading of the works on PCs or CD-ROMs. On access to works, over 63% of writers were neutral on their works being accessed from college/university computers or password-protected use by eligible students. Access to anyone via college/university Web sites was opposed by 64%.

Some comments from the survey are worth recording:

- "As different forms of e-learning develop, education at all levels will want to offer access to books, journals, extracts etc. from them in electronic formats. Authors and publishers need to be prepared to agree such access. Equally, institutions and students will need to agree that this does not make the material free and must be paid for."

- "The integrity of text is of prime importance to a writer or translator. On no account should this be altered or amended in any way."

- "I am happy for my work to be available providing it is *not* tampered with, it is properly attributed, and it is used for legitimate study. I do not wish it to be abused by people copying and circulating it at my expense in order to save them cost and time. Authors have to eat!"

- "Once I have published, I am happy for anyone to use my work *on condition I am given credit.* Naturally I prefer, where possible, to get monetary reward, but it is not my primary aim (sorry!)."

Once again, it is the way in which responses and general comments combine to give a picture of underlying needs and concerns that interests me, as well as the reactions to specific questions, and the way in which ALCS, as questioner, may have subconsciously influenced the response. For what is overwhelmingly clear is that this group of authors were very concerned indeed about issues that broadly fall under the heading of moral rights—and in particular acknowledgment for, and the integrity of, their work in a digital environment. And the reasons for those concerns seem to confirm the ALPSP results in relation to why academic authors publish—that is, communication with peers, personal prestige, career advancement, and funding—but, significantly for us as the questioner, add the need for remuneration in a significant number, but by no means all, cases.

In December 2003 ALCS also surveyed authors writing for a mixture of academic and professional journals on the specific issue of the rights that they had retained or assigned. The anger that spilled out into the space for comments took us by surprise, and although anecdotal, it seemed worth noting here since the ALPSP survey had already thrown up an indication of the way authors feel about copyright and specifically its assignment to publishers.

So what have I concluded from all this scouring of surveys and contracts, of open access bulletin boards and discussions with academic authors? Composites can be effective and they can be deceptive; but my initial reading between the lines over the last nine months results in the following summary:

1. Academic authors (indeed all authors) want to be recognized, acknowledged, and rewarded as the originators or creators of their published work. Most expect and want prestige, career advancement, and improved access to funding sources.

2. Not all want to exercise their right to direct financial remuneration. At certain stages in their careers—as research students or in retirement, for example—remuneration will be more important. It is also more important for those operating outside academic institutional structures or for some in the arts and humanities, where research funding is thin on the ground.

3. Access for peers, often as quickly as possible, is essential; wider access outside a peer group appears to be less important. Access for students appears to be seen as an institutional rather than an individual concern in many cases.

4. Copyright is not well understood by a significant number of academic authors, neither in terms of the implications of all rights or copyright assignment nor in relation to what constitutes legal or illegal copying. Those concerned with the protection of authors' rights can get a biased view of how important this is, we recognize, as we will tend only to hear from those authors who have suffered as a result either of assigning rights unwillingly or refusing to do so. In the academic community, copyright may often be seen as getting in the way of access. I am inclined to feel that this is not the fault of copyright itself but of those who exercise it. There were, for example, cases in 2004—individual we hope—of universities requiring copyright assignment from students. Without copyright and the right to remuneration, authors of all kinds are left totally unprotected—I would cite here a Society of Authors survey that found that over 60% of working writers in the UK earn less than £10,000 a year.

5. Infringements of moral rights—inalienable in most of the European Union but not so in the United Kingdom or the United States—give authors real cause for concern in a digital world, even if the rights themselves are not fully understood. Derogatory use, plagiarism, and the widespread cutting and pasting of unacknowledged portions of text are seen as potentially the key concerns, although for the individual it is probably paternity—the right to be recognized and acknowledged as the author of a work—that matters most.

If our members are to be believed, plagiarism is increasing, while understanding of copyright and moral rights is decreasing. Students are rightly encouraged to use the Web for a wider range of sources. Free access to, and use of, information on the Web once an Internet charge has been paid is increasingly seen as a right. The need to acknowledge sources is not sufficiently emphasized. The more apocalyptic see recognition by one individual of the value and quality of the original work of another as being already at risk. Recognition of originality, and even of quality, may itself also be at risk. Not all are so doom-laden. Nevertheless, those authors who have thought about the issues do feel that there is a risk that they will be trapped between the Scylla of uncontrolled use of their work by the individual and the Charbydis of the constraints on access that are imposed by global digital rights management systems, producing acknowledgment and financial return for an ever-decreasing number of producers/publishers.

A View from an Academic Librarian

Carol Ann Hughes

Dr. Hughes has been associate university librarian for public services at the University of California Irvine since March 2002. Some information about her activities in the area covered by this section can be found at http://www.lib.uci.edu/libraries/update/ spring04_rights.html. She is writing up her part in the contribution for an "opinion piece," which should be available as a "guest opinion" at http://www.ucop.edu/lauc/opinions/index. html. The following is a record of her talk, edited from notes and citations provided by her for this purpose.

In my position I have worked with faculty on our campus who are interested in the e-Scholarship program of the UC system. My discussions indicate that faculty want three things from a publication: personal impact, professional use in the future, and social impact for their work. I have come to the conclusion that these three types of impact are best served by authors/scholars managing their own copyright.

There are a few "big picture" points that I would like to make before I discuss what individual scholars want and fear. The system of scholarly communication that we have now was intended to promote international open communication.

The very nature of the academy depends on open communication. The nature of teaching and research is a recursive process that requires the sharing of information and feeding it back into an open loop for others to work with. The American Academy for the Advancement of Science has an eloquent statement from July 2002: "One of the features of scientific information is that it increases in value as more people have access to it and add new insights into its interpretation."[6] A recent report from the Science Advisory Board poll indicates that 80% of their over 1,400 life science and medicine respondents found that the most frustrating thing for them was the inability to get full text.

The nature of public investment in scientific and scholarly communication argues for the widest possible access to this information. Public coffers provide many/most grants, facilities, graduate student stipends, and faculty salaries as they write, edit, and peer review articles.

The nature of information itself militates against being closed. Cleveland writes: "Information tends to leak, that is it is diffusive. The more it leaks the more we have—it expands as it is used."[7]

Proprietary interests have created price and permission barriers that are over-reaching the public good. The merger effect among scientific publishers has compounded the trend to create barriers, as has the scholarly societies' outsourcing of publication to commercial publishers. The Association of Research Libraries (ARL) has called this a "silent crisis" 40 years in the making.[8] As Michael Keller said in the opening keynote speech of the conference, publishers now want to use copyrights to preside over the life . . . or death . . . of information. The USPPI increased 11% per year from 1989 to 1999, while the cumulative price index increased only 3.1% per year in the same time period.

It is important to remember that copyright is not monolithic. It is a "bundle" of rights that can be separated from each other. Authors can retain some rights and totally cede others, they can keep all rights and cede only the first publication right to a particular publisher, and they can keep all rights and grant the educational community free rights to reproduce for non-profit purposes.

Having set the larger context, individual scholars are still looking for personal impact. The measurement of success is not just publishing in a prestigious title. It includes being cited by others. A recent study by Kristin Antelman indicates that open access increased citation rates from 45% to 91% in science/social science articles.[9] Steve Lawrence did a similar study of 120,000 computer science articles and discovered similar evidence.[10] Formerly, being published in the "right title" was a sure way to readership and citation, but the price pressures alluded to earlier have weakened the link between visibility and publication in one specific title.

As Bob Martin stated in the second keynote speech at the conference, we need to allow for unpremeditated and constructive repurposing of content that is unforeseen at the time of creation. Technology presents us with unexpected opportunities at times. For instance, years ago course reserves were photocopies that students often avoided. This fall at UCI, putting reserved articles online has increased electronic usage 42 times photocopy access. A recent study by the Educause Center for Applied Research indicated that 93% of students are positive about electronic course Web sites, and 25% of them value the ability to do online reading most of all.[11] Tenopir and King, in their CLIR study, indicated that personal subscriptions are declining so that faculty depend on library copies (which are declining) and the Web sites of their colleagues for information.[12] They also point out a study by Palmer and Sandler indicating that many faculty think that being able to send an article to a colleague is a major benefit of online subscriptions[13]—remember that research colleagues are most likely to be at other institutions rather than home departments, so local licenses don't cover this need.

All of these uses, which may or may not be easily foreseen, increase visibility and impact of a faculty member's work. Copyright agreements have to take these needs into consideration, and the SHERPA site (www.sherpa.ac.uk) indicates that many publishers are doing just that.

Scholars do care about social impact as well as personal success. The public investment in research was mentioned earlier. SARS, AIDS, and numerous other issues have immediate application to applied disciplines and the general public.

As scholars work together in professional societies, they make statements that reflect their social commitments. Recently such a statement was made by the Association of Independent Research Institutes (AIRI): "Making research results freely available through NIH's PubMed Central (PMC), six months after the study's publication necessarily enhances the efficiency and effectiveness of the biomedical research enterprise and provides the public with access to credible and timely information."[14]

Discipline-based servers are one answer that assists faculty in having social impact as well as keeping up with their colleagues.

Alternative publication models are being actively investigated in this time of price pressures, falling readership, and fewer personal subscriptions. Institutional repositories and scholarly Web sites are two new types of publication that serve multiple faculty needs outside the traditional scholarly communication system.

I mentioned that SHERPA is tracking "scholarship-friendly" partners. The recent ALPSP principles seem to indicate that authors don't care about copyright retention and that it "may not matter."[15] Well, it does matter.

The position of the ALPSP doesn't "jibe" with what Ian Rowlands mentioned about the feeling of "principled resentment" that 79% of his respondents indicated having about having to sign over copyright. This position doesn't address realistically the very nature of information. It doesn't address the needs of faculty for personal use of their own labor. And it doesn't address other important issues that must be solved in the near term, like digital preservation. A study by JSTOR in the Tenopir and King review article indicated that faculty are very concerned about archiving/preservation. If we cannot come up with a satisfactory long-term right to preserve information with current publishers, we in the library world may need to contact individual faculty to ask for inclusion of articles in secure repositories run by us.

The economic use of copyright for market share and profit does not serve the needs of the academy for open access, visibility, and citation. We have to make the system work globally, not just through individual campuses or consortia through individual license negotiations.

We have to stop managing copyright as a "just in case" resource under publishers' control and manage it as a "just in time" resource for the faculty who study, publish, teach, and repurpose information continuously.

A View from a Publisher

In the introduction to this contribution I explained the genesis of the panel and my aims in putting it together. My own relationship to this area of investigation is partly described by my short biography.[16] What this does not explain is that I am also a "real" publisher of learned journals, as the dentistry publisher for Blackwell on a part-time basis;[17] my thinking is informed by daily interaction with academic journal editors. It is not unreasonable for publishers to consider that they represent the academic community in their role as authors. I have argued this elsewhere.[18] I also feel strongly that publishers have as much ability as librarians to take an independent stance and seek to establish the truth, but, because all of us have vested interests, we have to be very careful how we handle surveys in particular. I shall return to this point, but see the thoughts of Jane Carr in a previous section. However, I should also add that I have prepared this chapter of the Charleston Conference Proceedings for 2004 as an independent consultant, and none of those for whom or with whom I work have any responsibility for it.

Let us begin with the purpose of formal scholarly publishing. This is ably explained by Michael Mabe.[19] He picks out the following key concepts: registration, certification, dissemination, and archiving. Authors want to register a discovery as theirs and made by them on a certain date. They want to get their research (and by implication, themselves) quality stamped by publication in a journal of known quality. They want to let their peers know what they have done. Finally, authors to leave a record of their research to posterity. To this one can add the concept of reward, as Roosendaal does.[20] One can delve behind these concepts. One of the few truly scientific works on the journal system, or at least part of it, was prepared by Professor Bryan Coles back in 1993.[21] Coles was both a distinguished physicist and the chairman of a publishing company. His study was based on a questionnaire rigorously applied. This volume is now not easy to access, but some key tables can be found in the work by Mabe cited earlier in this paragraph. Coles conducted an analysis of the motivation for publication, in which he emphasizes the second motive over the first. He makes the point that those filling in a questionnaire do indeed tend to write what they feel they should, but that the second motive is revealing of real intent. On this analysis the real drivers are improved funding (he is dealing with scientists), career prospects, dissemination, and ego.

For the purpose of this contribution and from the point of view of the publisher, the question of what authors want and fear can also be indicated by where they choose to publish and why. Mabe provides slides in the source cited above, one drawn from Coles and one from Elsevier research. Coles picks out habit, quality, collection (the specialization of the journal), and speed (i.e., lack of delay). Elsevier research has picked out from its author surveys the following reasons why their authors publish in a particular journal: reputation, refereeing quality, refereeing speed, impact factor, production speed, the editor and editorial board, the physical quality if the journal, and the services provided by the publisher. I have seen suggestions that the research of a large commercial publisher, if the raw data are not open to scrutiny, must be suspect. My argument would be that it is in the interest of any publisher to find out what its authors want. Publishers want to attract the best authors and, to do so, publish their journals and develop their author gateways to attract them. As far as I know the raw data of none of the surveys mentioned in this section are available, except that from CIBER. If the conflation of questionnaire results from so many authors of articles in so many journals intimidates, there is a fascinating survey by Karla Hahn of just two journals in ecology that gives much the same result.[22] There is a useful table (page 8) taken from the first of two surveys produced for the Association of Learned and Professional Society Publishers,[23] an analysis of submission decision factors for authors in the arts and science fields. For both groups the key factors, for both in order of importance, are the perceived reputation of the journal, the impact factor of the journal, the perceived international reach, and the inclusion in abstracting and indexing services. The last item might seem a surprising key factor unless it is understood for many respondents to mean impact factors. There are other problems of terminology, which I shall return to later. Jane Carr has quoted from this survey at length. She makes some comments about how far it really represents author views, with which I would concur. I would also add that the funding bodies were perhaps too closely involved in the drawing up of the questionnaire and the writing of the report to make it entirely independent, and the sample was significantly skewed as far as both subject area and source of author names are concerned. Finally, Tenopir and King have provided a table looking at the average importance rating of factors for astrophysics authors.[24] Speed of publication and "circulation" are at the top. Their book is the bible for all those concerned with online journals and digital transition. Unfortunately, they only have one short chapter on author (as distinct from reader) behavior.

There is not space here to go into the big question of copyright. Publishers should listen with care to what representative professionals like Jane Carr and Carol Hughes say. Authors appear not to bother too much about copyright as long as they can do what they want with their own papers. The CIBER survey seems to suggest this, and it is the experience of publishers. Nevertheless, copyright has a symbolic position that should not be ignored and appears not to be ignored. There are extensive studies of attitudes to copyright in the Romeo series of papers,[25] which show a certain level of publisher responsiveness. The very detailed work done by the Romeo team, now very available, should be read in the context of the nature of the funding and the reason for the exercise. Professor Harnad was chair of the advisory group.

It could be argued that all these surveys are pictures of a past world and that authors now want something very different. Academic authors have a long history (long in terms of online capabilities) of not taking advantage of the potential of the Web where it means changes in the scholarly communication system. Instances are the journal itself, article structure, and peer review. They have all been condemned as obsolete, but they flourish. That is one view. A different view is that even where the electronic journals have involved apparent opportunities to express one's message with more force (e.g., using multimedia), these opportunities are only just beginning to be embraced, contrary to what had been anticipated. This was one of the discoveries of the pioneering SuperJournal project,[26] now written up by the director David Pullinger.[27] It is the impression of this presenter, and those who quarry the Elsevier database, that there are few changes in attitude among scholars to questions established as being of key importance to them. One of the problems of coming to any sort of conclusion about the nature of transition is that there is a conflation (noted, for example, in the comments of the reports from the Wellcome Foundation) of electronic versions of journals, electronic-only journals, and journals with different business models (primarily open access). There are some hints in the second study for the ALPSP by Key Perspectives.[28] There is, for example, a table showing the relative importance of features of electronic journals when authors are considering where to publish their work. In this table the four features leading the list of those picked out as either very important or important are

The long term preservation of back volumes is guaranteed.

The journal is available in some format to readers in all parts of the world at favorable rates.

The electronic version is available free of charge.

Back volumes are available free of charge.

To this writer, not only is the wording in the description of some of these features odd (to say the least), but the responses are activated in a world devoid of business models.

We are of course getting inexorably drawn into questions of open access. At the 2004 Charleston Conference, open access was the topical concern underlying most sessions.[29] It seems to me that we do not yet have the evidence. The biggest survey yet is again by Key Perspectives. It has been written up as an article.[30] Yet there are only 300 respondents providing answers to questionnaires. It is possible that authors who publish in open access journals may have different motivations and demands, but I doubt it. The view of this writer is that most authors are not primarily interested in whether a journal is OA or not as long as the criteria established earlier in this section of the contribution are met. The debate from this point of view is about the business model and whether or not it works. This is indeed the view of many publishers.

The CIBER survey, cited early in this contribution, did elucidate some author concerns demonstrated in earlier surveys cited. What does "perceived international reach" or "audience size" really mean to actual or prospective authors? Publishers themselves have not always gotten this one right. It is clear from this survey that what authors want is to reach their peers. This is a clarification, not a new view of a new sounding, but it shows the danger of careless wording. Public exposure is not important to most academics. If they want to contribute to the public understanding of science, they write a different piece.

Publishers and author organizations (learned societies) should, however, not fool themselves that the sort of studies we are concerned with here have much significance in the bigger scheme of things. Many OA advocates do not, in the end, care much about what the scholarly author actually wants. The taxpayer argument is the central one, as Peter Suber has discerned.[31] It can be couched as an economic (cost effectiveness) or a moral (information wants to be free) imperative, but it brushes aside selfishness by the academic community. For examples see the various press releases and interviews by Dr. Ian Gibson, the chair of the now well-known Select Committee of the House of Commons on Science and Technology.

Academic publishers and (I would argue) academic librarians, part of whose justification for existence is as intermediaries between scholars, should want to know what academic authors want and fear. They should conduct surveys, but, as is indicated by what I and some of my collaborators on the panel have suggested, they should be conducted properly. Surveys should be framed and conducted by those who have the academic training to conduct proper surveys. The funders should not decide the content of the questionnaire or the way it is handled. The professionals doing the survey should write the report. The sample should be representative—of something. It should be properly sourced. One could go on. Let us hope we continue to find out more and do the job properly and with understanding.

Notes

1. See particularly Michael A. Mabe and Mayur Amin, "Dr Jekyll and Dr. Hyde: Author-Reader Asymmetries in Scholarly Publishing," *Aslib Proceedings* 54, no. 3 (2002): 149–57.

2. http://www.parliament.the-stationery-office.co.uk/pa/cm200304/cmselect/cmsctech/uc399-iii/uc39902.htm

3. http://digital.casalini.it/retreat/retreat_2004.html

4. http://www.nature.com/nature/focus/accessdebate/23.html

5. http://www.lboro.ac.uk/departments/ls/disresearch/romeo/

6. Third paragraph at http://www.aaas.org/spp/sfri/projects/epub/finalreport.html.

7. Harlan Cleveland, "The Twilight of Hierarchy: Speculations on the Global Information Society," in *Information Technologies and Social Transformation*, edited by B. R. Guile (Washington, D.C.: National Academy Press, 1985), 55–80; also available at http://books.nap.edu/books/0309035295/html/55.html.

8. http://www.createchange.org/faculty/issues/silent.html

9. Kristin Antelman, "Do Open Access Articles Have a Greater Research Impact?" *College & Research Libraries* 65, no. 5 (September 2004): 372–82; also available at http://www.lib.ncsu.edu/staff/kantelman/do_open_access_CRL.pdf.

10. Steve Lawrence, "Online or Invisible?" *Nature* 411, no. 6837 (2001): 521; or http://osc.universityofcalifornia.edu/manage/maximize_impact.html and http://www.neci.nec.com/~lawrence/papers/online-nature01/.

11. *ECAR Study of Students & Information Technology, 2004: Convenience, Connection, and Control,* vol. 5, by Robert B. Kvavik, Judith B. Caruso, and Glenda Morgan. (Place: ECAR, 2004).

12. http://www.clir.org/pubs/reports/pub120/pub120.pdf

13. Janet P. Palmer and Mark Sandler, "What Do Faculty Want?" *Netconnect* (Winter 2003): 26–28.

14. http://www.airi.org/federal/airi-statement%20%20on%20open%20access.htm

15. http://www.alpsp.org/2004pdfs/SFpub210104.pdf

16. See http://www.ucl.ac.uk/ciber/peoplewatkinson.php.

17. http://www.blackwellpublishing.com/Dentistry/contacts/

18. See Anthony Watkinson, "Scholarly Communication: What Do Scholars Want?" *LOGOS* 12, no. 4 (2002): 194–98; and Anthony Watkinson, "The Role of the Publisher in Scholarly Communication," in *International Conference on Scholarly Communication and Academic Presses*, edited by Anna Maria,Tammaro (Firenze: University Press, 2002).

19. Michael Mabe, "What Do Authors Really Care About?—What 50,000 Authors Tell Us Each Year" (presentation at Fiesole Collection Development Retreats 2003) [Online], available: http://digital.casalini.it/retreat/retreat_2003.html.

20. For the references to his work, see the longer explanatory summary of these concepts (page 9) in *Final Report from the JISC Scholarly Communications Group (SCG) to the Research Support Libraries Group (RSLG)*, 2002 [Online], available: http://www.jisc.ac.uk/uploaded_documents/rslg.pdf.

21. B. R.Coles, *The Scientific, Technical and Medical Information System in the UK* (London: The Royal Society, the British Library, and the Association of Learned and Professional Society Publishers, 2003).

22. Karla L. Hahn, *Electronic Ecology: A Case Study of Electronic Journals in Context* (Washington, DC: Association of Research Libraries, 2001).

23. *Key Perspectives, What Authors Want: The ALPSP Research Study on the Motivations and Concerns of Contributors to Learned Journals* (West Sussex, UK: ALPSP, 1999).

24. Carol Tenopir and Donald W. King, *Towards Electronic Journals; Realities for Scientists, Librarians and Publishers* (Washington, DC: Special Libraries Association, 2000), 155, table 12.

25. http://www.lboro.ac.uk/departments/ls/disresearch/romeo/

26. See www.superjournal.ac.uk/sj/.

27. David Pullinger and Christine Baldwin, *Electronic Journals and User Behaviour* (Cambridge: deodot press, 2002).

28. *Key Perspectives on Authors and Electronic Publishing: The ALPSP Research Study on Authors' and Readers' Views of Electronic Research Communication* (West Sussex, UK: ALPSP, 2002).

29. See my own comments published in the *Professional/Scholarly Publishing Bulletin* 5, no. 3 (Winter 2004): 4–5.

30. Alma Swan and Sheridan Brown, "Authors and Open Access Publishing," *Learned Publishing* 17, no. 3 (2004): 219–24.

31. See http://www.earlham.edu/~peters/fos/newsletter/01-02-05.htm.

S till an important part of collection development is the future of the book. At the 2004 conference discussions on book issues included a look at the growing field of book history and the decline of the monograph and its implications for library collections.

The Book

JOHN JAMES AUDUBON AND CHARLESTON: REPRINTING OUT-OF-PRINT BOOKS ABOUT AUDUBON AND OTHER NATURALISTS

Christopher Small, President, Zenaida Publishing, Amherst, Massachusetts

With the publication of *John James Audubon: The Making of an American* by the Pulitzer Prize–winning author Richard Rhodes, interest in Audubon and his art continues to grow. In 2004 alone, four books were published about Audubon's life and the making of the *Birds of America* serial, which Audubon published over the course of 11 years. Along with Bill Steiner's *Audubon Prints: A Collector's Guide to Every Edition*, published in 2003, these recent books represent significant contributions to the Audubon library.

However, many important Audubon books remain out-of-print, unavailable to librarians, scholars, and students due to the scarcity and high cost of the remaining copies.

Utilizing technology not available a few years ago, Zenaida Publishing republishes important, out-of-print books related to Audubon and his work. In 2005, it published an updated edition of *The Double Elephant Folio* by Waldemar Fries. First published in 1973 by the American Library Association, Fries's book is known as the "Bible of Audubon scholars." It is the only book that traces and catalogs the surviving complete sets of Audubon's great work, as well as many sets that have been broken up. The 2005 edition features a new appendix researched and written by Suzanne Low, author of *A Guide to Audubon's Birds of America* and an associate in the Department of Ornithology at The American Museum of Natural History. The new appendix updates the status of all known complete and incomplete sets, including information about sets that have been broken up, destroyed, or stolen.

Since out-of-print books are often too rare and valuable for libraries to loan out on a regular basis, Zenaida Publishing plans to reintroduce books such as *The Double Elephant Folio* at moderate prices so that they can once again be available to scholars, students, and enthusiasts. (The 1973 edition of Fries's book, currently priced at $300–$400, when available, will be reissued at approximately $75.)

Zenaida Publishing will follow *The Double Elephant Folio* with a book on Dr. John Bachman, friend of and coauthor with John James Audubon of *The Viviparous Quadrapeds of North America*.

For information on upcoming titles or to be placed on the mailing list, contact Christopher Small at Zenaida Publishing (zenpub@comcast.net).

BOOKS AND SERIALS: OPENING UP THE VALUE OF YOUR REFERENCE COLLECTION

Bonnie Hawkwood, Program Director, eBooks & Distributed Databases, Gale Virtual Reference Library, Farmington Hills, Michigan

I recently read an article in the September 2004 issue of *Against the Grain* in which Dave Tyckoson, head of the Reference Department at California State University in Fresno, waxed eloquent about his attachment to the reference collection outside his office, noting a certain comfort in the presence of books, which sit like "soldiers at attention, awaiting their latest orders."

Tyckoson went on to discuss how his department's shelving statistics show a drop, from 46,000 reference volumes reshelved in the 1994–1995 academic year to 11,000 in 2003. Tyckoson suggests that the future does not look good for reference collections or reference publishers, although he believes that reference librarians will be around to help people use whatever tools are available in the future.[1]

With such a grim prognosis for print reference, is e-reference a solution? The answer to that lies in the many possibilities to expand the use of electronic reference and the benefits offered through this format:

> Libraries may choose to purchase one e-book at a time or subscribe to a predetermined collection such as a resource center.

> Electronic reference has the obvious advantage of providing remote access, with answers delivered 24/7 whether or not the staff are available or the library is open.

> Electronic access allows the library to put its reference content into circulation.

> Electronic databases allow users to search across and within e-books, serials, and primary sources without having to query multiple sites.

> Libraries have the ability to create links from a library or course Web page via persistent URLs, linking the assets of the library to the point of use during completion of course assignments.

> Usage statistics can help drive collection development decisions, much as reshelving statistics have done in the past.

> Electronic reference tools reduce costs for reshelving, repair of damaged materials, and shelf space.

So considering all this, what can we do to open up the value of reference collections? I believe that all of us need to become reference collection evangelists. We need to continually preach the availability and many uses of these collections to end-users.

Academic institutions can do this by embedding these reference collections in curricula, coursework, and even the job placement pages of their Web site. Following are some examples of how librarians have become evangelists and have developed unique ways to open up the value of their reference collections.

Our first example is from Suffolk University[2] in Boston, Massachusetts. The library provides access to e-reference from campus and off-campus and has added e-book MARC records to the OPAC. When a student selects the link, the next screen is the "About this eBook" for that particular title. Here, students can read a description of the encyclopedia, access the electronic table of contents, browse the index, glance at the list of illustrations, or search the e-book.

The Jackson Library Reference Department at the University of North Carolina[3] in Greensboro, led by Kathy Crowe, lists appropriate e-references as well as print encyclopedias on its course guides. Crowe explained that "using the eBooks on the course guide has also been an excellent teaching tool. For years I've passed around print copies of encyclopedias. However, being able to have the class focus on a screen is much more effective. I can show them an entry and how it's useful for background information. Then I can choose a title from the bibliography and go to our catalog to show how to look it up."

The next example is from Washington & Lee University[4] librarian Dick Grefe, who has done an excellent job of integrating e-reference into the library. On their Web site, the library staff have created a page for each resource, with details such as:

Title

Producer

Service

Description

Table of Contents

Usage Tips

Searching

Printing

Descriptors

For example, the entry for *Encyclopedia of Russian History*[5] provides not just a link to a PDF of the table of contents, but also a description of how to use the electronic table of contents. Tools like these will drive usage of the content that the library has selected for its e-reference collection.

At the University of Massachusetts Amherst, Mike Davis, library director, has teamed up with Isenberg School of Management faculty member Gino Sorcinelli to build a curriculum portal for its School of Management (SOM) Course 210. As part of the laboratory assignments, Professor Sorcinelli requires students to select a public company to study throughout the semester. Following is an excerpt from the Academic Information Portal:

You will use a business database, *Business and Company Resource Center,* to conduct the research. Each week thereafter your team's lab assignment will utilize the database to locate reports and articles. Results will be posted in your Team Work Space and shared with other teams throughout the SOM 210 Academic Information Portal."[6]

Toru Chiba, electronic resources librarian at Fairmont State University[7] in Fairmont, West Virginia, was the first to provide detailed information about the eBooks the library had purchased on its portal site, with direct links to the *Gale Virtual Reference Library* platform.

So What Does the Future Look Like?

In my opinion, the publishing industry is doing its best to adapt to the changing usage patterns in libraries. I visit many libraries to talk with our customers, and merely by observing the number of public library patrons or students in the building, it certainly appears that libraries are thriving. Knowing how electronic usage statistics for our databases continues to grow each year, many libraries are using very creative methods to help their patrons access reference information.

Will the reference publishing business be discontinued any time soon? I don't believe so. The newly released statistics from the Association of Research Libraries[8] shows that we are merely shifting resources:

> The percentage of the average library budget that is spent on electronic materials has increased more than fivefold, from an estimated 3.6% in 1992-93 to 25% in 2002-03. 111 ARL university libraries reported spending almost $230 million on electronic resources in 2002-03.

So despite changes in the way people conduct research, and their format preferences, reference collections will always be invaluable, though always evolving.

Notes

1. DaveTyckoson, Dave, "Facts Go Online: Are Print Reference Collections Still Relevant?" *Against the Grain* (September 2004): 34–38.
2. http://library.law.suffolk.edu/search/t?SEARCH=Encyclopedia+of+Public+Health
3. http://library.uncg.edu/depts/ref/bibs/his340.htm
4. http://library.wlu.edu/
5. http://library.wlu.edu/details.asp?resID=257
6. http://www.library.umass.edu/subject/business/som210lab3.html
7. http://www.fscwv.edu/library/findit/subject.shtml
8. http://www.arl.org/arl/pr/suppl_stats2002-03.html

THE GROWING FIELD OF BOOK HISTORY

Ann Copeland, Special Collections Cataloging Librarian, Pennsylvania State University Libraries, University Park

Book history has become an increasingly popular interdisciplinary field of study over the past 20 years. Recent events in popular culture and the media point to this. *The Rule of Four*,[1] a book about two Princeton students who set out to solve the mysteries of the *Hypnerotomachia Poliphili*, a Renaissance text attributed to Frances Colonna, was on the *New York Times* bestseller list for weeks. National Public Radio's *All Things Considered* reviewed the British Library's new digital exhibition featuring 93 copies of Shakespeare's 21 plays in pre-1642 editions on September 15, 2004.[2] The exhibition was reviewed by NPR's film critic, Bob Mondello, because of its many wonderful features: stage history, audio portions of famous actors in soliloquy, information about the historical sources for the plays, and the ability to compare texts side by side. Oprah Winfrey's book club is often discussed in current scholarship on the contemporary reading club culture.

Recently, the following question posted on Ex Libris[3] received 30 responses in one and one-half hours: "I am teaching a rare books class and would like to mention rare books in film. I have so far come up with Name of the Rose, 84 Charing Cross Road, and the Ninth Gate. Can anyone suggest other titles?" (*Ex Libris Sun*, June 27, 2004). The first response was: "Unfaithful, where the public learns two things about the rare book trade: 1.) rare book dealers are sexy, and 2.) getting blood on the dust jacket of a Jack London first edition is a bad bad thing."[4]

Although I was impressed by the lively suggestions, I was concerned about how our library might support a request from a faculty member to obtain these films for reserves. This caused me to think about how libraries are supporting pedagogy in book history at our universities currently and how the growing interest in the field might be supported in the future.

When I was first given collection development responsibilities in the field of history of the book (HISBK fund), I quickly realized that my conceptions about the titles we would purchase and the amount of funds allotted were both limited for today's growing field of book history. This chapter looks at the expansion of the field over the past two decades, what it has meant in terms of publishing, and how we can support pedagogy in book history/book studies in our library collections.

Background

From the nineteenth into the mid-twentieth centuries book history was largely the domain of Anglo-American bibliographers. Analytical bibliography, as epitomized by McKerrow and Bowers,[5] concentrates on the book as a physical object. These bibliographers have looked to physical evidence to reveal the production of texts, striving to find the ideal copy. Therefore, book history in the early twentieth century concerned itself with printing and the related arts and technologies involved in the production of the hand-printed book—including papermaking, typography, illustration, binding, the book arts, book publishing, the book trades, book collecting, etc.

It wasn't until the middle of the century that academic historians began looking at the subject "as a key to social and cultural history."[6] In the 1960s in France, a new strain of book history developed, *Histoire du livre*. The pioneering text of this movement, *L'Apparition du livre*—translated as *The Coming of the Book: The Impact of Printing 1450–1800*[7]—ushered in the new field. The French approach consisted of quantitative social history, using mathematical formulae and drawing on detail to understand the role of books in society.[8] This study, concentrating on the most ordinary sorts of books and the literary experience of ordinary readers, could not have been more foreign to English-speaking bibliographers, who studied rare books and fine editions.

The Anglo-American bibliographers and the French social historians had little in common and were divided, until several American historians studying Europe saw the value of *Histoire du livre*. Two important books at the end of the decade—Elizabeth Eisenstein's *The Printing Press as an Agent of Change*[9] and Robert Darnton's *The Business of Enlightenment: A Publishing History of the Encyclopedie 1775–1800*,[10] related the development of the printed book to broader social and political movements.[11] Elsewhere in academia, discourse was changing. English departments in the 1970s were looking less at texts themselves and more at the responses of readers to those texts. American historians at this time were led by egalitarian impulses to examine the experiences of minorities, women, and urban workers, which "created restlessness with the text-bound outlook of intellectual history as well."[12]

In 1980 the Rare Books and Manuscripts section of the Association of College and Research Libraries (ACRL) held an international conference in Boston on the theme "Books and Society in History."[13] That conference resulted in the published *Boston Statement on the History of the Book,* which called for funding, new programs—seminars, workshops, and conferences—and research on an international scale. Significant in the statement is the explicit use of the expression "history of the book" to refer to all aspects of the history of production, publication, and distribution, from the stage of authorship to the impact of books on readers and, ultimately, society. This statement, drafted by international and esteemed scholars in the field, symbolized the coming together of the two opposing schools of thought and their desire to bring interpretations of book history into one international whole.

The meeting point was articulated by the esteemed bibliographer G. Thomas Tanselle. He noted that the very question posed by *Histoire du livre*—"Did the material basis of literature and the technology of its production have much bearing on its substance and its diffusion?"—is the same question that English bibliographers from McKerrow onward have been asking. "Their goal may have been the editing of a literary text but they have seen that they must investigate how the material processes in the transmission of a text affect the words and punctuation, that is, the content—of the text itself."[14]

By the time of this ACRL conference, the French-influenced field of book history was already two decades old. In 1982, in his famous essay "What Is the History of Books?" Darnton declared it to be such a rich and varied field of study that it was less like a field and more like a rain forest: "The explorer can hardly make his way across it."[15] Darnton wrote about running into an undergrowth of journal articles, a crisscrossing of disciplines: "The history of books has become so crowded with ancillary disciplines that one can no longer see its general contours."[16] To provide some means of organizing the subject as a whole, he proposed a model for analyzing the way books come into being and spread through society—a communications "circuit" that joins authors, disseminators, and readers. Darnton's model is still widely discussed today.

Programmatic Expansion

In 1984, the American Antiquarian Society (AAS) held a conference, "Needs and Opportunities in the History of the Book," which established an ambitious research agenda.[17] In 1991, the Society for the History of Authorship, Reading, and Publishing (SHARP) was founded. SHARP, the leading international scholarly association for historians of print culture, consisting of more than 1,200 book historians worldwide, has as its focus "the creation, dissemination, and reception of script and print, including newspapers, periodicals and ephemera."[18] The impact of SHARP, its journal, and its annual conference has been significant in spreading book history into other disciplines.

In the introduction to the first volume of *Book History*, SHARP's journal, in 1998, Jonathan Rose and Ezra Greenspan wrote about how book history is energizing established fields of study: history, church history (every religious denomination is also a publishing firm), classics, musicology, and Russian studies. Scholars in all these fields are looking to the role of print in their disciplines. Even "[l]ibrarians, once consigned to the margins of academia, are now venturing into the mainstream of social and cultural history, exploring the role of libraries in shaping reading tastes, assimilating immigrants, censorship, racial segregation, prisons, and the Nazi holocaust."[19]

How has this growth of interest in book history affected published scholarship? In "What Is the History of the History of Books?" Joan Shelley Rubin states that between 1985 and 2001, the *Journal of American History* alone ran roughly 60 reviews of monographs on subjects pertinent to the printed word.[20] She suggests that the output is so significant that historians of the book have even endorsed a classification system involving three rubrics to organize such works: production, distribution, and reception. Authorship and editing as well as technology and the economic forces that shape the business of publishing fall under production. Distribution refers to all the activities that bring print to people, such as advertising, bookselling, censorship and self-censorship, libraries, and schools. Reception, synonymous with reading or use, may be public, private, oral, silent, individual, or collective. Reception refers to how as well as why and what readers read.

Avalanche of Literature

Recently, Edward Goedeken in *Libraries and Culture* referred to the publishing record in this way: "The veritable avalanche of literature devoted to the study of print culture could aptly be described as the monster that ate Pittsburgh."[21] He noted that in one year, works on "Reading, Printing and Publishing" included histories of the paperback; the American newspaper; publishing in the old West; publishing in New England; and histories of reading, such as why and what we read, or did read, the reading habits of homefront Americans during the Civil War, African American literary societies from late eighteenth-century slave communities through the Harlem Renaissance, and the reading habits of Osage, Iowa, based on circulation records from the local public library.

I did a very quick, unscientific study, to see if I could quantify this publishing record in some way. A few caveats. I searched OCLC for a 30-year period in 5-year segments. OCLC didn't really get up and running until the late 1970s for libraries, so some titles with these headings may just not have been caught by OCLC in the early years. Since OCLC includes records contributed by members, keep in mind that catalogers don't always assign the same headings. I limited my search to books and excluded juvenile materials. Books in English are included in parentheses, and I have highlighted the top years for sheer number of titles. The years 2000–2004 are short because they don't reflect the full five-year term; not all publications from 2004 have been cataloged or cited yet.

Looking at the numbers, some trends are visible. Books with the LC subject headings "Book Industries and trade" and "Printing" were more plentiful in the late 1970s and 1980s. (See figures 1 and 2.)

	OCLC SH: Book Industries and Trade	
	Titles	(English)
1971-1975	429	(223)
1976-1980	686	(346)
1981-1985	**724**	**(390)**
1986-1990	**763**	(365)
1991-1995	669	(262)
1996-2000	697	(284)
2001-2004	382	(166)

Figure 1. Books about Book Industries and Trade.

	OCLC SH: Printing	
	Titles	(English)
1971-1975	1,404	(877)
1976-1980	**1,617**	**(1,060)**
1981-1985	1,504	(899)
1986-1990	**1,628**	(1,026)
1991-1995	1,526	(937)
1996-2000	1,329	(752)
2001-2004	674	(402)

Figure 2. Books about Printing.

Works on publishing were greater in number in the 1990s. (See figure 3.)

```
                      OCLC
         SH: Publishers and Publishing

                  Titles  (English)
         1971-1975    747    (449)
         1976-1980  1,113    (653)
         1981-1985  1,389    (752)
         1986-1990  1,723    (880)
         1991-1995  2,000    (939)
         1996-2000  2,129    (983)
         2001-2004  1,717    (862)
```

Figure 3. Books about Publishers and Publishing.

But compare these numbers with those for books on reading, which are considerably higher in the 1990s. (See figure 4.) There were 1,000 more books published on reading in the early 1990s than in the early 1980s.

```
                      OCLC
           SH: Books and Reading

                  Titles  (English)
         1971-1975  1,306    (894)
         1976-1980  1,975  (1,138)
         1981-1985  2,308  (1,402)
         1986-1990  3,302  (2,296)
         1991-1995  3,618  (2,560)
         1996-2000  3,750  (2,523)
         2001-2004  2,099  (1,443)
```

Figure 4. Books about Books and Reading.

And if we compare all four topics for the late 1990s, we see that books on the subjects printing, book industries and trade, and publishing are fewer in number than those on books and reading. (See figure 5.)

```
                OCLC 1996-2000

      Subject Headings              Titles       English


   •  Book Industries and Trade      697        (284)

   •  Printing                      1,329       (752)

   •  Publishers and Publishing     2,129       (973)

   •  Books and Reading             3,750      (2,523)
```

Figure 5. Comparison of Books about All Four Topics.

I also searched the MLA *Bibliography* for trends in publishing after 1980 on various subjects. There were many more citations for "Analytical/Descriptive Bibliography" in the 1970s than in all the years following. This agrees with the predominance of traditional Anglo-American bibliography in the earlier years, before the influence of *Histoire du livre*. (See figure 6.)

```
                MLA Bibliography
        Analytical/Descriptive Bibliography
                  # of Citations
        1970-1980*           771
        1981-1985             50
        1986-1990             51
        1991-1995             40
        1996-2000             25
        2000-2004             17
```

Figure 6. MLA *Bibliography*, "Analytical/Descriptive Bibliography."

The subject Printing History has been strong all along. (See figure 7.)

MLA *Bibliography*
Printing History

Years	# of Citations
1970-1980	49
1981-1985	151
1986-1990	144
1991-1995	140
1996-2000	**163**
2000-2004	118

Figure 7. MLA *Bibliography*, "Printing History."

But the growth in readership and authorship studies in the late 1990s is also very apparent in these numbers. (See figures 8 and 9.)

MLA Bibliography
Reading

	Readers	Reading	Readership
1970-1980	745	2434	11
1981-1985	536	2361	39
1986-1990	536	3695	55
1991-1995	625	4812	76
1996-2000	**838**	**5700**	**81**
2000-2004	581	3393	57

Figure 8. MLA *Bibliography*, "Reading."

```
                MLA Bibliography
                    Authorship
    1970-1980*          278
    1981-1985           495
    1986-1990           585
    1991-1995           721
    1996-2000           874
    2000-2004           556
```

Figure 9. MLA *Bibliography*, "Authorship."

In the increase of citations for authorship, readership, and print culture studies in the MLA bibliography, we may be seeing the influence of SHARP and the research agendas set out in the mid-1980s on scholarship in book history. (See figure 10.)

```
                MLA Bibliography
                   Print Culture

    1970-1980            1

    1981-1985            2

    1986-1990            3

    1991-1995            39

    1996-2000            144

    2000-2004            173
```

Figure 10. MLA *Bibliography*, "Print Culture."

A recent posting on the SHARP listserv asking for any new books on the history of reading since 1999 drew a long list by many authors scattered across disciplines. Classification numbers in the Library of Congress Classification System ranged widely, from PR—English literature and PN—Literature, general, to DA: History of Great Britain, Z1003—Books and Reading, and BR for Christianity. Some examples:

- Lori Newcomb, *Reading Popular Romance in Early Modern England* (Columbia) PR2544.P33N49 2002

- Bernadette Cunningham and Maire Kennedy, eds., *The Experience of Reading: Irish Historical Perspectives* (Social History Society of Ireland) Z1003.5

- Elizabeth McHenry, *Forgotten Readers: Recovering the Lost History of African American Literary Societies* (Duke) PS153.N5M36 2002

- Brian Stock, *After Augustine: The Meditative Reader and the Text (U Pennsylvania Press)* BR65.A62S746 2001

Even within one publisher series on a particular subject the classification numbers range widely. For example, in the Cambridge studies in publishing and printing history, there are at least nine distinct call numbers, from the Bs to the Zs. In terms of collection development, if we are to support book studies/book history at our institutions, we will have to keep an eye on the wide range of disciplines touched by print culture studies.

Engaging the Field

The selector will also need to stay abreast of SHARP and Ex Libris listservs, where publications are announced. Getting to know the movers and shakers emerging in this field will also be important, the scholars as well as the institutions. For instance, the American Antiquarian Society (AAS) has taken an active role in publishing, sponsoring publications and lecture series. Periodicals such as *RBM: A Journal of Rare Books, Manuscripts, and Cultural Heritage* (ACRL, Rare Books and Manuscripts Section), *Book History* (SHARP, published by the Penn State Press), *Studies in Bibliography* (Bibliographical Society of the University of Virginia), *Printing History* and *Publishing History* (American Printing History Association), and , *Libraries and Culture* (University of Texas Press) are essential to the study of book history. And an increase in monographic series from university presses on print culture and book history signals a welcome trend in scholarly publishing.[22] Major national histories of the book are in press and will be essential purchases for our collections as well.

The selector should take note of the numerous groups, meetings, workshops, and conferences nationally and internationally concerned with book history. Major centers and programs are institutionalizing book history in the United States and abroad, even as graduate and undergraduate degree programs, bringing new generations of academics into the field.

Book History Pedagogy

The more that book history is spread through the disciplines, the more libraries have an opportunity to be engaged with the field. A fine example is the digital exhibit at Wesleyan, *"Old Books, New Pedagogy: Special Collections and Archives in the Curriculum"* which "highlights new pedagogical uses for old books, as well as periodicals, archival collections, and other primary sources" (http://www.wesleyan.edu/libr/schome/exhibit/index.htm).

The teaching of book history itself is becoming a topic of study. Rare Book School in Charlottesville, Virginia, offers a course entitled "Teaching the History of the Book" ("aimed at academics and librarians who are currently teaching undergraduate or graduate courses dealing with the history of books and printing, this course will emphasize not history but pedagogy").[23] A volume on the teaching of book history (including analytical bibliography, printing, book design, collecting, connoisseurship, etc.) at the undergraduate and graduate level and in library school programs is underway.[24] And the publication of two titles—one a reader of classic writings in the field of book history[25] and the other a selection of texts, resources, and an image archive to aid in teaching American book history[26]—signals the coming of age of this field.

When Darnton wrote in 1983 about the field being so crowded that it was hard to see the contours with the "crisscrossing of disciplines," he might not have imagined the next big frontier—print on the Internet. What will this do to add to the "avalanche of literature" that is print culture studies? As publishers' archives remain a largely untapped source, there is no dearth of material for the scholar of book history. Libraries need to prepare for the critical role they will continue to play in support of the field as providers of both primary resources and secondary materials.

Notes

1. Ian Caldwell and Dustin Thomason, *The Rule of Four* (New York: Dial Press, 2004).

2. www.npr.org Archives

3. Ex Libris (an electronic news and discussion group for those interested in rare books, manuscripts, special collections, and librarianship).

4. http://palimpsest.stanford.edu/byform/mailing-lists/exlibris/2004/06/msg00133.html and thread.

5. Ronald B. McKerrow, *An Introduction to Bibliography for Literary Students* (Oxford: Clarendon Press, 1927); Fredson Bowers, *Principles of Bibliographical Description* (Princeton, N.J.: Princeton University Press, 1949).

6. Robert A. Gross, "A Text for Our Times" in *Perspectives on American Book History* (Amherst: University of Massachusetts Press, 2002), 2.

7. Lucien Febvre and Henri-Jean Martin, *The Coming of the Book: The Impact of Printing 1450–1800* (London: New Left Books, 1976).

8. Kenneth E. Carpenter, "Preface," in *Books and Society in History: Papers of the Association of College and Research Libraries Rare Books and Manuscripts Preconference, 24-28 June, 1980, Boston, Massachusetts,* edited by Kenneth E. Carpenter (New York: R. R. Bowker, 1983), vii.

9. Elizabeth Eisenstein, *The Printing Press as an Agent of Change* (Cambridge: Cambridge University Press, 1979).

10. Robert Darnton, *The Business of Enlightenment: A Publishing History of the Encyclopedie, 1775–1800* (Cambridge, Mass.: Harvard University Press, 1979).

11. Carpenter, "Preface," viii.

12. Joan Shelley Rubin, "What Is the History of the History of Books?" *Journal of American History* 90, no. 2 (2003): 556.

13. "A Statement on the History of the Book," in *Books and Society in History: Papers of the Association of College and Research Libraries Rare Books and Manuscripts Preconference, 24-28 June, 1980, Boston, Massachusetts,* edited by Kenneth E. Carpenter (New York: R. R. Bowker, 1983), xii.

14. G. Thomas Tanselle, "Introduction" in *Books and Society in History: Papers of the Association of College and Research Libraries Rare Books and Manuscripts Preconference, 24-28 June, 1980, Boston, Massachusetts,* edited by Kenneth E. Carpenter (New York: R. R. Bowker, 1983), xxii

15. Robert Darnton, "What Is the History of Books?" in *Books and Society in History: Papers of the Association of College and Research Libraries Rare Books and Manuscripts Preconference, 24-28 June, 1980, Boston, Massachusetts,* edited by Kenneth E. Carpenter (New York: R. R. Bowker, 1983), 5.

16. Ibid.

17. Rubin, "What Is the History of the History of Books?"

18. SHARP Web (http://www.sharpweb.org/intro.html).

19. Jonathan Rose and Ezra Greenspan, "Introduction," *Book History* 1. no. 1 (1998): ix–xi.

20. Rubin, "What Is the History of the History of Books?"

21. Edward A. Goedeken, "The Literature of American Library History, 1999–2000." *Libraries and Culture* 37, no. 2 (2002): 138.

22. For example, the University of Massachusetts (Studies in Print Culture and the History of the Book), the University of Toronto (Studies in Book and Print Culture), the University of Wisconsin Press (Print-Culture-History-in-Modern-America), the British Library (British Library Studies in the History of the Book), and Cambridge University Press (Cambridge Studies in Publishing and Printing History).

23. Rare Books School (http://www.virginia.edu/oldbooks/).

24. *Teaching Bibliography, Textual Criticism, and Book History,* announced on SHARP-L, February 13, 2004.

25. *The Book History Reader,* edited by David Finkelstein and Alistair McCleery (London, New York: Routledge, 2002).

26. *Perspectives on American Book History: Artifacts and Commentary,* edited by Scott E. Casper, Joanne D. Chaison, and Jeffrey D. Groves (Amherst: University of Massachusetts Press, 2002).

WHITHER THE BOOK: STUNTING THE TREE OF KNOWLEDGE?

Milton T. Wolf, Head, Collection Management, University of Central Florida, Orlando

As most everyone knows, there has been a significant decline in the number of monographs being added to academic library collections over the past 20 years (for the purposes of this chapter, the term "book" is used synonymously with "monograph," and references those publications that tend to provide a linear, in-depth analysis that contributes to scholastic research). What are its causes? Why the concern? What value to scholarship does the monograph have over a journal article? What is the proper balance among the various information formats that can be added to an academic library? And, if monographic acquisitions are not in balance, what can, or should, be done about it?

These were some of the questions that a panel at the 2004 Charleston Conference wrestled with, and its exploration of these queries, along with the audience's contributions, proved to be engaging, provocative, and insightful. While no "one-solution-fits-all" answer emerged, there was agreement that the questions posed were legitimate concerns and that, perhaps, a new definition of a "book/monograph" was being born at the very same time that a digital transformation and the economic remodeling of information containers were taking place. There was also agreement that during this disruptive transition phase the best solution might be one of watchful waiting and fine-tuning of the instruments already available to us.

The Economic Model

Although no one could deny that there appeared to be a coincidental link between the continuous escalating prices of serial subscriptions and the concomitant decline of book purchasing in academic libraries, the major problem appeared to have more to do with the economic model of "bundling" used to sell serials, the "Big Deal," than with the importance of journals/serials for research. In other words, librarians decried the extravagant expense associated with choosing only the individual serial titles that they needed compared to the only slightly less astronomical expense of purchasing the serial "bundle," which includes most everything the publisher produces—even if most of it has little, or nothing, to do with the research that the library is attempting to support!

Caught between this economic Scylla and Charybdis, the old budgetary formulae (of the 1960s through the 1980s) dictating a healthful balance between acquisitions of books and serials of 60/40%, later 50/50, and, finally, in the 1990s succumbing, in some places to 20/80, are no longer useful. (More recently, many libraries face the largely agreed upon unbalanced ratio of 10/90!) Obviously, if this imbalance persists we are perilously close to throwing the baby out with the bath water and will be adding few or no books to our collections.

Digital Dyspepsia

The last two decades have seen digital technology affect scholarly communication in both positive and negative ways. On the positive side is the introduction of the e-book, which has had more success as a way of quickly referencing parts of books than as a way of reading them; however, in the areas of history, particularly, the e-book has provided a new and valuable research tool that lends itself to exploiting that discipline's need and desire to "link" variegated formats of historical information. This makeover of the book puts forward a digital, cyber environment that borders, at times, on a virtual reality of information that is partly defined by the chosen interactions of the user.

While this newfangled "book" also contains the more recognizable linear text of its paper lineage, it sports an amazing number of technological updates that permit more interplay of text, graphs, maps, pictures, and so forth than previously available in the traditional monograph. Whether other disciplines will gravitate toward this new format, and whether the format will be given the imprimatur of promotion and tenure committees, will be seen; however, as an economic model it seems to have possibilities.

On the negative side, digital technology has largely become the preserve of multinational information corporations, who quickly seized the high ground by consolidating their hold on science, technical, and medical (STM) publications, turning a huge profit from their virtual monopoly on STM (and legal) publications, especially serials. Journal publications in the STM area and their rapid commercialization (abetted by congressional passage of the 1998 DMCA legislation, which ensures decades of copyright monopoly to journal publishers) have inundated the academic and research markets. Utilizing business models like "bundling" (similar to those foisted on the consumer in the cable industry), serial prices have been driven relentlessly higher while thoughtful selection of individual titles has been economically perverted.

This economic invasion has come, unfortunately, at the expense of library acquisitions in the humanities and social sciences, which rely more heavily on the monograph (it's the gold standard for promotion and tenure) as a vehicle for intellectual examination. While many serials (especially STMs) are generated for their income-producing capabilities, academic monographs are largely subsidized by university presses and provide but marginal profit for commercial firms, leaving monographic publishing in the humanities and social sciences ill-prepared to compete for space on the ever more commercial shelves of the academy. It appears that the monograph, as we have known it, is in need of some resuscitation if intellectual inquiry is to flower again within the present scholarly communication paradigm.

Although it is often true that as Science turns, so does the World, a university should be supporting more than just the sciences, whose serial subscription costs alone have largely bankrupted the library acquisitions budget and diminished the information resources of the social sciences and humanities to the point where many institutions are incapable of supporting both teaching and research in those areas. The collections of the humanities, in particular, have been ruthlessly pared down at the expense of "scientific progress," which may turn out to be not much progress at all, if intellectual inquiry has been put into the commodified traces of the convenient, digital sound byte of non-leavened thinking. The study of the humanities and social sciences, steeped as they are in expansive examinations of all of humankind's advances, declines, and uniqueness, provides a needed balance to the powerful tools sparked by science and generated by technology.

Cognitive Dissonance

Writing, and reading, a book requires attentive focus that is far unlike the digestion of "bytes" of information found in articles. The cognitive process is more severely challenged when concentrated attention is required to organize and imagine large quantities of information scattered over not only large swaths of history but also innumerable disciplines of thought (including the scientific method). Synthesis is more often needed to humanize analysis. "Botanizing on your mother's grave" is to miss the experience at hand, the very real experience of learning what we are, and can be!

Knowledge is built on mistaken paths, on argument, diversity, and conflict; it is always under construction. Ultimately, judgments have to be made. And woe to that civilization that has not come prepared to make choices, hopefully informed choices! And, to be so informed, a society will have to collect as much information as possible, in all fields of endeavor, to find the proper balance that takes data, facts, information, and knowledge and distills wisdom. To do this, libraries must contain more than just science, more than just serial subscriptions. In today's "info sphere," there must be a place, too, for the cognitive distillation known as the "book."

How Subscribing to Books Controls Serial Expenditures: A Modest Proposal

One of the options for protecting the acquisition of books in libraries is to acquire them the same way that serials are required: by subscription! At the beginning of every fiscal year, libraries pay astronomical sums to subscribe for the entire year to publications (e.g., *Nature, Science, Atomic Research*) that they have not even received yet, and whose content is largely unknown at the time of ordering. Then, as happens more regularly than ever before in the history of academia, when money is needed by the administration (be it the library or university), they take it from the "book budget." Because the money for serials has already been expended, it is truly only the "book budget" that gets plundered. Is it any wonder that there are fewer books in academic libraries?

So, just to get things back on an even keel, expend the "book budget" before you send off the majority of the acquisitions money for serials. If your state permits it, use a deposit account with book vendors. If not, consider using the same legal contract that you sign with serial publishers, only put in the name of a monographic vendor. (Hey, the information is only in a different format!) Remember, part of your sworn duty as a librarian is to "love, honor, and negotiate." Let them eat serials! They have been eating monographs for over 20 years now. You're just trying to restore some balance in information collecting.

Another idea, perhaps not so advanced as the last one, for beefing up the monographic collections, but nonetheless effective, is paying more attention to attracting gifts, especially books. Too many libraries only think of the Gifts area as a place for book sales to the local community. Listen, there is gold in all those old books that are dropped off regularly by faculty, students, and the local community, and with a little effort you can increase the take. Most books are only in print a very short time, so if you missed acquiring them (and you probably did), this is another chance—at a very reasonable price.

If you have a library development officer, get him or her into the act. You're not too proud to take gifts in kind (like books, serials, videos, etc.). And you never know what they might send over the transom next. And while you have that development officer's ear, how about handing out some flyers at the next game of football, basketball, baseball, volleyball (all those academic sporting events) asking all those fervid fans if they could support the old alma mater library by dropping off a few books. You'd be surprised by how many of them read, or at least have books!

Conclusion: You Can't Have What Won't Sell

Publishing academic books is economically inefficient, because they are 1) specialized subject matter (therefore only a small number of consumers are available), 2) relatively voluminous (thereby more expensive to produce), and generally provide information that does not meet the criteria of profit-motivated publishing organizations (in short, the research has little practical value in a material culture). In short, under the present economic paradigm the book, the academic monograph, cannot be sustained unless we come to a better understanding of its value to the university environment, of its relevance as a tool of learning, and of our complicity, unwitting perhaps, in its demise.

Already STM publishing, especially medical publishing, is coming under fire for its increasingly compromised research (it's hard not to emphasize certain aspects of your research, when you are being rewarded to support certain conclusions), and sometimes it's even harder not to come to those conclusions when the research databases only contain the information provided by the same multinationals that originated the research grants in the first place. More and more, other countries are building their own research facilities and databases in order to escape the information hegemony imposed on them by multinational corporations, and to explore other, more promising, research directions (e.g., global warming, environmental biology, alternative energy sources, cloning and stem cell research) not always available in global, commercial databases. Unless knowledge is decoupled from profit, there is little chance that the outcome will be socially salubrious, or that research will be untainted. And, although the book may morph into an electronic entity that fits the economic model of the moment, it may be that the real artifact in the future is pure research.

Bibliography

Books

Briscoe, Peter. *Reading the Map of Knowledge: The Art of Being a Librarian.* Grand Terrace, Calif.: Palo Verde Press, 2001.

Articles

Albanese, Andrew Richard. "Moving from Books to Bytes."*Library Journal* 126, no. 14 (September 1, 2001) 52–55.

Chodorow, Stanley. *The Once and Future Monograph.* Provost, September 11, 1997. http://www.arl.org/scomm/epub/papers/chodorow.html#fn2.

Foster, Andrea L. "Who Should Own Science?" *The Chronicle of Higher Education* 51, no. 6 (October 1, 2004): A33–A36.

"The Impact of Serial Costs on Library Collections." *ARL Bimonthly Report* 218 (October 2001), at http://www.arl.org/newsltr/218/costimpact.html.

Lynch, Clifford. "What Do Digital Books Mean to Libraries?" *Journal of Library Administration* 35, no. 3 (2001): 21–32.

Mann, Thomas. "The Importance of Books, Free Access, and Libraries as Places—and the Dangerous Inadequacy of the Information Science Paradigm." *Journal of Academic Librarianship* 27, no.4 (July 2001): 268–81.

WHITHER THE BOOK?

Myrna McCallister, Dean of Libraries, Cunningham Memorial Library, Indiana State University, Terre Haute

Wither the book? What about us: wither the librarian? In the *New York Times Book Review* in October 2004, Neil Genzlinger bemoaned, "Poor librarians. Soon, no doubt, to go the way of blacksmiths and town criers, their chosen field made obsolete by Internet search engines and self-perpetuating electronic databases. . . . What a pity that soon the only place to find one will be at the Living History Museum, alongside the mule skinner and the wheelwright."[1]

With all due respect to Genzlinger, I just don't see this happening anytime soon to either librarians or books, though in the longer run I suspect that both books and librarians are to undergo some significant evolutionary change. Just look at the tools an academic reference librarian uses today compared with those relied on just 20 years ago. Now, that's some serious change.

Change is occurring not only in the way reference questions are answered, but throughout academe. As in the past, libraries did not create the current scholarly communication paradigm, though they must operate within it. Scholarly communication, like communication and society in general, is becoming more and more market driven or capitalistic in nature.

Change, of course, is not new to scholarly communication or libraries, and it has not always been readily accepted. Plato decried the use of writing in lieu of memorization, fearing it would encourage forgetfulness and lead people to place their confidence in the external rather than their own minds.[2] Besides, he thought, writing would lead to a flood of information, much of it of dubious quality, and thereby lower the standards of true knowledge.

In the late fifteenth century Filippo di Strata opined: "The world has got along perfectly well for 600 years without printing, and has no need to change now."[3]

In 1492, Johannes Trithemius, in his delightfully titled *In Praise of Scribes,* reasoned: "Printed books will never be the equivalent of hand-written codices. . . . The simple reason is that copying by hand involves diligence and industry."[4] Though Trithemius hedged his bets by becoming involved in the new publishing industry, he felt that there would always be a place for hand-copied books because of the unique tactile relationship between manuscript and scholar.

Like Trithemius, libraries definitely need to hedge their bets. We've been collecting various data formats since the days of clay tablets, and we've been doing it pretty well. That's another way of saying that libraries are in it for the long haul, and we can't afford to be entirely dependent on monographs anymore than we could on handwritten codices or opaque micro cards. However, in my opinion the book and the monograph will remain a big part of our lives for quite a while.

Like Captain Smith ignoring ice warnings on the *Titanic*, no serious scholar even in 2004 can proceed safely upon the assumption that all data on any topic are readily available online. Without risking disaster, he or she cannot even assume that the best, most complete, or even most recent data on any topic are easily retrievable online.

Books continue to hold significant advantages over e-books and related screen-based, electricity-driven formats. For convenience, accessibility, ease of use, portability, durability, adaptability, dependability, and long-term maintenance, they still win out every time. Make no mistake; these are SERIOUS, BIG TIME advantages. Barnes & Noble, Amazon, Borders, and Alibris seem to be doing just fine. In fact, the book market has widened into a true worldwide operation. Students seeking secondhand copies of textbooks no longer have to just deal with the overpriced campus bookstore. They can buy and sell in a much broader market than ever before, and it's clearly to their advantage to do so. Libraries (and individuals) seeking OP titles are no longer confined to pawing through catalogs, traveling to used book shops, and cultivating special relationships with secondhand dealers. The Internet has opened almost limitless possibilities.

Put in here your own conclusions on what you find in the *Bowker Annual* regarding the output of academic book titles during the past five to eight years. Think about it now. How often does your library run out of books to buy? How many times have you had to hand money back to your director or provost because there just weren't any more monographs to buy? Is the printed word, the printed word on paper, a certified "endangered species" in 2004? Has our electronic, paperless information society advanced that far into the twenty-first century? Is e-book congestion making it difficult to find room for shelving the old fashioned paper monograph?

Just a few years ago Umberto Eco, writing in *The Future of the Book,* reported: "There are too many books. I receive too many books every week. If the computer network succeeds in reducing the quantity of published books, this would be a paramount cultural improvement."[5]

Now, I mentioned earlier that things are changing, and it seems clear that already certain types of books are on the way out. Ask any reference librarian how often he or she uses printed indexes and abstracts these days. If you have a good computer and good Internet access, do you really need to keep works like the *World Almanac* or *Encyclopedia Americana* at home for ready reference needs? It seems likely that the evolution of publishing and scholarly communication in the twenty-first century may substantially change the role of the monograph within academe and thereby within the library. This, of course, is nothing startling. Scholarly publication and communication have changed significantly since the Royal Society was founded in 1660. The types of monographs found on the shelves of a college library in 1790 or 1890 were quite different in many respects from those in college libraries today.

Earlier I said that libraries should hedge their bets. Perhaps "go with the flow" is a better cliché. I say this because libraries and librarians are inherently conservative. Witness the decades we spent arguing about the future of the 049 field while other information specialists were developing WWW, Yahoo, etc. What's the most widely used search tool today: the library catalog (representing several hundred years of tedious (and often painful development by libraries), or that latecomer, Google!?

The issue here really isn't so much monograph versus e-book or the printed book vis-à-vis the electronic journal. The monograph will survive for the foreseeable future, just as hand-copied books and printed books coexisted for quite some time, and those who were truly wise worked with the best of both formats. The development and spread of the mechanical printing press occurred during a historical period when other significant social, economic, religious, scientific, and political changes were also underway in the Western world. Little imagination is required to draw parallels with the social, economic, religious, scientific, and political changes occurring in our own world during what we call the information age. And little wonder that such changes result in discomfort and speculation within our own profession.

As Anne Keating observed in *The Wired Professor*: "The mechanical innovation of printing not only widened the audience for books, but also changed the act of reading. In the early sixteenth century, being able to memorize passages from essential texts was a critical part of education and an indispensable aide in argument and comparison. The invention of printing and the modern book, the proliferation of private libraries and begin to rely on the book's 'memory' rather than their own increased access to books meant that sixteenth century readers could begin to rely on the book's 'memory' rather than their own."[6]

Scholars communicate differently in 2005. New ideas do not have to be printed and distributed in paper journals or books to be publicized and debated throughout the world. The average citizen also communicates differently, from text messaging to Google. It's not so much the monograph that is changing, but rather information, information storage, and the way people read that are changing. The monograph is merely one part of this, and it's all something that we must do our best to try to keep up with.

Anne Keating refers to "the perceived purity of an old technology over a new one."[7] In the late fifteenth century, Vespasiano da Bisticci, in his memoir of Duke Federigo of Urbino, observed that in the duke's library "all books were superlatively good and written with the pen; had there been one printed book, it would have been ashamed in such company."[8] There were libraries before the printing press, and there will be libraries after the computer.

I do not advocate di Strata's view: "Thank you very much but no change is needed now." I know exactly what many of us mean when referring to monographs as the gold standard, and emotionally I am in their camp. However, we all remember what happened to the gold standard during the Great Depression. Libraries = books as an algebraic equation does not compute! Never has really. We cannot prevent the further evolution of the monograph any more than we could forestall the development of the printing press and the decline of the codex, nor should we. If and when the world moves on, we must do the same. "Wither the book?" is certainly an appropriate question to pose, but I think it's even more important to ask: "Wither information?" "Wither the library?"

Notes

1. Neil Genzlinger, "Review of *The Librarian* by Larry Beinhart" *New York Times Book Review,* October 17, 2004, 12, col. 2.

2. John H. Lienhard, "Reflections Upon Education in the New Millennium" (paper presented at the Conference of Southwest Foundations, Pre-Conference on Educational Reform, Santa Fe, NM, September 26, 2000), cited at http://www.uh.edu/engines/confswfound.htm (accessed August 25, 2005).

3. Bernard J. Hibbitts, "Yesterday Once More: Skeptics, Scribes and the Denise of Law Reviews," *Akron Law Review* 30 (Special Issue 1996): 267 (this edition enhanced and updated for the World Wide Web), cited at http://www.law.pitt.edu/hibbitts/akron.htm (accessed August 25, 2005).

4. Ibid.

5. Umberto Eco, "The Future of the Book" (paper presented at the July 1994 symposium "The Future of the Book," July 1994, University of San Marino), cited at http://www.themodernword.com/eco/eco_future_of_book.html (accessed August 25, 2005). This essay is also found in *The Future of the Book,* edited by Geoffrey Nunberg (Berkeley; University of California Press, 1997), which collects 12 papers from the symposium.

6. The Wired Professor: Book Companion Web Site, http://www.nyupress.org/professor/site/webinteaching2.html (accessed August 25, 2005).

7. Ibid.

8. Ibid.

WHITHER THE BOOK?—PUBLISHING, READING, AND THE ROLE OF LIBRARIES

Suzy Szasz Palmer, Public Outreach Librarian, Department of Rare Books & Photographic Archives, University of Louisville, Kentucky

Book production is in fact up. According to a news release from R. R. Bowker (May 2004), preliminary figures for 2003 showed a 19% increase. And along with increased production have been increased sales. But of what? Oprah resuscitated her book club, leading to Penguin (re)printing nearly 800,000 copies of Steinbeck's *East of Eden*; Simon & Schuster released Hilary Clinton's *Living History*, selling nearly 1.5 million copies; and the latest *Harry Potter* installment led Scholastic to set a first run of 7 million copies, with sales eventually reaching 12 million.

But compare the trend among university presses—for whom academic libraries are the primary customers. Here, production in 2003 was down 2.2% (constituting a mere 6.85% of total book production). Perhaps more significant, print runs of scholarly monographs are down, from an average of 1,200 20 years ago to half that in recent years. This in turn pushes prices up to the point where even the prime customer isn't buying. And as sales go down, print runs again go down, and prices go up again.

Perhaps it's the monograph, not the book, that's withering? Or perhaps it's the traditional scholarly versus trade book *model* that needs to wither. Witness the recent news from Smithsonian Press (*Chronicle of Higher Education,* October 13, 2004), which plans to split the academic and trade apart (creating "Smithsonian Press" and "Smithsonian Business Ventures") . This move comes only a year after the Press reduced the number of scholarly publications from 80% to 20%. The goal is for federal grants to subsidize the publishing of Smithsonian Press books, with an expected rise in the numbers produced.

So much for production—the business side of books. What about consumption? Sales may be doing well, and many libraries (including my own) report increased circulation of books. But apparently no one is reading. According to a National Education Association survey, "Reading at Risk" (July 8, 2004), fewer than half (46.7%) of Americans over 18 read literature, with only slightly more of those surveyed (56.6%) having read a book of any kind in the previous year. These figures have been consistently falling in the last 20 years—even among those with a college education or above, for whom the percentage of readers dropped from 82.1% in 1982, to 74.6% in 1992, to 66.7% in 2002.

Libraries, as we all know, have been steadily decreasing the purchase of monographs for years. According to the most recent ARL statistics, serial expenditures as a percentage of total library materials expenditures range from 82.9% (high) to 29.6% (low), with 66.2% the average; and monograph expenditures ranging from 47.2% (high) to 8.33% (low), with 24.5% the average. Along with this, and compounding the problem, is the percentage of the average library's budget spent on electronic materials, increasing from 3.6% in 1992–1993 to 25% in 2002–2003. Why have we all done this? There's more going on than the simple sciences versus the humanities problem. And there's more at stake.

I believe the library community has limited control over the publishing industry, and only somewhat more over reading habits. But only we can take control of our budgets and reverse the seemingly unstoppable trend to spend more and more of our dollars on serials and electronic materials (most of which in turn are serials) at the expense of monographs. If we don't, librarians a hundred years from now will be filling the gap with "TFCO"—the Twenty-First Century Online. Maybe by then e-books will be the only books—but only if we let it happen.

THE GRAPH

Bob Nardini, Senior Vice President/Head Bibliographer, YBP Library Services, Contoocook, New Hampshire

The most famous image in all of academic librarianship for the past 10 years or so has been a graph, that one from ARL that explains everything, showing monographs getting trounced by serials. When the graph was first published, I think the point was to raise an alarm, to illustrate a bad situation. That situation has existed for so long by now, though, that it's hard to sustain a sense of alarm. The graph just shows the way things are. Serials are pushing through the ceiling. Monographs are crawling across the carpet, like annoying rug rats the grownups have learned to step over and ignore.

Bad news for books. The graph's a Gutenberg Elegy. It's a Chapter 11. It's Bedtime for Biblio. Let's turn the lights out, please.

No one today sets out in an academic library, as ambitious librarians used to, to make a career by being a good "bookman," once a term of praise but now a word that seems not only sexist but also antique. Those librarians who do remain centered on books often seem marginalized, even peculiar. Why aren't they online? What about information literacy? What about the digital collection? So much else to do. Don't they know that hardly anyone uses books today?

But maybe those librarians aren't quite so medieval. Look at any issue of the *Chronicle of Higher Education*, as good a way as any to take the pulse on campus. You'll see lots of book listings and ads and plenty of coverage on noteworthy scholarship as published in recent books. Books remain the focal point of professional meetings in many academic fields. Books are still the way to get tenure in those fields. Books still line the walls of many faculty offices. Walk into your nearest Borders. Mine, anyway, is often packed. On campus there's always a strong constituency for the book.

Not always in the library, though. Or, not always obviously so in the library. New book shelves are less common and less visible than they once were. Library Web sites put the focus elsewhere. New buildings are more likely to showcase the learning lab than the book stacks. In BI sessions, serials will again, as in the graph, trounce the books.

What's happened in the library is that books became easy. Librarians, with a big assist from book vendors—with our approval and slip plans, our elaborate bibliographic categorizations, our bibliographic databases on the Web, our discounts, our management reports—commodified books and spent their time elsewhere. We, vendors, helped to make it the natural thing, to turn books into abstractions like LC classes, MARC records, return rates, ftp files, notification slips: all things that anyone can manage, and that nobody outside of the library cares about. If so many librarians are talking about everything other than books, why should the graph look any different than it does?

Does the book need "resuscitation," as Milton put it in framing this session? If so, maybe that's because we've turned off the patient's oxygen valve.

WHITHER THE MONOGRAPH?—IS THE GLASS HALF EMPTY OR HALF FULL?

Mary Sauer-Games, Director, Publishing, ProQuest, Ann Arbor, Michigan

When Michael Keller of Stanford spoke at the conference, he made reference to the choices academic libraries were making regarding the increasing costs of their serials purchases in STM, which naturally come at the expense of their expenditures on monographs, particularly in the humanities. In talking to librarians about this issue, I have heard one additional concern expressed as a result of this phenomenon, which is the library's inability to provide opportunities for new scholarship for students or faculty on their campus who are studying in the humanities.

I would like to offer a more positive view, one where the glass is half full as opposed to half empty. Although print monograph purchases are in decline, there has been an explosion of historical monographs that have been made available through electronic database collections. On the commercial side, examples include

- ProQuest's Early English Books Online (EEBO) (125,000 works),

- Readex's Digital Evans (36,000 works), and

- Thomson-Gale's 18th Century Online (150,000 works).

On the academic side is Project Gutenburg (13,000 e-books/ e-monographs)

I would like to propose to the institutions that have been able to make these significant commercial database purchases that scholarship at their institutions is not negatively affected, since they have been able to make significant additions to their collections. Albion College, which purchased EEBO this year, has a collection of 300,000 volumes. This one purchase alone increased their collection by a third! (I don't think that these e-monographs necessarily are included when institutions review their acquisitions of monographs, since these dollars generally come from separate budgets).

To support my argument for increased scholarship, I looked at the usage statistics of EEBO for the last three years:

- Overall, EEBO usage doubled, from 2002 to September 2004 (13.5 to 26.8 million accesses).

- This usage holds at the institutional level (75% of institutions saw 40% increase or better in usage during this same period).

Why this increase in usage? In talking to librarians at some of these institutions, the following reasons were given:

- Increase in usage among graduate students and faculty for research

- Increased usage for teaching

- Increased usage among undergraduates (Who can imagine an undergraduate seeking out microfilm to view and compare these older monographs?)

As a side note, they have heard faculty stating that with these kinds of electronic resources available, undergraduates can now do graduate level work.

In addition, we are seeing institutions that have never had access to the Early English Books microfilm purchasing the electronic format, which is expanding the number of people who have access to this content.

This leads me to conclude that as a community, we have been able to increase scholarship despite our shrinking budgets, and we have been able to increase our access to rare historical monograph content through databases like those listed above. An added bonus is that this new format allows us to research this content in ways that were never before possible. Imagine being able to search across a wide corpora of texts to find how words have changed meaning over time or to rediscover works that may be held in print format in only a handful of libraries worldwide.

As a final question, is there also a lesson to be learned here for the current print monograph? By looking at how digital access to historical monographs has breathed new life into and a demand for these works for teaching and research, is there a similar opportunity for the current print monograph?

Technology is changing the way libraries do business. These changes are coming quickly and sometimes without time to research or analyze them. The 2004 conference provided librarians with an opportunity to discuss technology issues such as portals, Googling, digital initiatives, and how to plan for the future.

Technology

PREDICTING THE FUTURE—A HIGHWIRE TECHNOLOGY PERSPECTIVE

Bonnie Zavon, Public Relations, Stanford University, HighWire Press, Palo Alto, California

Although I'd like to paint a rosy picture of a future incorporating a seamless flow of ideas for study, contemplation, and innovation in the "knowledge information world," caution leads me to remind you that there's a seamy side to seamlessness: unless there are major changes in the Big Deal, a whole lot of the flow will get stopped depending on whether the institution has or hasn't bought into it. This will gradually work to advance open archives so that readers and authors will have unlocked file cabinets online (institutional or funder repositories) where research can be accessed for free.

My rosy picture involves a natural, evolving move to change the traditional role of publishing (printing, binding, mailing, fulfillment, order processing) in order to foster a system of Web-based knowledge—where the role of the professional society shifts to that of the facilitator of peer-review, editorial, distribution, and support for their community of colleagues. When the hot air cools down, I predict that the society's role will expand, rather than decline, because their contribution to the process is crucial in the scholarly world.

As the world of information gets noisier and noisier, the emphasis on quality brands and services will increase. That is, the role of the intermediary becomes more important on the whole as the noise increases faster than the signal. However, new intermediaries emerge (Google versus PubMed; PubMed Central versus traditional publishers; library-based repositories versus aggregators/publishers). Computer-based intermediaries will become very significant (Google, OAI applied to distributed repositories).

I envision a new type of online publishing, one that embraces an electronic, interactive moderated forum: Where *authors* are able to concentrate on research. Where *reporting* their results isn't the final step of the cycle, but a contribution to science, or the humanities, or whatever they are focused on. Where articles are refereed and posted and would be ripe for comments, updates, rebuttals, and critiques to published research: the article as a "live" rather than static artifact. We have not seen this flourish in the public space in some fields, presumably because of fear that candid comments will spur retribution. For example, if I say that an article by Dr. X is crap, then if Dr. X is on an NIH review panel looking at my next grant application, that may prejudice his impartiality and he may vote it down.

As has been happening all along, there will be changes in the delivery process. We all will receive the information we need in different ways—PDAs and wireless will become really practical. It's not too outlandish to picture the single integrated unit that is readable—personalized, beamed to us, as needed—and brings together everything we need: voice, print, video, and audio.

Publishing is becoming more fluid in the sense that multiple versions of articles are out there (and there will be more if NIH gets its way), and that publication has broken out of issue-based containers. Looking through a really Pollyanna set of glasses, the traditional, *journal* issue production of information will morph into the concept of centralized, interlinked, *topic* databases—creating a shared, resource-rich knowledge environment with the definitive copy of any research article, easily found and easily accessible.

Editors in professional and learned societies will select the best of the research submitted to their fields and will establish *services* designed to assist authors and readers in their quest for knowledge. Publishers will manage papers on the authors' behalf, acting as curators to the definitive copy—a partnership between professional societies and researchers. New partners will emerge, offering services to summarize articles into laypeople's synopses for use by the general public in a centralized depository. In reality, however, I strongly suspect that STM publishers won't act this way, especially if the content of the article is on the NIH server in six months.

All things being equal, the costs of this process will continue to be borne in a balanced, diverse ecosystem of funding by both users and producers of information—fair, reasonably priced tiers of some sort, set according to a logical assessment of contribution, use, ability to pay, and support from those with an interest in the final product. However, if open access prevails, then one major part of the funding goes away, shifting the costs of that part will have a bearing on the remaining players. For example, research-intensive institutions will pick up a bigger share of the costs based on their publishing volume, while large consumers (including pharmaceuticals and biotech companies that read but don't publish much) will get the benefits.

Libraries will continue to pursue their long-held responsibility to be a place in which literary and artistic materials, such as books, periodicals, newspapers, pamphlets, prints, records, and tapes, are kept for reading, reference, or lending. In addition, and as time goes by, one thing that is certain to happen is that large collections (Stanford, and other major libraries) will be digitizing huge portions of their collections and moving them online. For those materials that are outside of copyright, this will bring about major advances in availability. You, as the librarian community, have a unique, "insider's" view of which information your particular set of users require, not by what they don't get, but by tracking access in this worldwide knowledge forum—designed and arranged for ease of use.

Working with the best of the secondary publishers (ISI, CSA, whoever emerges in this field in the future), you will be able to lend your expertise to guide, review, and interpret not only which products, but which systems will be in your future. Maybe these partners will morph into different kinds of keepers of quality and will become more important as referees and organizers of scholarly information.

Librarians will be able to tap into this brave new world as partners in this technological ecosystem. *Discovery* and *preservation* will continue to be key buzzwords of the art of the librarian—both for and with the institution or foundation maintaining electronic collections. You, as librarians, have a future role, not only in preservation, but in collecting and organizing as well. With all the digital information out there, who else will decide what's important to save and work cooperatively to divide the responsibility? Perhaps it's time for a new age Research Library Group Conspectus Project . . .

The rosy world I paint does have a caveat: I think it's important to understand that the balances in the system (some of which are undesirable) are being changed, and it is difficult to change just one thing without affecting the others.

EXPECTING THE UNEXPECTED: SUPER COOKIES AND THE MOBY DICK PORTAL

Michael Pelikan, Technology Initiatives Librarian, Penn State University, University Park

This submission for the *Proceedings* is an after-the fact rendering, in textual form, of the ideas illustrated in a verbal presentation by a set of PowerPoint slides that were my prepared portion of a panel discussion. I'll proceed by using the slide texts prepared for the panel as a cue to prompt written remarks. In so doing I'll be attempting to capture the ideas as presented at the time, although the written form may, as a result, take on a less formal appearance than might normally be expected of a chapter written for the *Proceedings.*

The focus of my remarks was the continuing evolution of the personal digital equipment that has become increasingly important to the academic library's primary patrons, the students and faculty of our colleges and universities, and how that technology intertwines with, runs parallel to, or diverges from the paths along which our own university systems are evolving, as well as the commercial offerings of our vendors to us, and of digital content providers in the larger marketplace and their marketing efforts directed at our patrons.

What's Evolving, and How Fast?

The desktop at work is office equipment.

By this I mean that the desktop computers we use at work have become our chief work appliances. They are office equipment, no less so than a cubicle or a white board. The computers themselves, their make and model, have become largely irrelevant as long as they meet our requirements for speed and capacity. They may be personalized to some extent, but the realm of our endeavor is in the information we wield and the software tools we bring to bear on the information. It can be observed that, for a fixed cost, speed, RAM capacity, storage capacity, and screen size are all increasing. We make increasing use of collaborative tools, and it has become increasingly common for us to share our work on large screens.

The laptop is the personal computer.

In the academic realm, the laptop computer is the primary computer used by our patrons. The "space" represented therein is truly personal, much more analogous to the dorm room or personal study than the institutionally provided office (especially when the equipment is personally owned). Wireless access to the Internet is accepted by our patrons as the norm, and expected to be reliable, speedy, and ubiquitous. Within our institutional nets the patrons expect to be challenged for authentication, although they become increasingly impatient (as they should) with being asked to authenticate repeatedly as they move within our space, especially when the need for such repetition results from the still-cobbled-together nature of our increasingly complex institutional Web spaces. They put up with such nuisance only out of necessity.

The cell "phone" is the fastest evolving form of personal computer.

On this point I have become convinced, and perhaps overinsistent, although beneath the obvious there lies, I believe, evidence of a deep shift in digital culture, one that is nearly generational in terms of how these tools are perceived by us and by our patrons.

It is essential to realize that the physical form the cell phones have taken is only "phone-like" by way of convenience and familiarity for the user. Make no mistake: these are digital devices interconnected by a vast and growing digital network, exchanging digital information in huge and increasing volumes, not all of which is the endless chatter of our undergraduates and ourselves. These cell phones are, in fact, comfortable personal computer systems that can exchange any information that can be digitized, a fact that has been overlooked, perhaps, in our planning, although I assure you not overlooked by the profit-driven world of content designers, packagers, and providers, whose economic model is as old as the disposable razor: "Give them the razor, then sell them the blades."

Client-Side Fascinations

MP3 players

DVD hardware and portable video

We see this economic model at work in the commoditization of the personal computer, the MP3 player, and the DVD machine: "Give them the machine, then sell them the content." For a while, audio files in MP3 format made up a huge proportion of the digital information whizzing among the networks of the academic institutions; now the exchange of video files, whole episodes, and movies accounts for a great deal of the volume on our networks. Much of this exchange is *sub rosa*, but all of it is visible. The expectations of our primary users can be summarized simply:

Multimedia = any medium

They might as well say, "I expect to be able to see or hear anything I might want, instantly or nearly so."

My stuff wherever I am.

"It shouldn't matter where I am or whose machine I'm on, I should have access to what I want, when I want it, wherever I want it."

Content: sometimes bought, sometimes "shared"

"I'll buy what I want if I need to, but I'll be just as happy if someone just lets me copy theirs."

My cell "phone" is a fashion accessory as much as an implement of utility. It's part of how I let the world know who I am.

"I want the latest phone. I expect to be able to access anything I want on it, whenever I want to and wherever I am. Anything that stands in the way of my having what I want when I want it is simply lame and essentially intolerable!"

They might go on to say, "I don't expect the university to 'get it,' and I certainly don't expect the librarians to 'get it,' but if I can get what I need my way, who cares? If I have to do it 'their way,' they're just trying to make me do it 'for my own good,' which is simply lame and essentially intolerable too! But what do you expect? They're a bunch of dinosaurs! They haven't got a clue that everything I need is already online!"

Content

The Industry

Meanwhile, from our side of the desk we fuss with organizing our Web spaces and rage and storm at usurious subscription rates to provide access to scholarly publications and get, we feel, no thanks or little appreciation for all that we do on behalf of our sometimes reluctant clientele. At the same time, the information industries are gloatingly working both sides of the table. Just as they continue to sell us mere access to what we used to receive in physical fact, they're also priming a new pump, preparing to break up what they've been selling us into smaller and smaller pieces and offer it in convenient, bite-sized chunks directly to a hungry audience (who'll likely pay just for the coolness and pleasure of not having to go through our Web sites, let alone set foot in our facilities!).

What form do these new offerings currently take?

Smaller and smaller atomic units

- news clips, alerts
- weather forecasts
- stock quotes
- Amazon book and song excerpts

And all of this has a name—it's called *microcontent*!

The Trends

The keepers of commodity information have become very skilled, very quickly at preparing their content once and then rapidly or automatically "repurposing" it, reformatting it on the fly, to stream out into as many different forms of presentation as may be desired by their admiring clientele.

In short, the content itself is increasingly independent of the form its presentation takes, and for that matter, is increasingly viewed "in place," that is, served out in small chunks at a time, rather than downloaded as work-length units of the sort we as institutions are used to purchasing.

When network access is ubiquitous, who needs downloading?

There are great advantages to the vendor if we aren't getting our digital hands on the whole thing they're selling us access to at once—they can discern and promote what's popular; they can gather information about time-of-day and regional variance in preferences; and best of all, their ownership and control of access are maintained!

I would expect to see more and more resources of the sort exemplified by Net Library and Safari, as well as the "free" services modeled by Amazon, providing access to excerpts, and by Google, with their towering ambitions to provide universal (for the time being) digital access to library content.

While the "big package" prices continue to rise for us in the middle, I expect to see for our patrons an increasing amount of "free" access to many of the very same resources we're currently subscribing to for them, paid for by some combination of advertising support and, increasingly, direct, albeit small, charges (and this to a greater extent as a more widely adopted system for micro charges gets ironed out—who knows? It could be PayPal . . .).

We may find ourselves asking each other why we're paying for this stuff when our users aren't coming to us to get it!

Libraries Getting into Scholarly Communication

The commercial content providers are years ahead of what most academic institutions are presently capable of building by their own means. For most institutions, digitization means special collections: trying to catch up a little with the enormous task of presenting our mountainous backlog of physical artifacts on the Web.

Meanwhile, it is a fact that virtually all new content produced today is already born-digital. While university presses are running on fumes trying to publish important books that sell hundreds of copies, and to keep alive their irreplaceable journals, barely supported by subscriptions, hopefully they and the libraries of their institutions can begin to collaborate in the process of bringing scholarly content to those who need it: those who need to publish it, and those who need it published.

DPubS

DPubs is an example of the type of collaborative efforts we see increasingly combining forces of academic presses and the libraries at their universities. DPubS is a collaboration between Cornell and Penn State Universities to develop a "general purpose publishing platform for scholarly literature in diverse fields."[1] The system will support peer review, incorporate extensive administrative functionality, be interoperable with repository systems such as Fedora and Dspace, and be made available for broad use under Open Source licensing.

What Should I Do If I'm in an Academic Library?

I phrase this question in the rhetorical form often favored by sports analysts, "If you're Dallas then you want to run with the ball!" So, what should I do if I'm an academic library? Let's continue in the spirit of contact sports:

- Separate content from presentation! Smash those Web pages up! Move into content management systems! Write once, then repurpose many times! Figure out a way to help your institutions organize their corpulent Web spaces into something resembling coherence (this will require influence, but hopefully not require control—a huge topic for another time!).

- Prepare to link everything! Smash barriers! Demand single-point authentication of your vendors and your institutional IT organization (or be deemed irrelevant and simply lame by your users)!

  It should be a completely transparent process for a student to go from his or her personal Web space, to the class space in the course management system, to a set of electronic reserves for that course, to a threaded discussion list managed by a subject librarian, to the ILL page, to their personal inbox where the article they asked for is waiting for them.

- Keep pushing to break the vendors' death grip on their interfaces! We should hope to keep moving toward scenarios in which vendors give us direct access to their indexing and content without our having to go through their individual interfaces, or better, that they let us index their content ourselves and form our own aggregation of resources.

  The current crop of linking products still leaves the institution on the hook, paying for monthly updates into perpetuity. If we could just crawl the vendors' content spaces (perhaps with a consortial crawler so as to be polite to their systems), index their content as we see fit, and then just pay for what each of us accesses (the myriad of pricing structure possibilities I leave for those whose eyes sparkle at such prospects), we'd all be the happier, for we wouldn't have to go through 50 vendors' front ends to search for the content we're paying for access to.

Expect Demands for Unexpected Forms of Access

I will not be caught predicting in print the diversity of forms of access that our patrons may be demanding in five years, but I will say this: the gizmos they'll be expecting us to recognize are moving from R&D to Prototyping to Marketing even as you read this. Hold on to your hats!

So—The Next Five Years

The Age of the Cell "Phone"

Never mind that you and I might think it's just a telephone. Our patrons know different, and so do the content providers. I'm not talking about a renaissance for telephone reference (although telephone reference will probably undergo something of a renaissance once the chat reference world blends with voice over IP![2]).

Rather, I think that were it left to our patrons and their preferences, they'd want somebody to figure out a way for them to do on their cell phones what we currently ask them to log into our systems to do. They will wonder why it should be any harder for them to do their "research" for their Psych 101 class on their device of choice than it is to order their supper; download the latest hit video; or get the latest sports, news, and weather of their choosing.[3]

The Rise of the Micro-Browser

I'm not sure that the handheld phone-like device we're used to today will predominate in the marketplace five years from now. The "coolest" current expression of the cell phone lifestyle to be found today is the wireless headset. You've seen them, striding down the sidewalk or waiting in the checkout line, appearing to be talking to themselves. It's entirely possible that the whole current gizmo will become componentized and wearable. A nubbin in the ear, a screen on the sleeve, ad hoc wireless networking with anyone you'd like to exchange files with, seamless integration of your personal file space (wherever that is) with whatever device you happen to summon it from—modes of these sorts are what we should be preparing for.

In short, I expect our patrons to call for immediate access to any network-accessible digital information on demand, anywhere, anytime, regardless of medium or ownership. I believe they will expect to be able to begin a transaction on one device (maybe their laptop at home), continue it on another as they ride the bus (by "phone," for example, whatever that term means for, again, do not confuse the device with the cacophony of services that they may use it to access), and then have the content they've asked for waiting for them, accessible by whatever device they wish to use, ready to move it into their personal file space. They will want self-service, but will expect human help to be available when sought.

Wild Cards

Here I must place a few crazy ideas (not that everything else I've gone on about will prove sage or timely!). These are things that are either already barreling down on us, or ought to be. Some are real, some are somewhat real, and some I'm making up.

Voice-to-Text/Text-to-Voice

This one is practically at our doorstep; I swear it—although it seems to have been stuck at our doorsteps for a long time. Perhaps it will arrive quietly. One of these mornings we'll wake up and realize that it has crept into our lives almost without our noticing.

But make no mistake: once voice-to-text and text-to-voice become ubiquitous, that will mark a passage across the Rubicon that will not be reversed! I do not predict the end of reading, although there will likely be a huge impact on the slippery slopes where the written word already finds itself. It's not too hard (nor too cheerful) to imagine how a paragraph dictated by some of our students (indeed, by some of our colleagues!) may read, but I need not predict; we'll all find out, soon enough. Voice access to menus and searching and transaction with systems by voice interface will change everything.

For our library systems, the impact will be simple: It shall be expected that anything that used to require keyboard and mouse will be accessible verbally, to be delivered in the manner and mode requested.

"Super Cookies"

This is a term I've made up (and not a very good one, really) to capture some of the ideas I've already discussed. Users will have personal file space. It will be on their laptops, or on the university network, or on an information appliance of some sort that they keep some-where—it does not matter where. They will expect to be able to dump things into this space from anywhere, and to retrieve anything that is there from wherever they are when they need it. I used the term "super cookie" to capture the notion that "who I am" and "where my stuff is" will follow me around and be machine-knowable by any device I happen to use. You might also think of this as an extension of the "shopping cart" metaphor already broadly accepted.

Expect a transaction that goes something like this:

Library, this is me. I need three scholarly articles about underage drinking and peer pressure, so find me a dozen or so to choose from. Read me the abstracts when I call you from the bus and then I'll chose which ones I want delivered to my file space. Bye.

The Moby Dick Portal

So what will our "holdings" be? I don't know the answer to this, and it will certainly dif-fer from institution to institution (as, indeed, the shape of the institutions themselves will evolve). Will our accreditation swing on what we "hold," or on what we have access to? Clearly, if academic libraries are to evolve into something more than museums for books, we need to figure out what it is that we do that is truly irreplaceable and put it front and center fast. I continue to believe that the role of the librarian will be that of both mediator and teacher, providing assistance with choices and advice and instruction for both the informed and the overwhelmed, each according to need.

In a hyper-hyperlinked world, all that has been published about a particular thing may well eventually be discoverable and accessible from within that thing itself. It's not too diffi-cult to imagine Moby Dick as a portal, accessing not just Melville's deathless narrative but also the rendered redaction portrayed by Gregory Peck and critical interpretation by hosts of scholars and persons with expertise in fields ranging from naval architecture to theology, per-mitting side trips into scrimshaw, shanties, or commentaries on the allegory as form. In short, the musings of a thoughtful person making his or her way through a field or a work ought to be entirely aided by the best marriage we can make of information technology and human understanding.

If what we as librarians can continue to be known for is that we help our patrons to make sense out of a dizzying universe of choices in the realm of human knowledge, that will be a suitable outcome for all that we strive toward.

Notes

1. More information can be found at http://dpubs.org.

2. The novel aspect to this coming "revolution" in VoIP Reference will be that reviews of the literature that extend back only as far as much of our electronic indexing goes may well miss the seminal articles on the use of telephones to provide reference services that appeared nearer to a century ago, citations to which can readily be found in the print indexes we still have on our shelves today!

3. As before, I must leave for another time and place the ever-simmering screed that is ever-developing, never far from my mind, regarding our understanding of the term "information literacy" as it compares to our students' understanding of the term, not to mention the understanding and expectations of our faculty relating to this matter!

PARTNERSHIP MAKES IT WORK—CREATING THE SEAMLESS TRANSACTION

Anne Deacon, Head, Acquisitions, Library Technical Services, University of Western Ontario, London
Andrejs Alferovs, Vice President, Sales, Coutts Library Services, Niagara Falls, New York

Dwindling Resources—The Imperative for Workflow Review

As are many institutions, the University of Western Ontario is facing budget constraints and dwindling staff resources. The university library's operating budget has been cut by 3%; however, on the positive side the acquisitions budget has been increased by 5%. Another welcome factor is that as a Canadian university, the strength of the Canadian dollar on the world market has given far more buying power to the Library.

So the gap was increasing—more buying power, with less staff resources to spend the budget! From an acquisitions perspective we had to completely review how we were going about our operations.

Start, Stop, Do Differently

START: Dealing with the issues and make our process more efficient.

STOP: Thinking we could do the same amount of or more work with fewer people by burying our heads in the sand, thinking we could continue to operate business as usual and, in the end, jeopardizing staff morale.

DO DIFFERENTLY: I would like to add besides the DO also THINK differently.

The key for the team was to be willing to do things differently, to take risks, try new things, and strategically recognize that *access* is number 1—not perfection.

How—Develop Relationships with Vendors

To overcome the hurdles we faced, the Library could not go it alone. Working in partnership with vendors was the key to accomplishing our goal. Western uses Innovative Interfaces Millennium system, and the university has also developed and expanded its relationship with Coutts Library Services. Coutts traditionally supplied the library with paper slips for new title notifications.

During the past two years Coutts has developed a new Web application to help with collection development, *i*approve. Now the collection librarians can view the Coutts slips electronically and select what they want to order, indicating their fund on the electronic slip. This information is then automatically forwarded to the acquisitions department and so begins the seamless ordering procedure.

From a Dream to Reality

Whereas other institutions developed a way to have the order record added to the brief bibliographic record when it was downloaded from the Coutts system, OASIS, Western wanted to go one better. Why couldn't we have a full level bibliographic record with an order and circulation record attached?

Coutts quickly manipulated its system to provide us with full MARC records. In discussing the objectives with the Library's systems team, their response immediately was "why not?" Two of the Library's team members received Innovative Loader training, and the dream soon became a reality.

With Coutts having over 3.5 million titles in its database, we asked" why couldn't we use the Coutts system instead of outside resources for harvesting bibliographic records? After doing some testing and discovering that 99% of the titles that were being firm ordered by the acquisitions staff were in the Coutts database, we knew we were halfway there. The complete process is simple: Search by ISBN (Coutts provides an option to search multiple ISBN numbers), download the full level bibliographic record, then save the MARC download file and run it through the Innovative Loader, and an order and circulation record are automatically added.

Benefits

1. Western receives a good-quality record at the start of the process, which benefits our catalogers and means the record is available faster on our system.

2. The saving in staff time is enormous.

3. It eliminates overall paper shuffling.

4. Less staff time is required to input an order from scratch.

5. There is faster turnaround time from title selection to placement of order and delivery of a book and catalog record.

6. The overall benefit is to our users.

The Flow Process

- Using the multi-ISBN loader in OASIS (see figure 1), lists of ISBNs can be copy pasted (up to 250), with results searched and ready for ordering. Under Western's previous procedures the order process took three days. Now within 24 hours the order has been sent to the vendor.

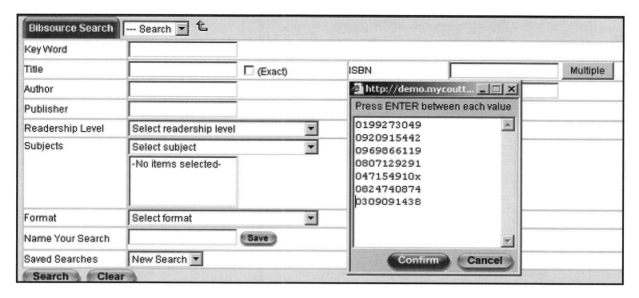

Figure 1. Coutts Multi-ISBN Loader.

- Once selected, the titles are placed in a shopping cart ready for ordering. As illustrated in figure 2, rather than placing the order online, the library has the option to download the MARC record, including any local information, and then place the order with Coutts by EDI.

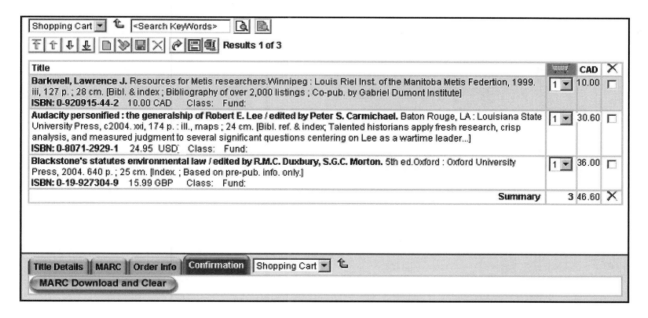

Figure 2. Preparing Selections for Download.

- The metadata is then loaded into Western's Innovative database—including the subject heading. (See figure 3.)

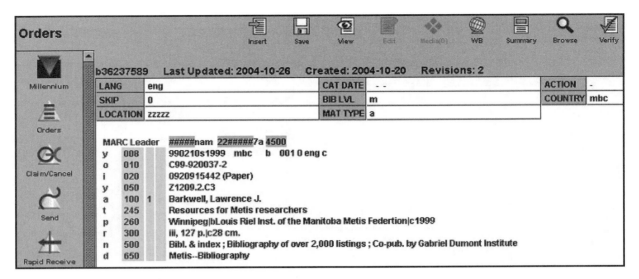

Figure 3. Full Bibliographic Record Loaded into Western's Millennium System.

- Western Library has created a load table for Coutts records. When Coutts records are loaded through that table, order and item records are generated into the Millennium Acquisition system. (See figures 4, 5, and 6.)

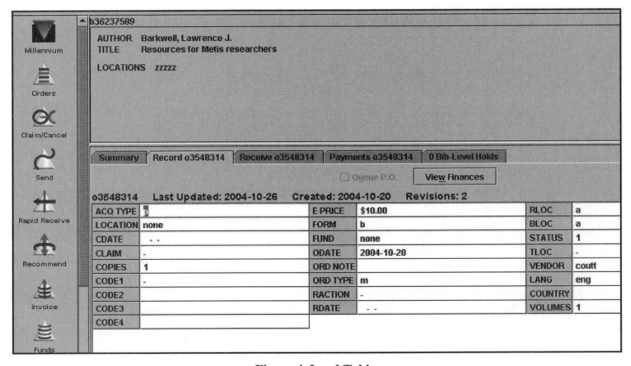

Figure 4. Load Table.

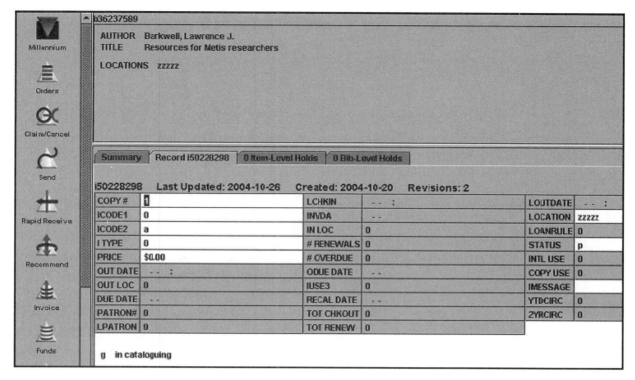

Figure 5. Load Table.

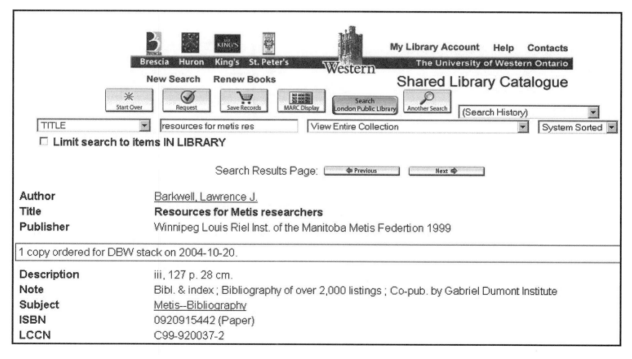

Figure 6. WebOpac View.

Creating the Application for Seamless Integration

As part of the process described, Coutts has developed an application—OASIS (On-line Acquisition and Selection Service) that interfaces with library systems. The example provided is with Innovative; however, the same principles apply with all of the major library systems that have the ability to bring in external MARC data seamlessly and have full EDI facilities.

In order to put the process and the positioning of book vendors such as Coutts in being able to deliver these integrated services in context, figure 7 is a review of the current supply chain for monographic information flow.

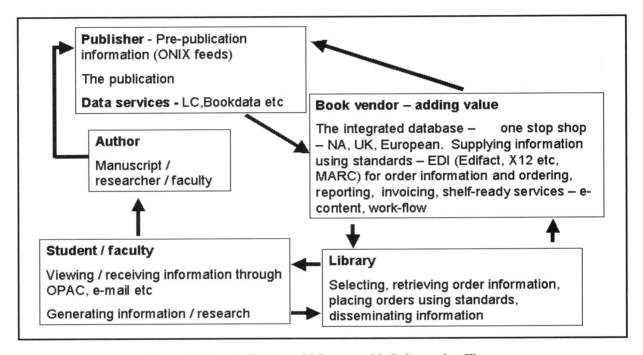

Figure 7. Supply Chain and Monographic Information Flow.

The vendor is in a position to provide significant value added and to act as a facilitator with the publisher or distributor, the library, and the library systems vendor.

In creating the application all these elements were kept in mind; the data sources include

1. Publisher ONIX feeds to facilitate book images, descriptions, and book jackets.

2. Third-party data sources to facilitate all of the above plus bibliographic records.

3. Coutts records to provide enhanced MARC for full shelf-ready services

After identifying these requirements, Coutts produced an application that would give libraries access to the system at various levels—for selectors to select, acquisitions to authorize, and administration to enable the system to work within a library's workflow.

The power of the multi-ISBN loader has already been demonstrated when creating firm orders through a standard database search. The application is further enhanced through selection support tools, such as Coutts's new title notification service, *slipstream*.

A typical flow would go from the selection process, through ordering, to receipt of book, with the following steps (see figure 8):

1. Collection development makes selections (or forwards items for recommendation to faculty) online.

2. The selections are seamlessly forwarded electronically to acquisitions.

3. Acquisitions carries out further bibliographic checking and duplication control (which the Coutts system also does across the firm orders, approvals, and standing orders) and adds local information that is mapped to the Coutts system for downloading.

4. Using Coutts's one-key download, a full MARC record, including LC class and subject headings, is loaded into the library system (a simple embedded order record can also be downloaded for acquisitions purposes).

5. The Innovative system automatically adds the purchase order number.

6. Bibliographic and item records are noted in Innovative.

7. An EDI order is sent to Coutts and recorded on OASIS.

8. On receipt of books, MARC records can be further enhanced with book in hand if required and transmitted via FTP together with an EDI invoice.

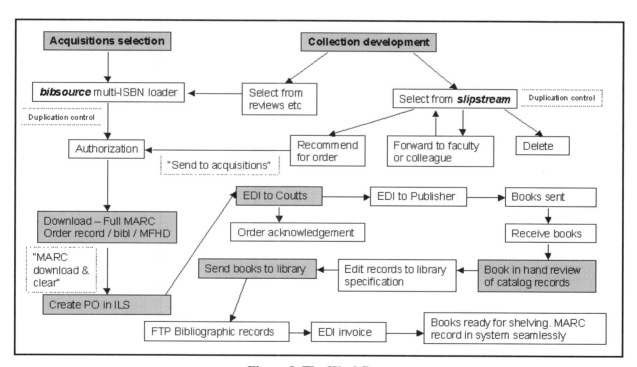

Figure 8. The Workflow.

Figures 7 and 8 give an illustration of how the acquisitions team can identify titles and place these on order (follow the flow above: Collection Development—Select from review—*bib source* ISBN multi-download).

The flow is slightly different from a collection development perspective, in which the collections librarians receive online slips from Coutts. Following the flow from "Collection Development" through "Select from slipstream," the process is illustrated in figures 9 through 12.

- The selector receives electronic slip notifications through *slipstream*. As well as having the ability to view the title detail, the MARC tab allows the selector to view the MARC record. All *slipstream* output will have been provisionally cataloged, giving a high-level initial record.

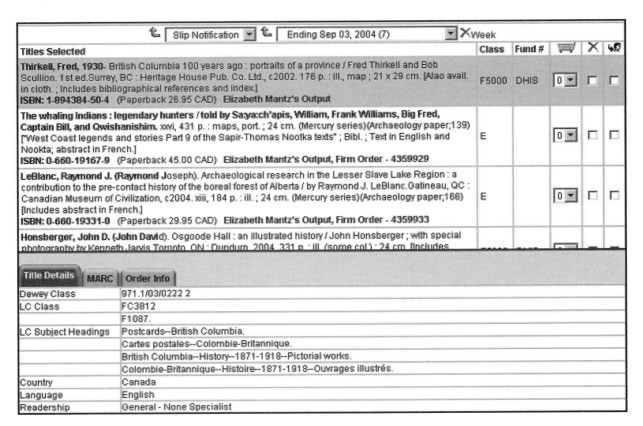

Figure 9. Electronic Slips.

- The selection is then forwarded to acquisitions through a one-click process, ready for acquisitions to review the order and detail. The record is then loaded into the Innovative system, as illustrated in figures 3 through 6. The library system then automatically allocates the PO reference, and the order is then transmitted to Coutts via EDI.

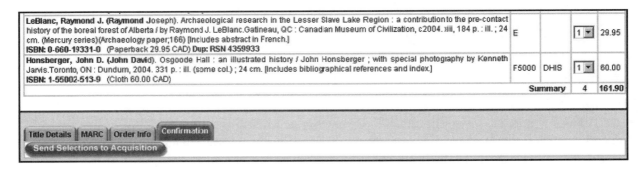

Figure 10. Sending Selections to Acquisitions.

• The administration function within the Coutts system is key to the smooth flow of information. The library administrator who controls this function can set various access levels, from read only to full authorization; route specific information to colleagues; add information to the MARC download feature; and set the order flow, giving the library total control.

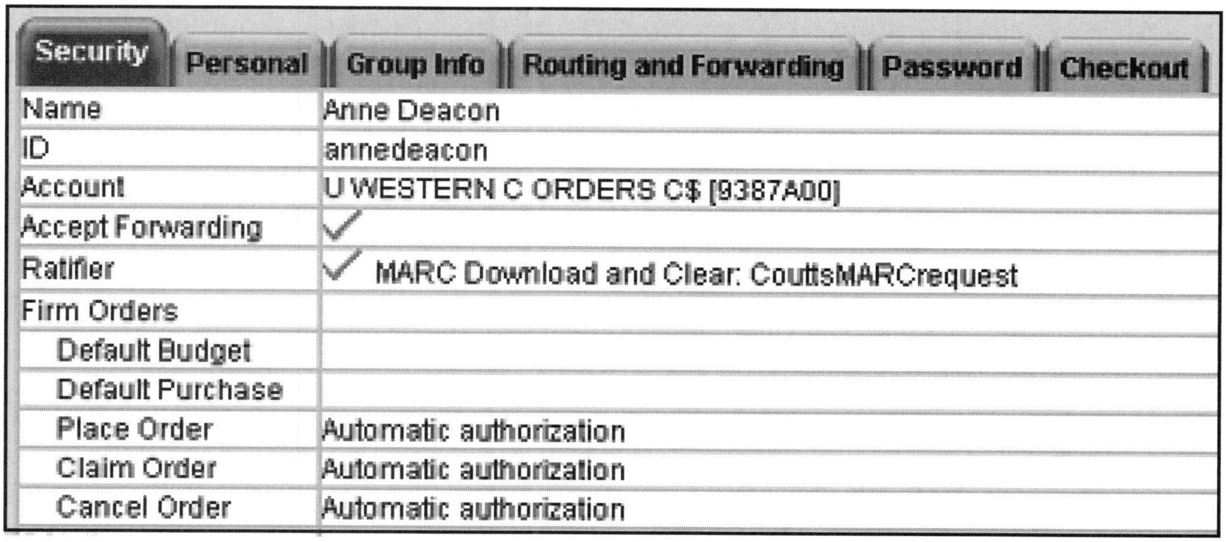

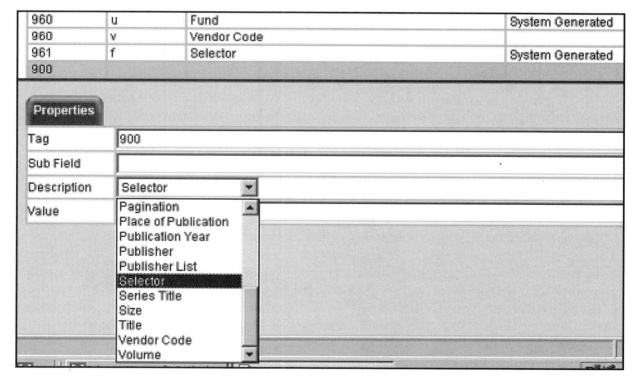

Figure 11. Setting Access Levels and Authorization for Workflow.

Figure 12. Setting the Fields for Adding Local Information to a MARC Download.

Establishing the Order Flow

1. Place the order directly online.

2. Download an order ready or a full MARC record in preparation to resubmit the order via EDI from the library system.

3. Download an order ready or a full MARC record and place the order directly online.

The methodology adapted by the University of Western Ontario using Innovative's Millennium system is option 2. (See figure 13.) This option creates the most seamless route for the library.

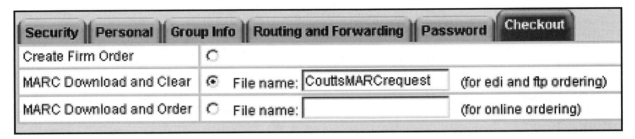

Figure 13. Order Information Workflow Options.

Benefits and the Future

These procedures have saved the library demonstrable time and money:

1. *Time:* Almost a week has been shaved off the previous cumbersome order process.

2. *Productivity and cost:* There is a considerable increase in throughput with less resource applied.

3. *Process:* The result is a full shelf-ready service, with the books arriving fully cataloged, processed, and invoiced, and with all the records automatically fed into the system.

So what of the future? Well, we are already in mid-development of Z39.50 searching across the database, working on this functionality with Innovative and Coutts. This will enable us to carry out automatic holdings checks as well as make it easier for Coutts to review shelf listings as part of the cataloging process.

From a selection perspective more information is becoming available electronically, such as more detailed descriptions and tables of contents. Coutts is already working with publishers on the production of sample content as well as the provision of full content online. The opportunities for seamless information provision are endless, and we are growing more and more efficient by working with our key partners—Innovative Interfaces and Coutts—integrating the application, searching across databases for holdings, or using the library database as the selection tool post-download.

PLAGIARY, GOOGLING, AND THE MOUSE: IS THE INTERNET KILLING OUR ABILITY TO DO RESEARCH?

William M. Hannay, Attorney, Schiff Hardin LLP, Chicago, Illinois

One morning a couple of weeks ago, my wife called our local high school looking for our son, who is a junior. He needed to see a doctor about a (fortunately, minor) health problem. It turned out that there was an opening in the doctor's schedule that morning, so she was trying to find him quickly. Well, to make a long story short, everybody was playing "Where's Waldo?" but nobody could find our son. It wouldn't have been like him to ditch school, but where was he? People got worried. Finally, he appeared of his own accord, and the answer proved to be that he had been in the school library. It was—and this is the takeoff point for my remarks today—the last place anybody thought to look. It was a surprise, not because young William is a bad student, but because "everybody" knows that "nobody" at Barrington High goes to the school library anymore.

Certainly the notion that "nobody" uses our high school library is an overstatement, but I don't think it's that much of an exaggeration. And I don't think that this phenomenon is unique to our local high school. My sense is that it is a phenomenon repeated at secondary schools throughout the United States, and increasingly at colleges and even graduate schools. When "they" say that nobody goes to the school library anymore, what "they" mean is that students are not using library *books* anymore to do research. Students are allowed, even encouraged, by their teachers to substitute online "research" for the more traditional process of delving into, for example, hard-cover histories or biographies, books of literary criticism, or monographs on the social sciences. Indeed, I'll tell you frankly that I don't know *what* my son was doing in the library because I seriously doubt that he has ever learned how to do research there. I suspect he was just looking for a quiet place to get some homework done. Nothing wrong with that, of course, but there's a lot more that libraries offer to the intellectual process than just a lack of noise. And I worry that, as a society, we are developing a generation of students who don't know how to do "book" research.

This summer I read about an online survey conducted by the Electronic Publishing Initiative at Columbia University in New York. The study concluded that electronic resources have become the main tool for university students gathering information.[1] Here are the principal findings of the survey:

- 99% of student respondents said that they were far more dependent on electronic resources than print resources for their schoolwork.

- The results show that undergraduate students, in particular, are heavily dependent on the Web.

- When going online to do work for a course, undergraduate students are more likely to use an Internet search engine (46.5%) than to go to a library-sponsored electronic resource (21.9%), by a factor of more than two-to-one. Graduate students are more likely to use library-sponsored electronic resources, however.

- Finally, although the physical library is still an important destination for students to retrieve articles and books, undergraduates are more likely to use the library as a study space, for the computing facilities, or for Internet access.

Commenting on the significance of the survey, Kate Wittenberg, director of Columbia's Electronic Publishing Initiative, said: "Students' research habits, and their preference for using Google and other search engines as their first stop rather than the library, is part of a more general cultural and social change and I am not sure that there is much that libraries, or anyone else, can do to change this pattern."[2]

I hope that this assessment is wrong, and that we can change the pattern of increasing dependence on Google and other search engines as the principal research tool for students. For it seems to me that there are at least three serious academic flaws that flow from this situation. First, reliance on Web browsing feeds an unwholesome tendency toward what one commentator has called "passive learning and grazing for information," rather than an active and questioning search for truth. Second, relying only on the Web denies students access to the vast majority of useful knowledge, for the simple fact is that the millions of pages of information on the Internet represent only a tiny percentage of the disciplined thought and writing available in books. Third, Web-based research provides students no guideposts or framework for analyzing the importance, acceptance, or even veracity of the information they electronically stumble across. (Is some unknown person's blog, for example, a valid and worthwhile authority to cite in a paper . . . in the same league as peer-reviewed journals or well-recognized treatises?)

Moreover—and I come now to the main issue I want to discuss—it is undeniable that the Internet has become the single greatest tool for academic dishonesty ever made available to high school and college students. With a well-chosen Google search and a few clicks of that devilish little mouse, a student can find and download portions of articles or even whole term papers and pass them off as his or her own. Plagiarism is not new, but it used to be a physically more difficult crime to commit when you had to write it all out by hand if you wanted to copy. The increasing tendency of students to resort to the electronic form of cheating has been monitored in the past few years by several academics. One of the better known scholars in this area is Rutgers professor Donald McCabe, the founder of the Center for Academic Integrity at Duke University.

Professor McCabe reports, for example, that in a survey of 14,000 college students at 23 schools, more than one in five students admitted to cheating on a test in the past year.[3] Moreover, according to McCabe, the fastest growing form of cheating is taking information from the Internet and passing it off as one's own work.[4] While 10% of college students admitted to Internet plagiarism in 1999, that number rose to around 40% in 2003, McCabe stated in a telephone interview with the *New York Times* this summer.[5] "Students are more liberal in their interpretation of what's permissible and what's not," he said.[6] Many students simply crib what Google dredges up free, but McCabe estimates that 2% of students purchase papers online.[7]

And it is not only in academic studies and surveys that evidence of the problem can be found. ABC's *Primetime Thursday* aired an hour-long report on cheating in school on April 29, 2004. Primetime's investigation found cheating on campuses everywhere—from top public high schools and colleges to Ivy League universities. Students described the powerful temptation to cheat, telling ABC they are under intense pressure to get good grades—and to keep up with peers who cheat on exams and papers. "It's unfair on your part, if you're studying . . . so many hours for an exam and everybody else in the class gets an 'A' cheating," said Sharon, a college student. "So you want to get in the game and cheat, too."

Comments from several of the students ABC interviewed indicate that the cheating trend may reflect a deep-seated cynicism among students that getting an education is more about learning to "work" the system than learning math and history.[8] Cheating in school, they argue, is good preparation for a career in the business world, where some do whatever's necessary to get ahead. (The *Primetime* report struck a nerve among parents and teachers. Hundreds wrote in after the show, concurring with the existence and enormity of the problem. See http://www.charactercounts.org/pdf/Primetime_post-show_comments.pdf.)

Why is this happening? Why don't all students recognize that, for example, cutting and pasting text from the Web without attribution is plagiarism? One scholar attributes some of the difficulties in teaching ethics to students to "the values of a generation that has no problem downloading songs off the Internet."[9] If copyright laws are perceived as irrelevant when it comes to music on the Internet, the ethical leap from failing to pay for music to failing to credit sources may not be far.[10] One possibly apocryphal but wonderfully amusing anecdote illustrates the moral tone-deafness of many students:

> A professor had a student come to his office to argue for an A on a paper instead of the C he received. When the professor asked the student to explain why he should get an A, the student appeared flustered, then replied, "Because the student I bought it from got an A."[11]

Another scholar finds a more global explanation, suggesting that students are dishonest "because their role models (parents, instructors, doctors, lawyers, clerics, police, and society in general) offer little to stimulate principled action" and that "[c]onsequentialist ethical theories that care more about results than principles take precedence over traditional moral thinking."[12] As a result, he argues, "unethical activity becomes acceptable when it is convenient or whenever one can get away with it."

And plagiarizable information is exceptionally "convenient" to find. Not only is it easy to find articles or Web sites from which students can cut-and-paste a sentence or a paragraph, but from a variety of so-called term paper mills, students can find entire papers, probably on the very topic the teacher has assigned. To test this convenience, I did a little experiment. On November 4, 2004, I ran a search on AOL for "free term papers"—I got 55,115 hits.[13] These included three sponsored sites, which were not exactly "free" but would undoubtedly have sounded appealing to a desperate student:

- www.monsterpapers.com, offering access to "1 Million Term Papers and Essays" for only $9.95.

- www.serve.com, offering "Term Paper and Research Paper Service"—it was at pains to note that "We are NOT a free service but our prices are low."

- www.papersonline.us—obviously a highly ethical and patriotic operation—it offers "Non-plagiarized term paper writing services from USA" at "Only $8 per page" for four days' delivery with a "Money-back guarantee."

There were also innumerable "non-sponsored sites" that were indeed "free," including:

- Term Paper Sites.com, with "Only the highest quality sites on the net" and "Thousands of free and searchable Term papers!"

- And a site billing itself as the "Home of teens for free term papers [and] homework" where you can also "Chat and Hangout." Its name? True gentle ladies and gentlemen, I ask you to please close your ears. It's www.schoolsucks.com.

Just to see what kind of papers were available for "free," I plugged in a Google search for "free term papers and The Scarlet Letter." (William, my son, is reading it for his English class, and I was curious what temptations might lie in the path of him and his classmates.) I got 29,900 hits. So I looked at a couple of them. They looked like pretty realistic high school papers: turgid, bewildered, tuneless . . . but probably worth a "B" in most high school English classes.

So it is convenient—terrifyingly convenient—to find tons of material to plagiarize in whole or in part. And, at least until the past couple of years, it has been woefully easy to "get away with it." As the dean of one college journalism school comments, "Many of the students think that their professors are too lazy, too busy, or too dumb to catch them. Some of those students and others have gotten away with it before, certainly in junior high school and high school, sometimes in other college courses."[14] It would be difficult for the typical teacher to catch such Internet plagiarism, but enlightened entrepreneurship seems to be coming to the rescue. An increasing number of computer-based detection tools are now available to academic institutions to catch the cheaters.[15]

One of the most successful is Turnitin.com, a California-based company formed in 1996 by a group of researchers at the University of California at Berkeley who created a series of computer programs to monitor the recycling of research papers in their large undergraduate classes. It is reported that over 3,500 institutions license Turnitin's plagiarism prevention system, including hundreds of high schools, submitting as many as 20,000 papers daily.[16] The software compares a student's essay to all text publicly available on the Internet, to various books and academic journals, and to millions of essays already turned in to the service, and within five minutes can issue a report that highlights each passage that matches another source.[17] "Approximately 30 percent of the 20,000 papers we check a day are less than original," the CEO of Turitin's parent, iParadigms LLC, is quoted as saying. "Our system doesn't detect plagiarism, it detects verbatim copy. It is up to the instructor to determine if plagiarism has occurred."[18]

Northwestern University has announced that it began using a similar Internet service in fall 2004. The one selected by NU is called SafeAssignment and allegedly not only searches for exact phrase matches but also looks for similar wording in cases where a student was savvy enough to change a few words in the lifted material. The university's associate provost for undergraduate education is quoted as saying that the service is necessary to combat a "significant" 10% to 20% rise in academic dishonesty.[19]

But one Web site concerned with the plagiarism plague warns that plagiarism detection services are not a complete answer:

These services don't catch "custom essays," and they don't catch plagiarism when the original work isn't already in the digital domain. If you rely on detection, you are doing a disservice to your students. . . . The fact is, detection services help to catch the cheaters who fall into the "not so bright" category. Smart cheaters can skate circles around these services.[20]

Moreover, the use of detection services carries with it a risk of being wrong. Consider, for example, the report of a University at Canterbury student in England who admitted downloading material from the Internet for his degree after the school began to run a pilot program of plagiarism-detection software to analyze students' work. He was advised, just before his final exams, that he would get no credits for his course work and is now suing the university for negligence. The student, 21-year-old Michael Gunn, claims that Canterbury officials should have warned him that his actions were against school regulations.[21]

So what is the answer to plagiary and the too-easy use of Google and the mouse? Professor Lawrence Hinman, director of the Values Institute at the University of San Diego, identifies three steps that institutions can take: "Our first and most important line of defense against academic dishonesty is simply good teaching. Cheating and plagiarism often arise in a vacuum created by routine, lack of interest and overwork. . . . The second remedy is to encourage the development of integrity in our students. A sense of responsibility about one's intellectual development would preclude cheating and plagiarizing as inconsistent with one's identity. . . . Third, we must encourage our students to perceive the dishonesty of their classmates as something that causes harm to the many students who play by the rules."[22]

Certainly the positivist approach suggested by Professor Hinman is vital in the long run. But in the meantime, it is just as important to use the available legal and academic sanctions against student plagiarists when they get caught. Honor codes and school policies against plagiarism must be emphasized and enforced by both secondary and postsecondary institutions, and the discipline meted out should be publicly disclosed so that an example can be made of those who have violated the codes or policies.[23] Where the academic institution has taken such disciplinary action, the accused plagiarist all too often turns to the courts of law in an attempt to avoid the loss of degree or, in the case of teachers, loss of job. Invariably, judges reject the plaintiff's effort to have the court second-guess the academic institution's procedures.[24]

The publicity given to the numerous instances of famous or near-famous "adults" who have been found guilty of plagiarism is highly salutary, both because it shows that people do get caught and also because it shows what a devastating effect committing plagiarism can have on one's life and career. Here's a quick list:

- In late September 2004, Lawrence Tribe, a distinguished Harvard law professor, admitted that he had copied without proper attribution portions of a 1974 book by Henry Abraham entitled *Justices and Presidents*.

- Notorious journalism scandals have recently come to the surface, such as those involving Jayson Blair (*New York Times*), Jack Kelley (*USA Today*), and Richard Judd (*Hartford Courant*).

- Historians Stephen Ambrose and Doris Kearns Goodwin used entire passages from other publications in their books without indicating from whence the material came.

- Huang Zongying, an associate professor of English at Peking University, was fired after a Chinese graduate student brought his misconduct to light.

- Roger Sheperd, an arts professor at New School University, resigned after admitting plagiarism. Portions of Meredith L. Clausen's book, *Pietro Belluschi: Modern American Architect,* appeared without attribution in Sheperd's book, *Structures of Our Time: Thirty-one Buildings That Changed Modern Life.*

- In September 2004, Mostafa Imam, a Saudi Arabia-based researcher, was accused of plagiarizing photographs of various organisms previously published in micropaleontology articles by other authors. Shortly thereafter, Imam died of a fatal heart attack.

- Tony-nominated playwright Bryon Lavery has been accused of plagiarizing passages from a 1997 *New Yorker* article by Malcolm Gladwell about Dr. Dorothy Otnow Lewis and her book *Guilty by Reason of Insanity*. Lewis and Gladwell say that a number of passages in Lavery's play *Frozen* are taken directly from their own work.

- In March 2004, the president of Central Connecticut State University, Richard Judd, was accused of plagiarizing materials for an op-ed piece that appeared in the *Hartford Courant* the previous month. A few days later, he announced that he would retire at the end of the school year.

Importantly, there are various legal weapons available to academic institutions to fight plagiarism committed by the student or academician as well as the aiding and abetting of such misconduct by online term paper mills. With respect to the latter, for example, 14 states have enacted laws that prohibit and, in most cases, criminalize the sale of term papers, theses, dissertations, or other written material where the writer knows or should reasonably have known that such written material is to be submitted by another person for academic credit at any institution of higher learning in the state.[25] Unfortunately, neither academic institutions nor prosecutors have proven to be interested in pressing such cases.

With respect to the plagiarists themselves, academic institutions seldom press for legal sanctions against the perpetrators other than internal disciplinary measures. Nevertheless, sanctions under various legal theories are in fact available.[26]

In the end, teachers are the first line of defense in both detecting and deterring plagiarism, and there is much good advice available on the Web about how to do just that. For example, an excellent set of guidelines, *Anti-Plagiarism Strategies for Research Papers,* prepared by Mr. Robert Harris in 2002, is available at http://www.virtualsalt.com/antiplag.htm. The guidelines provide helpful and workable details on how to apply the general goal of "mak[ing] the assignment and requirements unique enough that an off-the-shelf paper or a paper written for another class or a friend's paper will not fulfill the requirements" so that only a newly written paper will suffice.[27]

I do not know the extent to which your own academic institutions formally attempt to inculcate in their students, teachers, and researchers a deeper respect for book research versus online research as well as an unfailing sense of academic honesty and integrity, nor do I know the extent to which our institutions consciously and intentionally include library professionals in either the broader challenge of teaching intellectual rigor or the process of detecting and deterring plagiarism. But if the institutions do not redouble their efforts to inspire academic honesty, and if they do not include library professional in these efforts, those institutions are leaving themselves on a collision course with the present trends toward lazy and dishonest scholarship. Addressing these issues is not a "luxury" that can be postponed until a better time, notes Professor Lawrence Hinman. "It is a short step from dishonesty in schools and colleges to dishonesty in business."[28]

Notes

1. See Carol Power, "US Students Let Google Do Their Homework," *The Irish Times,* July 23, 2004, 53.

2. Ibid.

3. A case in point is reported in the *Boston Globe* for March 3, 2000, B1 (63 students in introductory computer science class at Dartmouth were charged with plagiarism on a homework assignment).

4. See *Chicago Sun-Times,* July 25, 2004, 16.

5. See *New York Times,* August 22, 2004.

6. Quoted in *Chicago Sun-Times,* July 25, 2004, 16.

7. "These days, stressed-out perfectionists and lazy no-goods alike can Google their way to an astounding array of plagiarism Web sites." Suzy Hansen, "Dear Plagiarists: You Get What You Pay For," *New York Times,* August 22, 2004, sec. 7, col. 1, 11 (reviewing samples of essays from online paper mills).

8. The report featured the results of an ABC News poll about the attitudes of kids toward cheating in school (http://abcnews.go.com/sections/primetime/US/cheating_poll_040429.html).

9. University of Georgia associate professor Barry Hollander, quoted in V. Whitehouse and J. Nicholls, "Inside These Hallowed Halls: How Journalism Schools Are Confronting Student Plagiarism," *The Quill* 92, no. 6 (August 1, 2004) 14.

10. Ibid.

11. Related in Theresa Winslow, "The Cheat Is On," *The Maryland Gazette,* June 5, 2004, C1.

12. Robert Hauptman, "Dishonesty in the Academy," *Academe* 88, no. 6 (November-December 2002) [Online], available: http://www.aaup.org/publications/Academe/2002/02nd/02ndhau.htm.

13. The same search for "free term papers" on Google came up with 5,090,000 hits. By contrast, a search for "plagiarism detection" came up with only 36,000 hits on Google and a mere 7,107 hits on AOL.

14. Dane S. Claussen, director of the journalism and mass communication graduate program at Point Park University in Pittsburgh, quoted in Whitehouse and Nicholls, "Inside These Hallowed Halls."

15. One article makes the disturbing suggestion that some term paper mills "have ties to plagiarism detection software companies." For example, detection software companies PlagiServe (http://www.plagiserve.com) and EduTie (http://www.edutie.com) have connections to term paper sites like MightyStudents (http://www.mightystudents.com), Essaymill.com (http://www.essaymill.com), EssaysOnFile.com (http://www.essaysonfile.com), and TopEssays.com (http://www.topessays.com).

16. See *The Irish Times,* July 23, 2004, 53.

17. Ibid.

18. Jordan Muhlestein, "New Technology Harbors New Era of Cheating," *The Daily Universe,* Brigham Young University, May 11, 2004.

19. Quoted in *Chicago Sun-Times,* July 25, 2004, 16.

20. See http://www.plagiarized.com/index.shtml.

21. See *The Irish Times,* July 23, 2004, 53.

22. Lawrence M. Hinman, Editorial, "How to Fight College Cheating," *Washington Post,* September 3, 2004, A19.

23. It would be surprising if any educational institution did not have such a code or policy. A quick Web search turned up numerous examples online. It also turned up the curious anomaly of one state university library Web site that included both the school's honor code as well as an extensive list of hyperlinks to fee-based and "free" term paper mills. One wonders about the wisdom of providing such information. As one legal commentator observed when encountering a similar situation on another university library's Web site, "[w]hile such information is not difficult to find, I consider it unethical to provide links to businesses that are explicitly violating the law." Ronald B. Standler, *Plagiarism in Colleges in USA,* 2000, http://www.rbs2.com/plag.htm.

24. See *Chandamuri v. Georgetown University,* 274 F. Supp. 2d 71 (D.D.C. 2003), a case in which an American student of Indian descent sued Georgetown, alleging unlawful discrimination on the basis of national origin and retaliation after the university sanctioned him for plagiarism. The court dismissed the complaint, concluding that the plaintiff offered no evidence that the disciplinary hearing was not conducted in accordance with the procedures published in the university's honor code. Moreover, the honor code clearly set forth the definition of plagiarism, and the hearing board's decision not to exercise its discretionary power to adjust the sanction was not a violation of the sanctioning guidelines.

25. See California Education Code §§ 66400–66405 and the following state education code sections: Colorado § 23-4-101-106; Connecticut § 53-392a-e; Florida § 877.17; Illinois ch. 110, §§ 5/0.01–5/1; Maine 17-A § 705; Massachusetts ch. 271, § 50; Nevada 207.320; New Jersey 18A:2-3; New York Education Law § 213-b; North Carolina § 14-118.2; Pennsylvania title 18, § 7324; Virginia § 18.2-505; Washington §§ 28B.10.580–584.

26. See Stuart P. Green, "Plagiarism, Norms, and the Limits of Theft Law: Some Observations on the Use of Criminal Sanctions in Enforcing Intellectual Property Rights," *Hastings Law Journal* 54 (2002): 167; Standler, *Plagiarism in Colleges in USA.*

27. One section of Mr. Harris's guidelines gives practical details on how to detect plagiarism. Rule number one is to "[l]ook for the clues." As you read the papers, he advises, look for internal evidence that may indicate plagiarism, such as mixed citation styles, lack of references or quotations, unusual formatting, off topic discussion, signs of datedness, anachronisms, anomalies of diction, anomalies of style, and smoking gun blunders.

28. Hinman, "How to Fight College Cheating."

PLANNING FOR A DIGITAL PROJECT

Rebecca L. Mugridge, Head, Cataloging Services, Pennsylvania State University, University Park

L. Suzanne Kellerman, Judith O. Sieg, Chair for Preservation and Head, Preservation Department, Pennsylvania State University, University Park

Many of the decisions that library staff must make in the context of a digital project are the same or similar decisions that must be made when handling more traditional library formats. Digital items, like traditional materials, must be acquired, described, and made accessible. In this chapter we describe and analyze those decisions and the steps that institutions must take to implement a workflow for digital projects, touching on standards and staffing issues as well. Penn State's experiences with digital initiatives are used to illustrate some of our points.

Background on Digital Initiatives at Penn State

The University Libraries' first undertaking to convert analog paper content to digital content occurred in 1992, just as digital technology was emerging. As a member of a consortium of eight academic institutions eager to develop the necessary digital technology for libraries, the University Libraries secured funding from the Commission for Preservation and Access to test the viability of digitizing archival materials. Two archival collections were targeted for the test project—the Pennsylvania Agricultural County Agent Extension Reports, consisting of over 350,000 pages, and the Steel Workers' Organizing Papers, a collection of roughly 3,000 individual manuscript pages.

Problems plagued both projects from their inception. Not only were library staff literally cutting their teeth on how the technology worked and how to scan a variety of formatted objects, but they were working with fragile, brittle materials that required special handling. Needless to say, the day-to-day work on both projects was demanding, tedious, and challenging. There was very little interaction with any other library department except for the University Archives unit that held ownership of the collection.

In addition to the challenges posed by the materials, the file structuring technology was proprietary. All objects scanned were converted to a proprietary file format, which in the end proved difficult to use or access.

By 2001 the University Libraries had launched its digital library initiative with funding support from the state of Pennsylvania. Internally, the Libraries formed a digital project leaders group and started investigating, evaluating, and installing digital collection management tools, such as CONTENTdm, Prime Recognition's PrimeOCR, and eventually Olive software for historic newspapers. It was important for the Libraries to build the necessary infrastructure, a platform of software tools to accommodate all formats of collections, from single pictures, to multi-page monographs, to newspapers.

Currently the Libraries' digital initiatives have evolved to include a "decentralized centralized" program methodology. A centralized production capture unit has been created in the Preservation Department with a decentralized project management team. The organizational structure of the project oversight includes five levels of management—from library administration for planning, funding, and library resources to library faculty and staff who directly oversee specific components of each project.

Administrative Organization of Digital Projects

Administrative oversight of the Libraries' digital initiatives resides in the Libraries' Information Technologies (IT) Priorities Group, not only for digital projects but for all technology needs of the Libraries. IT Priorities' main charge regarding digital projects is to review and approve or reject project proposals. Librarians interested in proposing a digital project must prepare a project proposal form, which involves obtaining support from relevant units, and submit it to the IT Priorities group for approval.

Because all digital projects have an impact on the "collection" as a whole, either expanding it with new content or creating content in alternate formats, the assistant dean for collections and scholarly communication has often been the first step for librarians in obtaining support and approval for a new digital project. Because of the plethora of ideas and proposals, the assistant dean formed a group representing many of the key stakeholders in the digital project environment. These stakeholders include selectors, catalogers, programmers, technicians, and librarians from our information technology unit. The main charge of the group is to select, prioritize, and push forward development of digital initiatives. To this end, the group meets monthly to discuss and review display and navigation options and to demonstrate and comment on software applications being reviewed or designed.

For each individual project that is active, the University Libraries forms a project team to manage its development and progress. This "decentralized centralized" approach to the management of digital projects includes assigning staff from four library departments (IT, Preservation, Cataloging, and DLT) as the core staff for each digital project. In addition to these members of the project team, there is a project leader, usually a selector or subject specialist, and others as needed:

- *Preservation digital staff* provides scanning of source documents, performs quality control on the images, maintains the file inventory, processes files for ingest into the software of choice, creates archival copies, and ships those to off-site storage.

- *Cataloging faculty and staff* provides the initial strategy for metadata requirements for the project, establishes a template of fields to capture data, provides oversight and review of metadata, and loads batched metadata into software such as CONTENTdm.

- *IT* provides software review and testing, loads the image repository, may develop programming to facilitate ingest, designs Web the interface, writes search and navigation instructions, and provides training.

- *DLT* provides network and server support and provides security and tape backup.

Administrative Management of Digital Initiatives

As mentioned previously, at Penn State we're taking a "decentralized centralized" approach to the management of digital projects. Much of the workflow is managed by the Preservation Department; but there is also significant participation by selectors, catalogers, the systems office, and our information technology unit staff. However, this approach is not without its challenges. For example, with a decentralized approach to management, when the staff who are working on a given project come from different divisions of the organization, who has overall oversight of the project? Who has the authority to light fires when they're needed? How are priorities set when there are competing projects from different constituencies? When resources are limited, *and all of our staff resources are limited*, how do we portion them out to support multiple projects? Finally, how does evaluation of the success of the organizational structure take place? Is it determined by the number of completed projects per year? Through surveys? By comparison with peer institutions? By the amount of publicity received? These are all questions that have to be considered on an ongoing basis.

It's essential to determine a general workflow for digital projects. How do they begin, progress, and end? Although we've been involved in digital projects for over 10 years, we're just beginning to establish a clear workflow for digital projects and all of the steps that must be considered for any project. It's critical to determine who is responsible for what aspects of a given project, and agreement must be reached when participants are from different units of the library. One of the key differences between traditional materials and digital materials is that the digital items do not create an obvious backlog (i.e., one that can be seen visually.) It's easy to see when monographs are piling up, or journals aren't being checked in, but when a digital project has stalled, it may not be clear. Digital projects require a more diligent oversight than traditional materials, if we want to ensure their completion. One way to master the digital project process is to develop a conceptual framework that helps everyone understand how the process works. We've done this at Penn State in implementing the following digital project workflow:[1]

- *Selection* is key to a successful project. The bottom line is to build a product that is useful and useable. It's critical to keep the audience in mind; give them what they will use and build a product that brings something new to the collection by adding value.

- *Copyright* is an essential part of a digital project workflow. It's necessary to determine whether you have the legal right to make digital surrogates and disseminate the images; the answer to this question is a major consideration to weigh during the selection decision-making process.

- *Funding* needs should be determined up front. Projects often take longer to complete and cost more than expected.

- *Material preparation* should occur prior to image capture; the source documents should be reviewed and stabilized.

- *Catalog records* may be created at various points of the workflow, depending on the origin of the metadata and project needs.

- *Digital image production and quality control best* practices for image capture abound. Excellent resources are available through the *Digital Library Construction Tools: How-To Manuals* compiled by the British Columbia Digital Library.[2]

- *Content representation on the Web* is a critical step in the digital project process. Much staff time can be spent designing and reviewing the pubic display; the goal is to make useful and useable sites.

- *File management and image database* maintenance is essential, knowing what you have and where it's stored. It's critical to have a backup plan for items mounted on local servers, but it's also important to have a preservation plan for archival files.

- *Delivery* of the digital content can be in many forms, such as the Web, CDs, DVDs, archival copies stored off-site, etc.

- *Publicity* for your digital collections is the final step in the process. After all the work that has gone into creating a digital collection, it's important to share the final product through press releases and in other ways. New ideas might include a "book" launch—inviting the public, special guests, library staff, donors, and prospective donors to a special event in the library. Another idea is to send postcards with images from the collection that has been digitized. Such promotional activities might encourage future financial support for additional digital projects.

Types of Projects

Materials selected for digitization can include a wide variety of formats:

Pictures

Monographs

Newspapers

Archival materials

Journals and periodicals

Cartographic materials

Sound files

Each of these formats presents a different challenge for material preparation, image production, cataloging, and content representation.

The metadata needs for different types of projects can be very different from what we're used to supplying for traditional materials, and also very different from each other. With pictures, we're often digitizing them and providing metadata for them at an item level, whereas in the online catalog we would be much more likely to catalog them as a collection. The metadata for monographs is usually already available and can be converted from MARC records, although there is still often a fair amount of data manipulation required. Metadata for newspaper projects was simpler, as the newspapers are digitized and OCR'd, and the full text serves as its own metadata.

Penn State's Pennsylvania German Broadsides and *Frakturs* Collection

We have several collections of *frakturs* in our Special Collections Library. Most of them are unique items and should prove to be a useful resource for researchers. This collection includes more than 250 images from the holdings of the Rare Books and Manuscripts unit in Penn State's Special Collections Library.[3]

An example of one of the *frakturs* that has been digitized is a birth certificate of a resident of Pennsylvania from the mid-nineteenth century (figure 1).

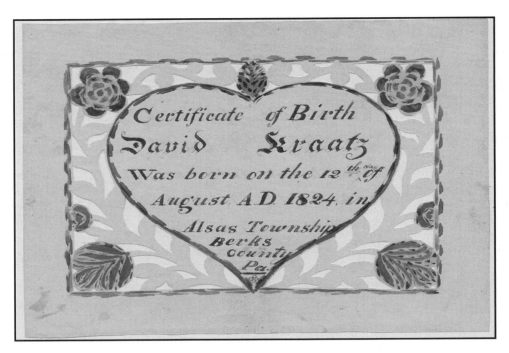

Figure 1. Digitize Nineteenth-Century Birth Certificate.

Penn States Mira Lloyd Dock Glass Lantern Slide Collection

Another exciting digital project that has been completed at Penn State is this collection of digitized images of the flora of Pennsylvania.[4] The glass lantern slides presented a challenge for preservation because they needed to be handled very carefully as they were thoroughly cleaned and then scanned. Figure 2 is an example of one of the slides.

Figure 2. Digitized Glass Lantern Slide.

Penn State's *Digital Collegian Archive*

OCLC's Olive software for historic newspapers was our software of choice for providing access to backfiles of newspapers. The Web site directing library patrons to our digitized student newspaper, from 1887 to 1940, is illustrated in figure 3.[5]

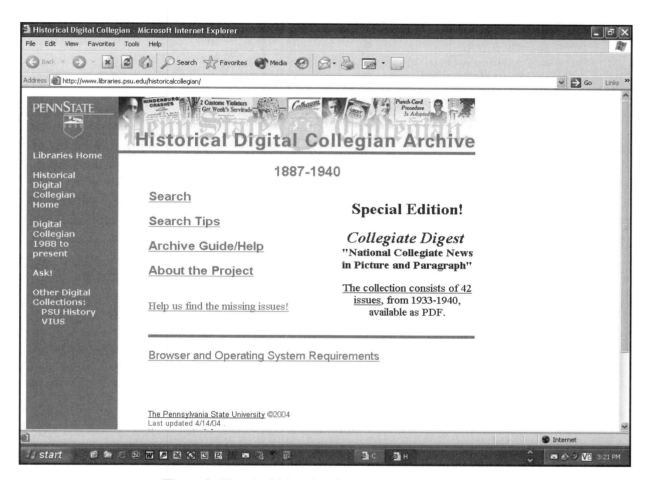

Figure 3. *Historical Digital Collection Archive* Web Page.

Cataloging Workflow

With each digital project, it's necessary to work with the selectors to determine metadata needs, such as what subject thesaurus should be used. The source of the metadata may be the cataloger, but depending on the project, it may also be supplied by a subject specialist, it may be purchased, or it could be converted from existing metadata such as MARC records. Finally, the metadata should be reviewed for quality and consistency before it is mounted and made publicly available.

Metadata Issues

One of the most difficult issues for us to deal with in the digital environment is that there are so many different standards to choose from (e.g., DC, VRA, EAD, MODS, TEI, FGDC).

Often parts of different standards are combined to create a metadata schema for a particular project. There is a general consensus that standards development will *not* settle down any time soon; they will continue to evolve at a rapid pace. We can't wait for them to settle, but when you do pick a standard, it's best to stick as closely to it as possible, and when you do veer from it, be sure to document what you decided and why. Another observation is that cataloging expertise is needed for effective metadata. There's a reason why catalogers chose the profession they did: they like the work! Selectors and others may not want to create metadata and may not be good at it when they do. On the other hand, most cataloging departments are not staffed to provide metadata for thousands of digitized photos, things that we would normally just create one MARC collection-level record for, so a compromise may be needed. Catalogers with expertise could define the metadata needs and design a template/spreadsheet, but they may need to train others to do the input and possibly hire people with subject expertise to help out as well. Catalogers should always be responsible for the quality of the metadata and have some review and/or oversight responsibilities for it. Finally, many have acknowledged that authority control is one area that needs to be explored. We have authority control pretty much figured out for traditional materials; but we're at the infant stage for digital projects. A lot of work has to be done in this area, and the Library of Congress has begun to explore this with MADS.

Figure 4 represents a catalog record in CONTENTdm for the first *fraktur* picture we showed earlier. We cataloged most of the *frakturs* on separate MARC records, then used the MARC records as the basis for the metadata in CONTENTdm, which I'll show briefly later. One reminder of how important standards are is that our use of line breaks for display purposes in the subject field has caused our records to not validate for OAI purposes. We're participating in a CIC OAI project, and the project manager will be able to correct the problem on their end, but it was a reminder to us that even though CONTENTdm is OAI compatible, the data you store in CONTENTdm also have to be OAI-compatible. Another thing we did that was not recommended in the OAI standards was that we put all of the subject headings in one subject field (again, for display purposes), which we'll probably avoid next time around.

Title:	Certificate of birth : David Kraatz was born on the 12th day of August A.D. 1824 in Alsas Township, Berks County, Pa., 1824.
Author:	
Other Title:	
Publication Information:	
Physical Description:	1 p. : col. ; 13 x 17 cm., on sheet 17 a 20 cm.
Notes:	In Rare Books and Manuscripts, University Libraries, Pennsylvania State University, University Park, Pa. (#F160.G3P463/Box 1 Item 25/Vault).
Summary:	Hand-crafted birth certificate for David Kraatz, b. 12 Aug. 1824. Text in heart-shaped border, with floral designs and cut paper decorations. Flowers and borders brightly colored.
Acquisition Source:	Gift of E. K. Hibshman.

Finding Aid:	Online finding aid for all Penn State Pennsylvania German broadsides and Frakturs available at http://www.libraries.psu.edu/speccolls/FindingAids/fraktur.frame.html
Subject:	Kraatz, David, b. 1824 Birth certificates—Pennsylvania—Alsace (Township)—Specimens
Genre:	Cut-paper work; Frakturs (documents).
Contributors:	
Collection:	Pennsylvania German broadsides and fraktur, 1750-1979
Permitted Uses:	This image is posted publicly for non-profit educational uses, excluding printed publication. Other uses are not permitted. For details please see: http://alias.libraries.psu.edu/vius/copyright/publicrightssc.htm
Image Size:	923 x 768
File Format:	JPEG

Figure 4. Catalog Record in CONTENTdm.

Figure 5 is a metadata record from one of the Mira Lloyd Dock slides that we showed earlier. You can see that the metadata includes family, genus, and species name, which we would not have been able to supply in Cataloging. This is the part that we hired a specialist to supply. Our electronic resources cataloging librarian worked with the selector to design the metadata template. The selector input most of the metadata, and the specialist provided the very detailed subject metadata.

Collection:	Mira Dock Forestry Lantern Slides
Title:	**Black walnut (Juglans nigra), Chester Co., Pa., TF 109**
Location:	Chester County (Pa.)
Description:	Bare tree with split rail fence in background
Photographer:	
Processor:	Pennsylvania Department of Forests and Waters
Date of Photograph:	n.d.
Topic:	Trees
Family Name:	Juglandaceae
Genus Name:	Juglans
Species Name:	nigra
Common Name:	Black walnut
Penn State Collection:	Mira Lloyd Dock Glass Lantern Slides
Source:	Mont Alto Campus Library, The Pennsylvania State University
Permitted Uses:	This image is posted publicly for non-profit educational uses, excluding printed publication. Other uses are not permitted. For details please see: http://alias.libraries.psu.edu/vius/copyright/publicrightsdock.htm

Accession Number:	MLD069
Object Type:	Glass lantern slide
Color:	Black & white
Size of Original:	4 X 3 1/4 inches
Image Size:	924 X 768 pixels
File Format:	JPEG
Digital Processing Notes:	

Figure 5. Metadata Record.

Workflow

Figure 6 compares simplified workflows for traditional versus digital material. It all begins with selection. Whereas with traditional materials the next step is to acquire the item, with digital we often have the item in hand, whether it's a picture, newspaper, microform, or what have you, and the parallel step is the digitization process. That, of course, could be done in-house or outsourced, depending on the nature of the project. The next step is to provide the cataloging or metadata for the collection or items. The main difference, and it is a big one, is that for traditional materials, there's not a lot of ambiguity about how we will catalog something. There might be a question of whether to catalog something as a set or as individual monographs, or to class something together or separately, but for the most part we know what we're doing! With digital materials, we often have to negotiate with selectors or other interested parties about how the metadata will display, what aspects we want to bring out, who will do the metadata input, etc. The next step is to physically process traditional materials, with the mounting of files and metadata the analogous step in digital projects. The physical item has to go to the shelf, and the digital item has to be made accessible through some public interface. Finally, with traditional materials, there is some ongoing work, such as integrating resources or serials maintenance. Most digital collections are integrating in nature, in that we can digitize a collection of pictures, such as our *fraktur* project, and then the selector can acquire another 20 at an auction and ask that they be added to the collection (as has happened recently).

Traditional	Digital
Selection	Selection
Acquisitions	Digitization
Cataloging	Cataloging
Physical processing and binding	Mounting of files and metadata
Shelf	Provide access via WWW
Some materials are integrating in nature	Most collections are integrating in nature

Figure 6. Simplified Workflows for Traditional Versus Digital Material.

Trends

Our experiences with digital projects has led us to the conclusion that the role of technical services staff is expanding in several ways. First of all, it's necessary to understand many more standards than just MARC and AACR. The number of metadata standards is exploding, and those standards are evolving rapidly, with the result being that we have to keep up with much more change than ever. Another difference is that with traditional materials, it's not necessary to negotiate and plan their cataloging the way we have to with digital projects. The standards are accepted, cataloging policies are established, and they are not often questioned. With digital projects, the standards are much more fluid, or at least they appear so. And the display of information is driving a lot of the decisions, so technical services staff involved in digital projects are involved in project management to an extent that just doesn't exist with traditional materials that have established policies, procedures, and workflows. The need for collaboration across library units is growing, and that is not just in technical services, but also in technology support units, systems offices, and collection development. Finally, it's clear that ongoing education is critical. We are truly in a learning environment, and we have to be lifelong learners in order to keep pace, and even more so to be leaders.

Just as the roles of tech services staff are changing, perhaps even more so is the technology world—both software development and new products, as well as new equipment options. Other trends that librarians need to continually monitor are open source solutions; the development and need for migratable file formats; the changing relationships and roles of vendors, publishers and libraries; and new trends in scholarly communications.

In conclusion, the rapid changes associated with digital projects are presenting significant challenges to libraries. As digital project management within libraries matures, with an established administrative oversight and prioritization of projects, established and reliable standards, and consistent and dependable funding sources, digital projects will become a standard and unquestioned part of our acquisitions, cataloging, preservation, and public services routines.

Notes

1. Adapted from *Handbook for Digital Projects: A Management Tool for Preservation and Access* (Andover, MA: Northeast Document Conservation Center, 2000).
2. www.bcdlib.tc.ca/tools-manuals.html
3. The collection is available at http://content.libraries.psu.edu/cgi-bin/buildPSUpages.exe?COLL_SRC=PAHist&COLL_ALIAS=Frak.
4. The collection is available at www.lias.psu.edu/preservation/mld/.
5. http://www.libraries.psu.edu/historicalcollegian/

ONLINE RESEARCH RESOURCES (ORR)—UNIVERSITY OF ILLINOIS AT URBANA-CHAMPAIGN'S INTEGRATED MANAGEMENT SYSTEM FOR ELECTRONIC RESOURCES

Wendy Allen Shelburne, Electronic Resources Librarian, University of Illinois at Urbana
Michael Norman, Head, Serials Cataloging, University of Illinois at Urbana

On June 1, 2004, the University of Illinois at Urbana-Champaign (UIUC) Library went live with its own electronic resources management system, known locally as the Online Research Resources page or ORR. Through the work of user surveys, several access task forces, implementation groups, and the Library's Electronic Resources Work Group (ERWG), the Library identified that our users, as well as librarians and staff, desired more comprehensive electronic journal representation, immediate access, better publisher and coverage data, simplified searching functionality, and the ability to effectively use and display multiple access points for all our electronic resources, particularly our e-journals.

Prior to the construction of the new ORR, it was clear that the Library was providing access through the previous Electronic Resource Registry (E-Registry), which was a manual entry system constructed in 1999, for only a small portion of the e-journals and databases purchased each year. At its highest levels in May 2004, the database contained a total of 7,149 unique serial titles and 296 different databases. Although the Library was paying for full text access for thousands more serial titles that also included online access (Oxford, Cambridge, Emerald, World Scientific, Taylor and Francis, Walter de Gruyter, etc.), aggregated databases (EBSCO, Gale, Wilson, Proquest, Lexis-Nexis, etc.), and publisher packages (Elsevier's ScienceDirect, Wiley's Interscience, Blackwell's Synergy, SpringerLINK, Kluwer, etc.), there was no way to maintain accurate access points to these titles in a manual system.

The Library's collection of electronic resources receives tremendous use, with well over a million hits per month on the Library's Gateway and nearly two million downloads of articles per year from such e-journals such as *Science*, *PNAS*, *Nature*, *Tetrahedron*, *Physical Review Letters*, *Angewandte Chemie*, and many others. To take full advantage of the Library's significant investments in electronic access, the Library needed to construct a system that revealed to the Library's user community all available access points full text. The Library also wanted a system that helped keep information about serials accurate and current, including URLs, titles added/dropped within the various aggregators, ISSNs, title changes, and information on indexing and abstracting for individual titles.

What Is the ORR?

The ORR is a SQL Server database containing multiple interconnected tables with various data about each resource. It uses PHP and PERL scripts to push this information to the public interface making the most current and accurate information and URL link possible about an individual serial title or database available to the user (see figure 1). The database is populated with data from TDNet, UIUC's Voyager Integrated Library System (ILS), EBSCO, Ulrich's, and several other sources to produce a knowledge base populated with as much complete and accurate information as possible about a serial title or database. With the Library's user community always at the forefront of our thoughts concerning the best way to present this information, we combined a powerful search engine, virtually creating a mini-OPAC of electronic resources, into an interface that allowed keyword, start of title, and abbreviated title searching capabilities. We additionally provided display functionalities for an A-to-Z list of all titles, which can be further refined by subject categories. The interface created combined the best aspects of both (see figures 2 and 3).

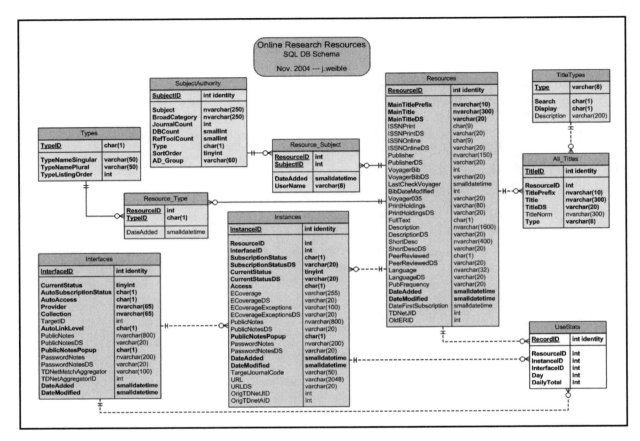

Figure 1.

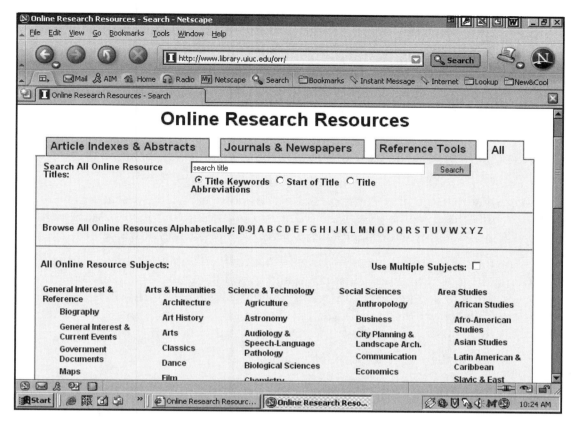

Figure 2.

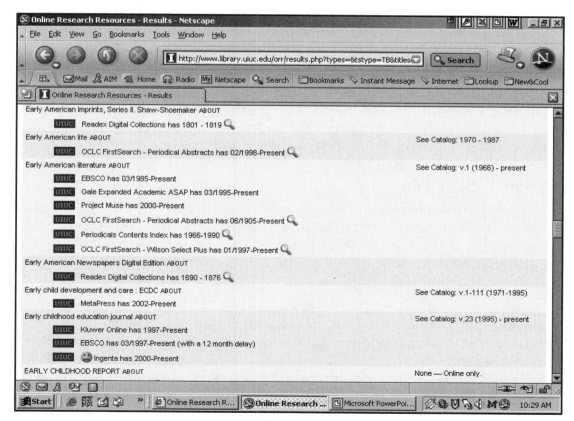

Figure 3.

What data are included in the ORR's knowledge base?

314,502 data records,

313,952 different instances of e-journals,

51,527 unique journal titles,

440 different aggregator packages, and

6,345 titles not associated with an aggregator or publisher package.

It must be mentioned that not all of these records are displayed in the public interface, rather, through automated updates and a set of permissions assigned to various staff for activation purposes, only the resource titles we have access to through our paid subscriptions and publisher packages, free resources, and open access serial titles are viewable.

Currently, the ORR provides access points to more than 27,000 unique e-journal titles, 43,567 different instances of those same titles, and over 440 databases and digital image repositories. An efficient component of the ORR is that when access is purchased to a new aggregator or publisher package (also called provider), the serial titles associated with that provider package can be turned on through an automated procedure.

Where do we get these data to keep information current and accurate?

- *TDNet:* The Library gets a weekly feed from TDNet of their complete database, which includes all 314,502 data records, informing us of changes that have occurred (such as URL, e-coverage, and titles added/dropped. TDNet data records include journal title, print ISSN, e-ISSN, URL, dates of coverage, the provider of full text, and a unique tracking number that helps us identify each separate instance of individual titles. The Library did not contract to receive publisher name, subject categories, or MARC records.

- *EBSCO:* The Library has access to nearly ten different aggregator databases through EBSCO including Academic Search Elite, Business Source Premier, Professional Development Collection, Health Source: Nursing/Academic Edition, Military & Government Collection, and several others. EBSCO provides a data feed that allows the consolidation of all EBSCO links into one single, earliest full-text coverage link and also allows the Library to list embargo information when a title does not have access to the most current issues.

- *Ulrichsweb:* Through several projects, the Library gained current information about publishers, peer-reviewed status, ISI Impact Factors, and ISSN (both print and electronic) for serial titles. Keeping this information current and accurate is vital to link resolver implementation and DOI or OpenURL deep-linking at the article level.

- *Voyager Integrated Library System:* To give users the greatest possibility to find the e-journals and databases the Library have access to, standardized information concerning title information, such as main, abbreviated, and alternate/variant titles had to be established. The title information we pulled from TDNet, EBSCO and Ulrichsweb was not uniform in nature. The Library determined that the bibliographic records populating our Voyager Integrated Library System would be the best source information. We also pull in additional data from the bibliographic record including ISSNs, OCLC number, frequency, subject headings, call numbers, where a title is indexed and abstracted, title change information, etc. Presently, the Library is working on creating the situation in which information is kept currently simultaneously in both the ORR and the Library's ILS.

Data within the ORR include

main title,

abbreviated title,

variant/alternate titles,

all ISSNs associated with the work,

URLs,

whether it peer reviewed,

ISI Impact Factor if applicable,

where it is indexed and abstracted,

title change history,

e-coverage,

print coverage,

current publisher information and publisher history,

targeting information,

subject categories,

the OCLC number,

LC Subject Headings,

LC & Dewey call numbers, and

current usage data.

The Library is in the process of adding 1) purchase order information; 2) pertinent licensing information such as ILL terms, simultaneous users, and course pack restrictions; and 3) additional usage statistics for collection development purposes.

Goals for the Future

The UIUC Library has been delighted with the progress made through the creation of the Online Research Resources (ORR). For the first time, the Library's user community has had comprehensive access to all the serial titles purchased by the library. Improving this home-grown system will be an ongoing process. The Library has established several important goals for the system as we move into the future including:

• Make maintenance of the e-resource ORR as automated as feasible to improve timeliness, consistency, and accuracy.

- Incorporate more data directly from the Voyager catalog and acquisitions modules to improve consistency between these databases and to maximize the benefits of library systems, acquisitions, and serials cataloging efforts.

- Use these assorted data feeds to help us keep information in bibliographic records as current as possible.

- Integrate ORR and SFX knowledge bases to create an enhanced system that grants our users current information and accurate links to full text content for our electronic and digital resources.

- Continue to improve the interface to make it easier to use and find what users need for their research.

The Online Research Resources (ORR) is a powerful and robust system for the Library and will continue to be enhanced in the future. The Library's new electronic resources management system has given us the ability to provide efficient and effective access to all our electronic resources, especially our e-journals, and presented the UIUC Library the chance to move forward in utilizing current technology. (To view the UIUC Library's Online Research Resources, go to www.library.uiuc.edu/orr/.)

Today librarians have to deal not only with collection development issues such as changes in technology and how resources are provided, but also with how these changes affect personnel. Library personnel issues such as coping with change and being more assertive as a manager were addressed at the 2004 Charleston Conference.

CHANGING CHANGE TO MAKE A CHANGE

Mary E. (Tinker) Massey, Library Technical Assistant, University of South Carolina, Columbia

The conference session was designed to be for a small group of supervisors trying to find answers for working with their employees. The major stress in libraries today is on coping with the rapid and numerous changes brought about by changes in personnel, structure, workflow, and technology. This workshop was woven from the threads of personal and environmental adaptations that help individuals and libraries make those changes. Our first discussion was about all of the stresses each person incurred getting to the conference (personal, weather, transportation, etc.). We all shared those experiences and talked about how we solved problems and how we felt about our solutions. We talked about the impact of stress on our health and lives and began to examine stress releasers. Exercise, meditation, relaxation methods, food, music, and other factors were explored in determining our ability to cope with change. Once we decided that we could manage the stress in many ways and on many levels, we talked about using changes to create more change that was also manageable.

A large part of the discussions centered on how to motivate and positively direct staff into those new changes. It was shown that as human beings, we must be given a chance to vocalize our losses, similar to the grief process, and take part in exchange sessions in which people can offer ideas about the impact of the changes and what they mean to them. Then, using the staff's ideas, new ways of coping could be found so that the staff would be able to buy into the new programs and workflows. Key to learning and accepting change is the "buying in" process. We decided that we needed to establish short-term goals that could be met quickly, as well as long-term goals for the ultimate and final targets to attain. Each short-term goal is a step toward the long-term goal and a piece of the coping process. It is important to never lose sight of our dreams, too. If we lose our dreams, we lose the courage to change and develop in our profession.

As an example, we used my simple personal dilemma, that of becoming a professional librarian (goal). Our "positives" were the motivation to become a librarian, having a B.A. degree, job experience, people skills, publications, speaking engagements, and running organizations (all professional activities and skills). The negatives were the lack of an MLS, lack of supervisory skills, lack of time, and the cost of going to school. To move from the starting point, we need "actions." With no time or money, we need to make time and find a source of money. Supervisory activities would not be available to most paraprofessionals, so that is one thing to delete from the "worry list." The MLS is the greatest stumbling block. You need a good GRE score and a decent resume and recommendations. You study for the GRE, take it, and pass, or you take the Miller's Analogies Test and pass it. The resume and recommendations I had already acquired over an extended working life. School was started and is now nearing completion. That entire process took other participants a short time. For me, it took three years, but the process will be completed shortly and everyone can see the step-by-step procedures necessary for completion.

By breaking change or stress down into its realistic factors for completion, we enable ourselves, our libraries, and staff to cope, adapt our lives, and establish new habits for dealing with the differences. The anxiety and fear come from the massive dark cloud of change, but the droplets of water in that cloud are far easier to deal with. I believe we all left the room with more positive feelings, and many handouts. Thanks go to the participants for their good-hearted interaction.

ASSERTIVE MANAGEMENT FOR LIBRARIANS (OR HOW I LEARNED TO STOP WORRYING AND LOVE CONFLICT)

Glenda Garbutt, Acquisitions/Serials Coordinator, DePaul University Libraries, Chicago, Illinois

> *Librarians are inclined to serve, not fight. . . . But unless librarians develop more fighting spirit, their services will suffer even more than it has.*
> —Robert R. Douglass, *The Personality of the Librarian*, 1957

This fascinating, non-intuitive statement highlights the inextricable relationship that exists between "good service" and what the Japanese call "kanjou" (khan-Joe), or "fighting spirit." The consummate library professional must be, as James Wyer so aptly noted,[1] intelligent, accurate, dependable, courteous, imaginative, adaptable, cooperative, etc. The "for-profit" service industry has long known, however, that customer service excellence and organizational success dependent on staff who are more than just capable, diligent, or nice. Today's library professionals must be everything that Wyer advocates and more. They must eagerly embrace change, confidently communicate their ideas, and fearlessly face conflict. Of the 27 traits Wyer listed, he deemed "intelligence" to be the most important to the profession of librarianship, with what he termed "forcefulness" coming in only twentieth-sixth place.[2] A great deal of literature has sprung up around the issue of competency, while "so little seems to have been published about understanding and managing conflict in libraries."[3] Yet conflict is as prevalent in libraries as it is in any organization. In 1957, Douglass examined the stereotypic characterization of the librarian in his thesis, *The Personality of the Librarian*, in which he repeatedly found librarians described by both "laymen" and librarians themselves as fearful, harmless, introverted, defensive, nonaggressive, inhibited, unadventurous, spineless, timid, nonconfrontational, passive, shy, meek, and nonargumentative.[4] Although these librarians may have been in all other respects excellent employees, the continuous depiction of librarians as "wallflowers," "shrinking violets," and "nervous Nellies" should not be dismissed as antiquated or obsolete, particularly where "conflict is now recognized as a necessary part of change."[5] This chapter considers the issue of conflict management in light of this persistent stereotype. First I consider the origins of the stereotype. Then I provide a definition of conflict and conflict management and discuss the costs and benefits of conflict. Finally, I explore the behavioral strategy of "assertive management" as an effective tool for coping with conflict.

"Marion the Librarian"

At the turn of the last century, one of the few professions a respectable gentlewoman could pursue besides that of teacher was that of librarian. In fact, today 84% of the CEOs of Ontario's public libraries are women (www.library.on.ca). Women still dominate the profession of librarianship. What impact does this gender domination have on, for example, management style? Do men and women manage differently? The answer is an unequivocal and resounding "Yes." "Until the 1960's, men and women received different signals about what was expected of them. . . . [W]omen have been expected to be . . . cooperative, supportive, understanding, gentle, and to provide service to others . . . .While men have had to appear to be competitive, strong, tough, decisive, and in control."[6] In the case of management styles, societal expectations have resulted in women adopting "nontraditional leadership" practices. For example, men tend to describe themselves as "transactional" leaders, who "view job performance as a series of transactions with subordinates—exchanging rewards for services rendered or punishment for inadequate performance."[7] Women describe themselves as "transformational"[8] leaders. "Transformational" leadership involves "getting subordinates to transform their own self-interest into the interest of the group through concern for a broader goal."[9] Rosener noted that perhaps the key difference between male and female managers is that "women actively work to make their interactions with subordinates positive for everyone involved."[10] Thus, given society's expectations of women, transformational leadership is characterized (not surprisingly) by managerial behaviors that "encourage participation, share power and information, enhance other people's self-worth, and get others excited about their work."[11] This brand of nontraditional leadership has a much more positive impact on an organization's climate compared with, for example, a more traditional management style such as the "coercive" or authoritarian style in which "leaders demand compliance."[12] However, given that the majority of library management is female, how do the traditional societal expectations and the nontraditional management styles of women affect conflict management?

Managing Conflict

"Despite librarians' silence on the subject, conflict is alive and well in libraries, just as in other complex entities,"[13] and although librarians may run from it, they can not hide. "Conflict exists whenever there are important unresolved differences among people, groups, or departments."[14] According to Allred, "management theorists have outlined three basic approaches to conflict: traditional, behavioral, and interactionist."[15] Traditionally, conflict was viewed as "a sign of failure, unnecessary and essentially destructive."[16] Thus organizations needed to avoid conflict at all costs. A behavioral approach to conflict, while acknowledging its organizational inevitability, cast a more neutral light on conflict, with an emphasis on "resol[ution] or eliminat[ion]."[17] However, "conflict resolution is the limited view that conflict is bad for the organization: thus it focuses only on techniques for dealing with unresolved differences."[18] The interactionist notion holds that "the elimination of conflict is as undesirable as it is unrealistic."[19] Today, astute managers realize the irrefutable necessity of conflict in helping to "solidify and maintain the relationships between individuals and groups . . . [as] . . . respect for individuality is fostered through disagreements, and interpersonal ties are developed and strengthened through agreement."[20]

At its best, "conflict can be invigorating, challenging, and absolutely essential to the effective functioning of a vital organization."[21] The benefits of "constructive conflict"[22] include improved communication; increased creativity; tension and stress release; and objective, goal, or mission re-evaluation. Not all conflict, however, is created equal. "Uncontrolled . . . or dysfunctional"[23] conflict can wreak havoc within an organization. "When conflict gets out of control, it can . . . poison the work environment, disrupt normal communication, and lower productivity and job satisfaction."[24] Allred notes that, at its most destructive, conflict most often results in "lowering of morale; creation of a climate of distrust and suspicion; stress and the toll it takes physically and psychologically . . . ; diversion of energy from work goals; a deepening of differences and an increase in distance between people; polarization of individuals and groups; obstruction of cooperative action; presence of irresponsible . . . behavior; [and] extension of the hostilities . . . to others not directly involved."[25] The literature, much to the chagrin of every librarian, recognizes no end of causes. According to Pettas and Gilliland,[26] conflict can be caused by any of the following: personal differences, differences in values, communication problems, competition for scarce resources, differentiation or specialization, line-staff conflicts, ambiguities of responsibility, role dissatisfaction and burnout, job-related issues, technological change, bureaucracy, and management style. So, what is a poor librarian to do? How is she to manage conflict effectively given her perceived propensity for non-confrontational behavior, societal expectations, and a plethora of causes? Needless to say, smelling salts will have no place in the ensuing discussion.

"The Assertive Librarian"

To begin to effectively manage conflict, library management and staff must fully acknowledge its crucial nature. "Organizations that permit and even at times encourage dissent adapt better to change."[27] Needless to say, librarians do not want to spend all their time managing conflict, but they must not avoid it or be frightened by it. Hulbert points to "three basic styles of [conflict] intervention . . . passive, aggressive, and assertive management."[28] Passive or "nonassertive people show deference, timidity, and meekness; have difficulty dealing with feelings of anger; make efforts to suppress their feelings; and feel frustrated much of the time."[29] Passive management is characterized by "avoidance behaviors, silent acceptance, self-denial, and over toleration."[30] Caputo notes that the passive individual is "prone to suffer hurt feelings, resentment, low self-esteem, and psychosomatic illnesses."[31] Passive management can have devastating effects on staff because it promotes distorted communication, frustration, negativity, low morale, and inconsistent treatment of staff members.[32] Nevertheless, "society encourages passivity [especially among women] by advocating such concepts as 'turn the other cheek' and by teaching people not to express feelings openly for fear of offending others."[33] Librarians, for the most part, have been societally and professionally conditioned to be passive. Of course, self-evaluation is critical in discerning whether or not one's own management style can be deemed passive; however, I would argue that most women probably engage in at least one if not more of these counterproductive behaviors from time to time. Suppose that a female library manager undertakes a scrupulous examination of her own managerial habits and finds, for example, that she regularly avoids expressing disapproval or disagreement. What options exist to help her modify or eliminate these unwanted behaviors?

As mentioned above, there are two other management styles from which she could choose—aggressive and assertive. To a passive individual, the attributes of "aggressiveness" and "assertiveness" may carry negative connotations, but are they the same? Hulbert acknowledges that in its most positive light, an aggressive management style characterizes "forceful, energetic people who stand up firmly for their own rights."[34] So what is wrong with standing up for your own rights, one might ask? Certainly this must be the forcefulness that Wyer espoused so many years ago (or is it)? While aggressive managers may appear confident and strong on the surface, often what underlies this managerial style is "a lack of respect for alternative points of view and . . . anger."[35] "Aggression is standing up for your rights without concern for the violation of others' rights."[36] Aggressive management is characterized by a quickness to "draw conclusions . . . , ascribe blame . . . , express dissatisfaction . . . , overreact . . . , insist on their own point of view, . . . and eschew negotiation and compromise."[37] Caputo explains that "the usual goal of aggression is domination, or winning, . . . [which] is ensured by humiliating, degrading, belittling, and overpowering other people."[38] Although "aggressive people often exhibit assertive behaviors such as honesty and clarity,"[39] the underlying motivation is manipulative and hostile. Thus Hulbert is quick to point out that "at its worst, aggressive behavior creates a climate of mistrust, demoralization, hostility, and antagonistic behavior."[40] Also, more often than not the aggressive management style acts to further fan the flames of conflict, offering little if any resolution.

Caputo draws attention to an intermediate style she calls "passive-aggression,"[41] which Hulbert does not include in her list. The clinical definition of passive-aggression is "a mechanism of defense, or a maladaptive pattern of coping behavior."[42] As a mechanism of defense, "passive-aggressors . . . are unaware of the aggressiveness of their intent."[43] This is to say that they see themselves always in the role of the victim and are highly adept at hiding their real feelings from both themselves and others. As a "maladaptive pattern of coping behavior," however, the passive-aggressor is fully conscious of his or her aggressive intent. Regardless of whether the intent is known or unknown to the passive-aggressor, the behaviors are more or less the same, and they include "dawdling, procrastination, intentional inefficiency, stubbornness, and forgetfulness."[44] This individual is the consummate saboteur whose every action seeks to undermine the organization or group's goal achievement. While Caputo does not speak to its specific management application, it is interesting to keep this style in mind. Although there may be few librarian managers who are passive-aggressors, there are probably many staff who display this type of behavior. In light of the prevalence of a passive management style, most librarians would not be well equipped to deal with passive-aggression.

In the end, our passive librarian in search of effective change is left with "assertive management." The primary difference between the assertive and the aggressive manager is that the former "confronts problems without personally attacking the beliefs and rights of others,"[45] whereas the latter does not. "*Assertion* is standing up for your rights without violating the rights of others."[46] Assertion is the middle road. "Assertive people attempt to strike a balance between passive and aggressive behaviors that emphasizes their self-responsibility."[47] In addition, assertive management is characterized by open, honest, direct, and non-defensive communication tempered by feelings of empathy, sensitivity, and respect for others. Thus, according to Hulbert, the assertive library supervisor manages conflict efficaciously using the following techniques:[48]

1. *Effective listening,* which includes an organized plan to discuss the problem in an appropriate meeting place; the use of active listening skills, which include "eye contact, facial expressions, gestures, and posture" and are key to assertiveness; direct questioning for suggestions regarding improvements and solutions; and paraphrasing to ensure accurate communication.

2. *Expectation clarity* which involves the elimination of "management by assumption," whereby objectives, goals, and tasks with timelines are clearly established and the resulting feedback is direct and neither vague nor misleading.

3. *Focus maintenance,* which involves correcting or solving problems at the time they occur, as well as the use of such organizational aids as agendas when facing problems in a group.

4. *Contextual limitations,* attempts to stop conflict before it begins by clearly explaining the true nature of, for example, "the extent of . . . responsibility, the level of . . . authority, . . . budgetary constraints, the political climate, and reporting hierarchies" in any given situation.

5. *Compromise and negotiation,* which stress the "assertive solution," which is always a win-win scenario, by reducing opposition and threat through the art of compromise and negotiation.

6. *Persistence and patience,* which try to minimize the stress, tension, and anxiety caused by change.

7. *Positive reinforcement,* which includes "intangible [staff] rewards," such as advice seeking, opportunity provision, reporting mobility, and contribution recognition.

8. *Effective criticism,* which involves the implementation of "interactive leadership"[49] whereby "problems are . . . described specifically, calmly, and objectively, without the use of charged language or sweeping generalizations."[50]

These eight techniques are not particularly earth shattering in their novelty, but neither is assertive management, which is why I am so often surprised by how little it is used. Because assertive managers are honest, objective, accurate, respectful, tolerant, and self-expressive, their ability to effectively manage conflict is all but ensured.[51] "The assertive librarian can face conflict with an investigative assurance that problems can be solved and decisions can be made through an appropriate analysis that allows respect for human rights."[52] This should simply be a matter of common sense. If this stereotypical depiction of librarians remains even remotely true today, however, the customer service success of libraries is tenuous at best. As passive and aggressive management styles involve the denial or suppression of another's rights (e.g., in the former the manager's and in the latter the staff's), the only style of management that is appropriate during situations of conflict is the assertive style. "You can be an assertive librarian: Your responsibility is . . . [to] effectively stand up for your rights while protecting and maintaining the rights of others."[53]

Notes

1. James I. Wyer, *Reference Work: A Textbook for Students of Library Work and Librarians* (Chicago: American Library Association, 1930).

2. *Ibid.*

3. Margaret A. Wilkinson and John P. Wilkinson, "Plotting Conflict," *Library Administration & Management* 11, no. 4 (1997): 205.

4. Robert R. Douglass, *The Personality of the Librarian* (Chicago: University of Chicago, 1957).

5. Jane M. Kathman and Michael D. Kathman, "Conflict Management in the Academic Library," *The Journal of Academic Librarianship* 16, no. 3 (1990): 145.

6. Judy B. Rosener, "Ways Women Lead," *Harvard Business Review* (November-December 1990): 124.

7. Ibid., 120.

8. Ibid.

9. Ibid.

10. Ibid.

11. Ibid.

12. Daniel Goleman, "Leadership that Gets Results," *Harvard Business Review* (March-April 2000): 80.

13. Carol B. Allred, "The Anatomy of Conflict: Some Thoughts on Managing Staff Conflict," *Law Library Journal* 79, no. 7 (1987): 7.

14. Kathman and Kathman, "Conflict Management in the Academic Library," 145.
15. Allred, "The Anatomy of Conflict," 8.
16. Ibid.
17. Ibid.
18. Kathman and Kathman, "Conflict Management in the Academic Library," 145.
19. John R. Darling and Dale E. Cluff, "Managing Interpersonal Conflict in a University Library," *Library Administration and Management* 1, no. 1 (1987): 17.
20. William Pettas and Steven L. Gilliland, "Conflict in the Large Academic Library: Friend or Foe?" *The Journal of Academic Librarianship* 18, no. 1 (1992): 25.
21. Allred, "The Anatomy of Conflict," 30.
22. Ibid.
23. Ibid., 9.
24. Ibid.
25. Ibid., 10.
26. Pettas and Gilleland, "Conflict in the Large Academic Library."
27. Doris Hulbert, "Assertive Management in Libraries," *The Journal of Academic Librarianship* 16, no. 1 (1990): 158.
28. Ibid.
29. Janette S. Caputo, *The Assertive Librarian* (Phoenix: Oryx Press, 1984), 4.
30. Ibid., 5.
31. Ibid.
32. Caputo, *Assertive Librarian.*
33. Hulbert, "Assertive Management in Libraries," 159.
34. Ibid.
35. Ibid.
36. Caputo, *Assertive Librarian,* 3.
37. Hulbert, "Assertive Management in Libraries," 159.
38. Caputo, *Assertive Librarian,* 5.
39. Ibid., 6.
40. Hulbert, "Assertive Management in Libraries," 159.
41. Caputo, *Assertive Librarian,* 6.
42. Ibid.
43. Ibid., 7.
44. Ibid.
45. Hulbert, "Assertive Management in Libraries," 159.
46. Caputo, *Assertive Librarian,* 3.
47. Ibid.
48. Hulbert, "Assertive Management in Libraries," 160–61.
49. Rosener, "Ways Women Lead," 120.
50. Hulbert, "Assertive Management in Libraries," 161.
51. Hulbert, "Assertive Management in Libraries."
52. Caputo, *Assertive Librarian,* 4.
53. Caputo, *Assertive Librarian,* 216–17.

Recommended Reading

Allan, Jane. "The Power of Persuasion." *Management Accounting-London*, 74, no. 11 (1996): 26.

American Library Association. *Racial and Ethnic Diversity Among Librarians: A Status Report.* 1998.[Online]. Available: http://www.ala.org/ala/ors/reports/racialethnic.htm.

Anonymous. "Assertiveness: More Than a forceful Attitude." *Supervisory Management*, 39, no. 2 (1994): 3.

Ash, Stephen. "How to Make Assertiveness Work for You." *Supervisory Management* 36, no. 7 (1991): 8.

Babcock, Linda, et al. "Nice Girls Don't Ask." *Harvard Business Review* 81, no. 10 (2003): 14–16.

Branden, Nathaniel. "Our Urgent Need for Self-Esteem." *Executive Excellence* 11, no. 5 (2003): 14–15.

Broughton, Diane. "When Being Nice Is Not Enough." *Library Management* 14, no. 6 (1993): 21–23.

Byrd, Richard E. *A Guide to Personal Risk Taking*. Edina, Minn.: Richard E. Byrd Company, 1994.

Davis, M., et al. *The Relaxation and Stress Reduction Handbook*. Oakland, Calif.: New Harbinger, 1988.

Diener, Marc. "Bully for You." *Entrepreneur* 27, no. 10 (1999): 183.

Dorgan, William, J. "Defensiveness: How Managers Can Be Assertive." *Modern Machine Shop* 71, no. 1 (1998): 122.

Eiring, H. Larry. "Dynamic Office Politics: Powering up for Program Success." *Information Management* 33, no. 1 (1999): 17–25.

Haddock, Patricia. "Communicating Personal Power." *Supervision* 63, no. 1 (2002): 13.

Haddock, Patricia. "Communicating Personal Power." *American Salesman* 48, no. 6 (2003): 30.

Janice, Elizabeth. "Assert Yourself: How to Put Your Foot Down Without Stepping on Others." *Black Enterprise* 25, no. 4 (1994): 71.

Kirwan-Taylor, Helen. "Don't Just Stand There Say Something." *Management Today* (2001): 66–69.

LeMon, Carl. "Motivating Adult Employees to Grow Up." *Employment Relations Today* 27, no. 3 (2000): 89–98.

Levy, Mike. "Stand Up and Be Counted." *Director* 52, no. 5 (1998): 15.

Levy, Philippa, and Bob Usherwood. *People Skills: Interpersonal Skills Training for Library and Information Work*. Cambridge: The University Press, 1992.

Lindenfield, Gael. "How to Say Sorry." *Management Today* (2001): 101.

Lwehabura, Mugyabuso. "Effective Library Management: Issues for Managers and Subordinates." *New Library World* 101, no. 1158 (2000): 263–68.

Mental Help Net. *Assertiveness Training: Standing up for Your Rights*. 2004. [Online]. Available: http://mentalhelp.net/psyhelp/chap13/chap13e.htm.

Ontario Library Service. *Ontario Public Library Email Addresses*. 2000. [Online]. Available: www.library.on.ca/CEO%20address%20listing/emailhead.html.

Raupsepp, Eugene. "Are You Properly Assertive?" *Supervision* 64, no. 5 (2003): 18–20.

Reynolds, Keith. "How to Feel Bad about Yourself Nearly All the Time." *Management Accounting-London* 77, no. 8 (1999): 86–87.

Schullery, Nancy M. "The Optimum Level of Argumentativeness for Employed Women." *Journal of Business Communication* 35, no. 3 (1998): 346–67.

Total Success. *Assertiveness*. 2004. [Online]. Available: http://www.tsuccess.dircon.co.uk/assertive.htm.

Zuker, Elaina. *The Assertive Manager*. New York: AMACOM, 1983.

Appendix 1: Assertive Bill of Rights*

1. The right to be treated with respect.

2. The right to say no without feeling guilty.

3. The right to experience and express feelings.

4. The right to take time to think.

5. The right to change my mind.

6. The right to ask for what I want.

7. The right to do less than I am humanly capable of doing.

8. The right to ask for information.

9. The right to make mistakes.

10. The right to feel good about myself.

11. The right to be listened to and taken seriously.

12. The right to choose not to assert myself.

* From Janette S. Caputo, *The Assertive Librarian* (Phoenix: Oryz Press, 1984); and Elaina Zuker, *The Assertive Manager* (New York: AMACOM, 1983).

As good custodians of our collections budgets, we all need to be concerned about making responsible decisions. Budget/fiscal matters continues to be an ongoing topic at the Conference, and quite rightly so. So many of our decisions, in all realms of librarianship, are based on economics.

Budget/Fiscal Matters

MARTHA, ROSIE, AND CONRAD: FIDUCIARY TRUST AND THE EGO-DRIVEN PUBLISHER

Bruce Strauch, Associate Professor, Business Law, The Citadel, Charleston, South Carolina

Fiduciary trust is the ethical standard of the firm. When you enter into employment, you are automatically bound by it. It is a relationship of the highest trust and is enforceable by law as a breach of contract and in the most egregious cases by criminal prosecution.

Breaching fiduciary trust is not unique to the publishing industry, but with three such terrific examples in recent news, it's hard to not want to address the publishing mentality in this regard.

Picture yourself having a revolutionary notion in publishing, a new angle never-before seen. You start a company and build it with a solid niche in the market. It's a publication that expresses your very essence, so you love living with it every day. You're doing well, realizing your justly deserved fame. There's nothing as heady as seeing your product in print on a regular basis.

You want to grow, so you do a public offering. With good advice from the investment bankers, you structure the stock so you control the board. The company still seems to be yours. Your pals on the board party and vacation with you. The company skyrockets. The world fawns. You did it all. And then you do something really dumb.

You lose sight of the fact that you have a fiduciary duty to those other shareholders, even if their votes amount to nothing.

The Martha Stewart Saga in Short

Helen Gurley Brown taught that sex sells and completely revolutionized women's publishing. Even the homeliest homemaker magazines began telling women how much noise to make during sex.

But Martha Stewart was out there with a dream, not of homemaking, but of being a fabulously wealthy doyenne of many mansions. Without mentioning the word sex, she laid out a world of luxury that vibrated like a tuning fork in the psyches of America's female magazine readers in the "aspirational demographic." People laughed at the elaborate crafts, but the message was not that some poor reader would actually labor for five days on Halloween decorations. It was a dream of having an army of servants to do it. Or to order around some craftsperson. Or a caterer for those delightful little luncheons for 15 under the trellises of the vineyard in the Sonoma Valley.

And Martha became a household name. Martha Stewart Omnimedia (MSO) operates in publishing, television, merchandising, and Internet industries selling products blazoned with Martha's brand name. Martha did her IPO in 1999, selling class A shares with the right of one vote per share. Martha owns 100% of the class B shares, which are entitled to 10 votes, along with sufficient A shares that she controls 94.4% of the shareholder vote.[1]

And thus she controlled the board of directors, all close personal friends such as Darla Moore, high-powered banker married to a billionaire corporate raider, and Naomi Seligman, who also sits on the board of John Wiley & Sons.[2]

The enterprise was truly Martha's brainchild, and how sweet it was. In 2002, Martha got a salary of $900,000 and a bonus of $680,600. The board of course just knew she was worth it.[3] But that's not all. When you are the brand name, everything in your life is arguably a business expense: hair styling, massages, driver for an antiquing jaunt in New England.

And then there are those fabulous mansions. In 2003, MSO paid $2.5 million to a real estate management company owned by Martha to rent her mansions—the Hamptons, Westport, Maine—for the magazine and TV.

Need to get away for a weekend? Use the company jet to scout a locale for an article. Or entertain the advertisers. When the insider trading scandal erupted, Martha and a friend were cosseted in a $1,500 per night suite at the Las Ventanas al Paraiso resort in Mexico. Total bill excluding the staggering cost of the jet: $17,000, including kayak tour and dinners in the Sea Grill.[4]

Martha of course had her wealth wisely invested by Peter Bacanovic of Merrill Lynch. One of her stocks was in ImClone Systems, Inc., a biotechnology company with one key asset, a cancer-specific drug called Erbitux. ImClone's CEO Sam Waksal was a master promoter and pal of Martha's and one-time escort of her daughter.[5]

On December 25, 2001, Waksal learned privately that the FDA had rejected his application for Erbitux approval. A panicked Waksal dumped his shares on the market and tipped his father and daughter, who did the same. Curiously, Peter Bacanovic was broker at Merrill Lynch for both Waksal and Martha, and in turn tipped Martha to the news.

Martha was on the company jet with her friend and neighbor Marianna Pasternak, then in the process of getting a divorce from an M.D. husband. Marianna, mindful of where money comes from, tipped her separated husband. Martha sold her shares on December 27, and Pasternak sold on December 28. At the close of trading on the 28th, ImClone told the world the bad news.[6]

Any spike in trading before a big corporate announcement is investigated by the Securities and Exchange Commission (SEC). Merrill Lynch began its own internal investigation. A panicked Bacanovic and Martha Stewart apparently got together on a story that the sale was a prearranged stop-loss order if and when the stock fell to $60.

Waksal was caught red-handed, pled guilty, and is now in prison. Stewart was convicted of making false statements to the SEC in violation of 18 U.S.C. § 1001.[7]

At the trial, the media drama focused on Bacanavic's assistant ratting them both out and Martha's loyal servitor breaking down in tears as she described Martha erasing an e-mail message and then replacing it. One of the more intriguing bits of evidence was a list of Martha's stock, on which Bacanavic had made notes using one pen and then later made the @60 notation with another pen. The jury, curiously, did not convict on this.

Our self-obsessed Martha had equally self-obsessed celebrities like Rosie O'Donnell make cameo courtroom appearances to embrace her, apparently feeling that poor rubes on the jury would be so impressed by the celebrity parade that they would not convict. In fact, nothing seems more calculated to tell the jury how insignificant they are and how important a world Martha lived in.

Legal experts filled the air and print with the issue of Martha not testifying on her own behalf. The Occam's razor approach to this issue is that an attorney has an ethical duty to not put a client on the stand if he knows she is going to perjure herself. And Martha had already tried her lies with the SEC, to no avail. She also had a notorious temper.

The prosecution's key witness was Douglas Faneuil, assistant to Bacanovic. He said that on the morning of December 27, he learned that Waksal and family members were dumping ImClone stock. He got Bacanovic on the phone and transferred the call to Martha's assistant. Bacanovic instructed Faneuil that Martha would be calling later and to tell her about Waksal. Martha indeed called while in transit on the company jet to a luxury Mexican resort, and Faneuil did as instructed. She told him to sell.

Martha also phoned Waksal's assistant, asking what was going on with ImClone. These calls were verified. And if Faneuil's story was correct, Martha had traded on improperly obtained insider information. Not too bright for a former stockbroker, but vintage Martha.

When she returned, she went with her lawyers to be interviewed by the SEC, FBI, and U.S. Attorney's office. And there she told her lies. And did it again over the phone to the same parties on April 10, 2002.[8]

Martha dealt a real body-blow to the corporation's primary asset, her name, reputation, and associated goodwill. Already a woman either loved or hated, the media went into overdrive. Cartoons, tabloid headlines, late night comedian jokes—*schadenfreude* run wild. Ambushed repeatedly by media personalities she had once thought her friends, Martha had to discontinue TV appearances. MSO's stock fell 65%.[9]

This breach of fiduciary duty is remedied by a derivative suit, which is to say, damages go not to the shareholder but to the corporation. The shareholder only profits derivatively and may in fact still lose value in his or her investment.[10] The lawyers who specialize in this sort of litigation are always standing by, and suits have been filed.[11]

The irony of the whole situation is that Switzerland approved Erbitux, and ImClone's stock rebounded. And Martha is now behind bars with her loyal fans awaiting her return. MSO's stock is rising again, given that she will only be in the slam for a short five months, followed by house arrest in one of her many mansions, where she can continue her work.

And of course she still controls the board and through them can put herself right back to work.

Rosie O'Donnell and the Celebrity Tantrum

The Rosie O'Donnell case was one of pure hubris that only today's screeching and uncontrolled celebrities can get into. Execs in suits believed in her abilities, and she repaid them with anger and hysteria.

The giant Bertelsmann bought Random House and 75% of Gruner + Jahr (G + J), with the Jahr family holding the rest. In its conception it was going to be one of those media synergies once so highly touted.

Gruner + Jahr entered the American market in 1978, buying *Parents* and *Young Miss* (transmogrified into *YM*). It then published *GEO*—a more hip European version of *National Geographic*—for the American market. *GEO* closed two years later due to squabbles between German and American executives.[12]

In a bid to build a business magazine group, G + J way overpaid for *Fast Company Magazine*, and then the dot-com bubble burst.[13]

In 1994, G + J bought aged women's titles such as *Family Circle* and *McCall's* just as *Martha Stewart Living* and *O, the Oprah Magazine* set an entirely new paradigm in women's magazine publishing.

Struggling to meet the new female competition, G + J shut down the very fatigued *McCall's* and rebirthed it as *Rosie*, a showcase platform for talk-show host Rosie O'Donnell. It began with great hoopla and an initial 3.5 million circulation, but in the second year, Rosie savaged sex god Tom Selleck on the air over gun control despite the fact that her bodyguards went about armed. This got the conservative bloggers on her case. Then she announced her homosexuality, and for unexplained reasons quit her TV show.[14] In today's sensitive environment, she might get a pass on not staying in the closet, but G + J no doubt naturally assumed this was to be a multimedia deal like Oprah's.

The partnership fell apart in 2002 in a spitting contest between corporate and the raging celebrity and led to suit and countersuit. The point at issue was "editorial and artistic control." And you can imagine all the smiling assurances that were given Rosie that this was to be her magazine and of course she would be deferred to.

Then came a famous cover that Rosie was determined would show cancer survivors with their hair fallen out from chemotherapy. G + J saw the cover repelling buyers in the grocery store checkout line and nixed it. Rosie went berserk.[15]

There was another noteworthy spat over a photo of Rosie with the "Sopranos," run without her permission, which she claimed "made her look fat." Berserk encore.[16]

Pretty small stuff, but Rosie walked. When G + J threatened suit, she replied with a threat to ruin them.

As a stand-up comedian in her early days, Rosie had been known as "The Queen of Mean," apparently with good reason. During pretrial discovery, a lot of evidence of Rosie's tyrannical little ways emerged. She allegedly accused a cancer survivor employee of lying to her and said that "people who lie get cancer." She denied this under oath in a deposition but then admitted it was true at trial.[17]

Ordinarily this "liars get cancer" sort of charge is what clients use to bore their lawyers. He's a bad person. She's a mean person. And they can't accept that it has no bearing on the legal issues. In this case, however, it did. It went to the issue of whether Rosie really had any compassion for the cancer victims on her famous disputed cover or just got riled when she didn't get her way.

For the legal commentator voyeur, the case should have provided some interesting law about good faith behavior on the part of the celebrity editor, but two weeks into the trial G + J's case fell apart.

Under Rosie's contract, if the circulation did not hit a target level, either side could break off the enterprise without legal repercussions. O'Donnell claimed Gruner + Jahr had manipulated circulation figures, keeping them falsely high. Since the subscription list is verifiable, you inflate newsstand sales. The Audit Bureau of Circulations found a 32% overstatement by G + J.[18]

After a two-week trial, the judge dismissed both cases.

Conrad Black Loots His Company

"Greed has been severely underestimated and denigrated, unfairly so, in my opinion," Conrad Black to his biographer.[19]

Starting in 1966, Conrad Black and his buddy David Radler began putting together a small empire of local and regional newspapers across Canada. He had a brief period as a corporate takeover swashbuckler during which he was criticized for disregard of minority shareholders.[20]

A political obsession lured him back to his original business, and by all accounts he was a brilliant newspaperman. And what could be more marvelous than being a press baron?

Ownership of *The National Post* and every other big newspaper in Canada was not enough for his ambitions, so he went global. Black's holding company, Hollinger International, bought the *Telegraph* and the *Spectator* in Britain, the *Chicago Sun-Times, The Jerusalem Post,* and part of *The New York Sun* and *The National Post,* as well as a multitude of weeklies in the United States and Canada.

Just like Martha, Black held control through "super-voting shares," which allowed him 72.6% of the vote with 30.3% of the equity.

He hand-picked the board, filling it with folks like Henry Kissinger, uber-presidential advisor; Marie-Josée Kravis, wife of a corporate mergers giant; Richard Perle, famed neo-con; and billionaire Alfred Taubman, billionaire and owner of Sothebys.

Life was sweet. Black took an annual salary of $6.5 million compared to Arthur Sulzberger Jr.'s $6.3 million from an empire four times the size of Black's. And Black got $1.9 million in management fees for a management company he owned, but more about that later.

He had four homes: seven acres in the Bridle Path neighborhood in Toronto, Kensington in London, Park Avenue in New York, and 17,000 square feet in Palm Beach on Ocean Drive. And of course, so much of the expense could be charged to the company as necessary digs for a press baron on the go.[21]

The two company jets cost $8 to $10 million annually, and one was redecorated for $3 million. The company paid portions of the servants' salaries in all the houses and $100,000 annually for the Manhattan apartment.[22]

Lavish personal spending for Black and his wife Barbara Amiel included $24,950 for "summer drinks" and $90,000 to refurbish their personal Rolls Royce. They splurged on exercise equipment, handbags, and silverware for the corporate jet. An intimate 80-guest birthday gathering for Barbara at La Grenouille blew $42,870. Guests included Peter Jennings, Charlie Rose, and Barbara Walters. So it's business, right? But then Oscar de la Renta and Ron Perelman were there. Partially social climbing? What the heck? All of it was charged to the company.

But it just wasn't enough. So over a period of years, a company Black owned called Ravelston got $218.4 million in management fees, tens of millions of dollars above what direct management would have cost. The objective of course was "to shift cash to Black and Radler in amounts far greater than any direct compensation package could ever do."[23]

Yes, he was outsourcing management of the newspapers to himself.

With all that money being sucked out of Hollinger, they had trouble meeting their debt service. So they sold off $2.2 billion in assets. And in an incredibly brazen maneuver, Hollinger, run by Black, sold newspapers to companies owned by Black and his partner David Radler. In the most brazen maneuver of all, two very profitable weeklies were sold for $1 each.

The cat got out of the bag when the inky wretches toiling at their journalistic trade noticed that the same management team was coming around as before.

By 2000, the management fee was running to $38 million. Most of the Canadian newspapers were unloaded in that year. Since the business was now smaller, the board approved $19.4 million as a "break fee" to Ravelston since the business was now so much smaller and they would be getting less. Black and Radler also got board approval for $32.4 million in noncompete agreements.

Black was agreeing to not compete with the newspapers he had sold off. But the payment should have come from the purchaser, not the seller, and the money should have gone into Hollinger's, not Black's, pocket. Yes, the board was totally asleep.

An angry fund that owned Hollinger stock began demanding answers, which Black could stonewall only for so long. The board had to wake up and react.

A special Hollinger board committee filed a 513-page report with the federal court and the SEC charging that Lord Black and Mr. Radler "made it their business to line their pockets at the expense of Hollinger almost every day, in almost every way they could devise."[24]

What was the board's problem? It was either partying or engaging in conflicts of interest. Richard Perle, a former defense department official, received close to $3 million in loans to companies where he had ownership.[25]

The report said "the board Black selected functioned more like a social club or public policy association than as the board of a major corporation, enjoying extremely short meetings followed by a good lunch and discussion of world affairs."[26]

The lunch functioned more like a think tank or a high-society political salon than a board meeting. They would discuss China and the European Union, topics that allowed the members to wax philosophic and not confuse themselves with money matters.

The annual Hollinger Dinner was a $1 million, two-day gala at which directors rubbed elbows with Margaret Thatcher, Paul Volcker, and Joan Collins.[27]

Hollinger money was spread around among the directors' pet causes: a $15,000 table at the Museum of Modern Art dinner honoring board member Ms. Kravis; $45,000 to the Americas Society, for which Kissinger fundraises; and $152,000 to other Kissinger charities.

And then there was that nice investment of $2.5 million worth of Hollinger money in director Richard Perle's venture capital fund Trireme. Black also had an interest in this company. The investment was made without audit committee approval.[28]

With Martha Stewart, the board had no duty to monitor her personal affairs. They couldn't very well attach a spy to her jet to eavesdrop on phone calls to her broker. The company was otherwise well managed, and the board did its job.

But Hollinger's directors have liability under their fiduciary duties of care and loyalty.[29]

They seem to have flubbed these pretty royally.

Notes

1. *Monica Beam, derivatively on behalf of Martha Stewart Living Omnimedia, Inc. v. Martha Stewart et al.*, 833 A.2d 961, 2003 Del. Ch. LEXIS 98 (2003).

2. Ibid.

3. Matthew Rose and Emily Nelson, "Martha Stewart v. Martha Stewart Living: Probing a Gray Area," *The Wall Street Journal,* February 26, 2004, B1.

4. Ibid.

5. *Monica Beam.*

6. Ibid.

7. *United States v. Martha Stewart & Peter Bacanovic,* 323 F. Supp. 2d 606, 2004 U.S. Dist. LEXIS 12538 (2004).

8. Ibid.

9. *Monica Beam.*

10. *Abrams v. Donati,* 66 N.Y.2d 951, 953, 489 N.E.2d 751 (1985).

11. *Monica Beam.*

12. James Bandler and Matthew Karnitschnig, "European Giant in Magazines Finds U.S. a Tough Read," *The Wall Street Journal,* August 19, 2004, 6.

13. Ibid.

14. Matthew Rose, "Fireworks Are Likely at Start of *Rosie Magazine* Trial," *The Wall Street Journal,* October 27, 2003, B1.

15. Ibid.

16. Ibid.

17. Matthew Rose, "Gruner + Jahr, O'Donnell Finish Out of the Money," *The Wall Street Journal,* November 26, 2003, A1.

18. Rose, "Fireworks," B4.

19. Duff McDonald, "The Man Who Wanted More," *Vanity Fair* (April 2004): 293.

20. Ibid., 292–95, 333–39.

21. Ibid., 336.

22. Ibid.

23. Mark Heinzl and Christopher J. Chipello, "Report Slams Hollinger's Black for a 'Corporate Kleptocracy'," *The Wall Street Journal,* September 1, 2004, A4.

24. Ibid., A1.

25. Ibid., A4.

26. Ibid.

27. Robert Frank and Elena Cherney, "Lord Black's Board: A-List Cast Played Acquiescent Role," *The Wall Street Journal,* September 27, 2004, A1.

28. Ibid., A6.

29. See *In re Abbot Laboratories Shareholders Litigation,* 325 F.3d 795 (7th Cir. 2003); *In re Caremark International Inc. Derivative Litigation,* 698 A.2d 959 (Del. Ch. 1996); and *In re Baxter International, Inc. Shareholders Litigation,* 654 A.2d 1268 (Del. Ch. 1995).

BUDGETING FOR PRINT + FREE ONLINE

Robert Alan, Head of the Serials Department, The Pennsylvania State University Libraries, University Park

Introduction

There are at least several different publisher pricing models now offered for serial publications in print and online formats. One area of concern raised each of the last several years at Penn State Libraries has been the issue of funding for print subscriptions with accompanying free online access (print + free online). As user demand for 24/7 desktop access increased, the Libraries responded by quickly building a large, comprehensive electronic resource collection. Free online access accompanying print subscriptions was a preferred option when available. Selectors considered free online access that replicated print, a bargain that should not be passed up. However, it was always assumed that this pricing model was simply a way for publishers to introduce online access while developing their products and gauging user demand. Once user acceptance was in place, pricing models would change, and publishers would begin charging for online access.

Background

As background, Penn State has 23 campus locations across the state plus a growing distance education program. The addition of electronic resources has been especially beneficial to the many remote campus locations. Penn State requires that all electronic resources, with a few exceptions for specialized products, be licensed for all campus locations. Therefore, activation of free online access accompanying print subscriptions is contingent on open access to all Penn State users. On occasion, licensing terms cannot be agreed on, and the print subscription remains the sole source of access.

Transition from Print to Online

But there was also a perception that while free online access accompanying print was a good thing for the Libraries, there was a cost associated with maintaining this option. Are publishers going to continue to supply it for "free," or as we expect, is this model a precursor to charging for online access? Were selectors maintaining print subscriptions at the expense of other content due to the accompanying "free" online access?

To summarize, in 2000/2001 it was assumed that

- free online access accompanying print would eventually no longer be "free";

- online access would become the preferred medium, and print might only be available at an additional charge; and

- print + free online was still a model valued by subject selectors.

Better Planning Required

In 2000/2001 Penn State's serials budget was restructured with the goal of improving management of both print and electronic serials. Like many libraries, Penn State maintained separate funds for standing order and subscription commitments plus new orders, replacements, etc. A new category was established to keep track of print + free online access. When a selector requested that free online access be activated, the funding was changed from recurring print serial funding to the new category of recurring print + free online.

From a collection development perspective it was important to keep better track of print + free online. Like many libraries, Penn State Libraries has needed to continuously review its serial commitments and most often needs to reduce its serials base to accommodate budget increases that do not cover inflation. In addition, there are always new products (especially electronic resources) that require additional support. The budget category of print + free online ensures that selectors are aware that by canceling the print, the online access will also be lost. This is an important decision point for selectors as they need to be aware of the impact of each serial cancellation.

Transition Continued

By 2003/2004 there was clear evidence that more and more publishers were changing their pricing models and replacing print + free online with one of the following models:

- Free would no longer be free but would be offered at a surcharge (either dollar value or percentage of print [content].

- E-content would be charged for, with optional print available at a deep discount.

Between 2000/2001 and 2003/2004 several publishers did change their models away from free online access with accompanying print subscription (e.g., Cambridge and Oxford). While online access to Cambridge titles was continued at a reasonable surcharge, Penn State has yet to reach agreement with Oxford.

As the budget planning process for fiscal year 2004/2005 began, the issue of print + free online access was brought to the table. Three questions were asked at that point:

- Is the category of print + free online on the decline? If so, is the decline due at least in part to the shift in publisher pricing models away from print + free online?

- Are annual price increases for print + free online significantly higher than other categories (e.g., print only, online only, etc.)? Or is the category of print + free online within the same range of inflation experienced by other categories of serials?

- What strategies, if any, should be employed to better manage the category of print + free online?

Is Print + Free Online Becoming a Dinosaur?

Penn State began keeping track of the category of print + free online in 2000 and added the additional category "print + online access for an additional fee." Subscriptions were also converted to electronic content (content would be billed at 100% + access fee + possibly a percentage of the content fee for optional print).

Table 1 indicates the percentage of the overall collections budget assigned to 1) print + free online, 2) online access at a surcharge with print subscription, and 3) subscription converted to e-content only with optional print. The categories of e-content for additional fees (2000/2001–2002/2003) and subscription converted to e-content fees (2000/2001–2002/2003) were not tracked due to Penn State's migration to a new ILS system in 2000/2001 and a lack of individual order records for many of the print and electronic serial titles. However, available data indicate that the percentage of the collections budget allocated to print + free online remained constant. This means that while some print + free online products are being converted to other categories, publishers continued to support the print + free online model. There was no analysis of current sources of new print + free online titles being added that allowed the percentage to remain constant. However, it was concluded that many of the newer print + free online titles were from society publications and smaller publishing houses.

Table 1. Collection Budget Analysis.

Collection Budget Analysis (% of total collections budget)					
	2000/2001	2001/2002	2002/2003	2003/2004	2004/2005
Complementary E-Content with Print	4.8%	6.8%	6.7%	6.6%	6.7%
E-Content for Additional Fees[a]	0.0%	0.0%	3.1%	5.0%	7.3%
Subscription Converted to E-Content Fees[a]	0.0%	0.0%	0.0%	14.2%	14.8%

[a] Separate funding categories for print plus additional surcharge for e-content not implemented until 2002/2003, and percentages of total collection budget not available.

The title counts appear in table 2. The counts also show a fairly constant number of print + free online titles maintained each year. But the table also clearly shows an increase in categories of e-content added for additional fees and titles converted to e-content. With Springer/Kluwer and Taylor & Francis announcing their intention to charge for content currently provided free with print subscriptions, the numbers will rise even further next year. Both Springer and Taylor & Francis titles are currently funded as print + free online.

Table 2. Collection Counts.

Collection Counts (titles activated and accounted for)	2000/2001	2001/2002	2002/2003	2003/2004	2004/2005
Complementary E-Content with Print	611	934	823	697	709
E-Content for Additional Fees	0	0	357	340	686
Subscription Converted to E-Content Fees	0	0	874	929	1,239

In response to the question of whether print + free online is on the decline, it can be concluded that it is. With the move of Springer and Taylor & Francis to a different pricing model, there may be 200+ fewer print + free online products within the next year.

Is "Free" Really Free?

Like many libraries, Penn State factors the predicted inflation rates for the upcoming year into collections budget projections. In 2004/2005 the question was asked whether we should factor in a slightly higher figure for print + free online titles due to one or both of the following factors:

- Annual price increases for print + free online may be higher than other categories, especially print only.

- An unknown percentage of print + free online titles will need to be converted to either the model of print + surcharge for e-content *or* e-content + surcharge for optional print.

In 2000 the results of a study on the effect of electronic journal pricing on print price subscriptions were published in the *Bulletin of the Medical Library Association*.[1] The study examined the rates of print journal subscription price increases for selected medical and medically related journals according to the type of available electronic access. The types of access included electronic priced separately from the print, combination print with "free online" access, and aggregated, defined by the authors as being electronic access purchased as part of a collection (e.g., Elsevier ScienceDirect). The authors analyzed the percentage of print price increases for 300 journals over a five-year period (1996–2000). (See table 3.)

Table 3. Five-Year Price History.

Five-Year Price History					
	% Increase 2000/2001 (compared to 1999/2000)	% Increase 2001/2002	% Increase 2002/2003	% Increase 2003/2004	% Increase 2000/2004
Various Print (59)	6.4%	8.6%	8.6%	7.1%	37.6%
Various Print + Free Online (247)	8%	8.9%	8.1%	12.2%	42.7%
Cambridge (62)	5.1%	7.7%	5.2%	9.9%	30.9%
Sage (63)	11.5%	12.9%	7.1%	17.6%	58.6%
Springer (67)	4.9%	5.2%	5.8%	9.3%	27.7%
Taylor & Francis (156)	11.2%	12.2%	9.9%	14.7%	57.3%

The results of this study indicate that print prices for journals with electronic access exceeded journals that did not offer an electronic option:

- Electronic priced separately averaged 3% to 5% higher than print titles, using both measures.

- Combination print with "free online" access had higher price increases from 1996 to 1999. In 2000 price increases for print + free online were about the same as for print-only titles.

- Costs for e-content that was part of aggregated packages consistently went down over the five years.

- Print journals with no online option had the lowest price increases.

In 2004/2005 Penn State identified 709 titles (6.7% of the total collections budget) in its collection that were funded as print + free online. Although a relatively low percentage of the total collection, the category of print + free online still amounted to a significant recurring expense each year based on the overall size of the budget.

In response, a study of print + free online titles was conducted that partially replicated the study published in the *Bulletin of the Medical Library Association*. The primary differences were that the sample included titles from all subject areas and only included titles currently subscribed to by Penn State. Since many of Penn State's electronic resources are part of negotiated packages based on the value of the title mix with a negotiated inflation cap applied, aggregated packages were not included in the study. Several major publishers who have changed models from print + free online to e-content with optional print were included.

Conclusions

This brief study based on Penn State's mix of titles indicates that there is no appreciable difference between price increases for print + free online and print or e-only. But there are other factors to consider:

- Price increases (at least based on Penn State's mix of titles) for print + free online have for the most part consistently been within normal inflation ranges each year from 2000 to 2004.

- Publisher price increases appear to exceed the average increase in the year a pricing model changes. This may be due to a number of factors, but it is an interesting observation at the very least.

- Given that Taylor & Francis and Springer/Kluwer plan to change their pricing models, there is an expectation that the category of print + free online will further decline. It now appears that most, if not all, of the major publishers have or soon will convert from the print + free online model to other models.

- Should libraries separately budget for print + free online access? Yes, it can be important to track this category of serials. Changing pricing models can have a significant impact on libraries if they do not plan accordingly.

Notes

1. F. L. Chen, P. Wrynn, F. L. Erhman, J. L. Rieke, and H. E. French, "Electronic Journal Access: How Does It Affect the Print Subscription Price?" *Bulletin of the Medical Library Association* 89, no. 4: 363–71.

The chapters in this section provide insight into what it means to buy and sell books via the Internet. This is a relatively new way of doing business, and one that has changed our libraries' workflows and procedures. Speakers provided guidance on this topic and confirmed that business transactions via the Internet are here to stay.

Books and the Internet: Buying, Selling, and Libraries

BOOKS AND THE INTERNET: BUYING, SELLING, AND LIBRARIES

Heather S. Miller, Assistant Director for Technical Services and Systems, State University of New York at Albany

Introduction

This conference session explored what it's like for publishers and booksellers to sell, and for libraries to buy, books (that is, real, printed books) via the Internet. Panelists included representatives from the publishing, bookselling, and library worlds. They delved into the pros and cons of this mode of doing business and provided some insight for others who might wish to use the Internet to buy or sell books. Time limitations necessitated very brief comments by the panelists, with the expectation that interested persons would follow up individually for specific advice.

The panelists agreed that buying and selling books over the Internet is here to stay and that it has significantly changed working practices. All noted tradeoffs, but the advantages and disadvantages differed among publishers, vendors, and libraries, and it was valuable for each sector to hear the others' points of view. Although it was apparent that the Internet has been an added means of buying and selling books, not a replacement for traditional means of doing business, Sherman Hayes expressed the most enthusiasm. Under his leadership, UNC's Randall Library has moved wholeheartedly into purchasing books via the Internet.

The comments of the speakers follow.

LIBRARY EXPECTATIONS AND INTERNET BOOKSELLERS

William P. Kane, Regional Sales Manager, Alibris for Libraries, Emeryville, California

To satisfy patrons' increasing demand for speedy fulfillment, libraries more and more frequently turn to Internet booksellers for nontraditional book supply—previously the exclusive realm of "traditional" jobbers and wholesalers.

Many, if not most, library patrons—including faculty and librarians—have grown up in or at least grown used to a world where instant communication is the norm; instant messaging, wireless e-mail, and cell phone cameras all purport to deliver the goods immediately, worldwide. Whereas information delivery via fax machine was not long ago considered state-of-the-art, today's library patrons are accustomed to (and already frustrated by) information delivery via express delivery, e-mail, and Web sites offering ready access to dynamic, real-time news.

To today's library patron, armed with desktop access to databases of tens of millions of books, each with stipulated real-time availability attached, a response from the library along the lines of "six to eight weeks" to a seemingly simple purchase request can seem laughably outdated—notwithstanding righteous explanations of contractual business agreements, shipping requirements, and library processing and notification time. Instead, patrons see can fairly easily see that the book in question is readily available "on the Internet," and expect immediate (if still unrealistic) results.

Indeed, libraries have stepped up to the challenge of providing up-to-date information immediately: The online catalog serves as the preeminent example of real-time inventory mega-database; liaison-driven collection development is finely tuned to anticipate and pre-satisfy patron demand; full text electronic journal subscriptions are obtained (at dear costs) to provide campus- and/or worldwide access to formerly hard-to-get-your-hands-on research; librarians are accessible 24/7 via "virtual" reference desks; and many patrons are empowered to perform formerly mediated library functions such as renewals/reserves/ILL at their convenience, rather than the library's.

Library suppliers of scholarly books have likewise reacted appropriately to increasing fulfillment time pressures: Approval plans are intended to get the books in the door before patron requests for same; some jobbers offer full cataloging and processing services, cutting critical to-the-shelf time; application development to coincide with integrated library systems can reduce paperwork and the time-consuming (and long-dreaded) problem of double-keying orders; and sophisticated customer service is routinely available across all time zones.

But not until the advent (and subsequent onslaught) of Internet-based booksellers did a book's bibliographic (including edition, subject headings, imprint, etc.) and extra-bibliographic (including condition, availability, price, discount, etc.) elements become intertwined, and equally transparent. The library can now verify a book's ISBN and immediate availability simultaneously, and across multiple and competing vendor platforms. The transparency of a book's whereabouts and price compels Internet and traditional booksellers to transform competition into partnerships—booksellers, no matter the stripe, are in the business of selling as many books as possible, and happily sell them to each other in order to serve the library customer faster. Therefore, it is not uncommon for libraries to place orders with "traditional" vendors for Internet bookshops' books.

Meanwhile, whereas "traditional" library booksellers can often boast of dozens of large (in terms of dollars) customers, Internet booksellers may claim thousands of relatively small customers—while traditional library booksellers succeed by selling large numbers of books to relatively few customers, Internet booksellers can also succeed by selling relatively few books to relatively large numbers of customers.

Unfortunately, the math is never that simple, but the trend is toward "sachet selling," and not away from it—there being many, many, many more sellers and customers and potential customers at the so-called bottom of the pyramid than at the top. To truly thrive, all libraries and Internet booksellers need do now is find each other.

THE INTERNET AND BARNES & NOBLE

Brian Buckley, Vice President, Professional Sales and Marketing, Barnes & Noble, New York City

The Internet has revolutionized our lives and has changed the way we do almost everything—from selling our "garage sale" items, to doing research on health issues, to communicating with friends and business associates around the world. As a bookseller, we, too, have seen our world change. In less than 10 years, online consumer book sales have grown to $3.4 billion, or 14% of all consumer book sales.[1]

Over the last few years, we have also seen bookselling and buying change for libraries. According to research conducted by Barnes & Noble.com, more and more public librarians are using consumer Web sites to help determine which books to add to their collections by reviewing sales rankings, and in some cases reviewing bibliographic information. These rankings and bibliographic information supplement a librarian's own personal experience and research with an up-to-the-minute view of what books, subjects, and categories are considered "hot." And many university libraries are now purchasing books, music, DVDs, and other products for their "rush orders" from online book vendors like Barnes & Noble.com, where they are finding very competitive prices, vast selection, Purchase Order Accounts, and most important, fast delivery, which in many cases is also free.

Barnes & Noble launched its Web site, BarnesandNoble.com, in 1997, targeting online consumers. In 2003, we launched our online Library Program (www.bnlibrary.com) to address the special needs of public, academic, and K–12 school libraries. We focus on rapidly fulfilling rush orders utilizing our in-stock inventory of over one million titles (the largest of any online bookseller), and we offer libraries an extra online discount on every purchase, free shipping on orders of $25 or more, and the option of charging orders to a Purchase Order Account. In addition, BarnesandNoble.com is currently exploring various value added library services, including processing and cataloging, standing orders, and integration with integrated library systems.

Note

1. Jupiter Internet Shopping Model (U.S. only).

THE UNPLANNED REVOLUTION IN LIBRARY BOOK AND MEDIA ACQUISITIONS: THE INTERNET, USED BOOKS, NEW PLAYERS, CREDIT CARDS, AND SPEED

Sherman Hayes, University Librarian, University of North Carolina at Wilmington

Revolution? In the last seven years our library has radically changed how it acquires books and media. It has purchased its materials at lower costs per item and received them in record time compared to 1996/1997. The vendors we use are both similar and very different. We accept, in fact we seek, used books as comparable to new books whenever possible. We buy paperback before hardback if there is a choice. We use the Internet for almost all of our popular media purchases. We buy fully two-thirds of our materials using a credit card and the Internet. While electronic ordering was common seven years ago, using the multiple vendors of the Internet was not. The credit card for state agencies was just a dream in someone's mind seven years ago.

I am uncertain whether "revolution" is too strong a word. Revolution implies that there was a plan proposed by someone to change the world. I think that there was no one plan, but a myriad set of forces that have come together to change how we do business. Perhaps a more appropriate "descriptor" of the change would be acquisitions departments "tap dancing" in the new world of Internet materials acquisitions as fast as we can.

Before I list the factors that created this "new world" (revolution or tap dance) for us, let me give you some disclaimers and statistical background. You should always put disclaimers up front, instead of in the footnotes! Randall Library at UNCW (University of North Carolina at Wilmington) represents one experience in the wide array of library acquisition programs. We are not totally representative of what may be happening at your institution. I think we are similar to academic libraries of our size and collection development philosophy. We do not have major approval plans such as the largest universities do. If we did, then our story would be different. We serve a wide variety of subjects, but do not buy extremely in depth in any one subject. We value quantity of materials purchased that support our specific curriculum. Those libraries that buy large amounts in very specialized subject areas such as science, foreign titles, rare books, and such will have different experiences than we had. We are not a public library that needs to keep up with best sellers immediately. The best you can do from following our narrow experience is to see if any subset of our particular case can help you understand the changes in the industry or even help you change voluntarily to improve your acquisitions program. You, of course, may throw up your arms (figuratively) and choose to avoid the changes we have made! Examples to run from are a good learning tool as well as modeling good practices.

Librarians who worked 10 years ago in acquisitions at our library would not recognize much of what we do today. In 1997/1998 we spent $450,000 on book and media purchases. This represented about 6,000 orders, of which 3,800 (63%) went to our main vendor, Yankee Book Peddler. We had no credit card purchases, nor did we use the "general Internet" for many purchases. Our remaining orders were primarily paper-based orders to the usual vendors available at the time. Fiscal 2003/2004 was radically different. We spent $500,000, on approximately 9,060 firm orders, of which only 611 were with Yankee Book Peddler (7%). Fully 6,373 orders (70%) used our VISA credit card (State of North Carolina issued). These credit card orders were by definition electronic Internet vendor orders. The major vendors we purchased from in 2003/2004 were Amazon, Barnes & Noble (online), Powells Books, Strand

Books, Alibris, and Abebooks. This next year we will be adding Baker and Taylor online as another competitor, primarily with Amazon and Barnes & Noble.

Through Alibris, Amazon, and Abebooks sub-vendors we generated hundreds of "direct electronic" orders. These are new vendors for us. Most of these vendors were not functioning as electronic companies, nor were the small bookshops or even individuals selling through the electronic jobbers and nets eight years ago.

Why did we change?

1. *Journal inflation*: We found that we desperately wanted to change because we felt that book and media purchasing was going to die unless we got better and could protect it from the crazy growth of journals. I know none of you reading this want to go over once again the most important ongoing shift in purchasing in academic libraries. However, the ridiculous increase in inflation of journals has and continues to put unusual pressures on other purchase opportunities for materials in other formats. Eight years ago we cut our journal subscriptions, and three years ago we cut our journal subscriptions. By buying into major aggregator sets and statewide networks and cooperatives, we have actually added to our total titles while we continue to cut individual journal and index subscriptions. We felt and continue to feel that we just have to buy books and media at the best prices possible to continue to build collections. The continuing pressure of journal price inflation has made us willing to try many new approaches.

2. *Used books:* We decided that used books were as good as new in most instances. We decided that binding paperbacks was unnecessary and discontinued that practice except for special occasions. We now automatically choose paperbacks if there is a choice.

3. *New collection needs:* Our collection development needs have been changing these past years, and the Internet has helped. We now set aside about $50,000 per year for "projects." These are buying efforts made by teaching faculty and library faculty to improve a narrow area of the collection that is deemed weak or that we anticipate needs to be stronger. Allocations are between $1,000 and $4,000 per project for books, media, or even microform sets. This particular type of purchase often looks backward, searching for noted titles, out of print, or classics. The Internet book networks are a natural for this type of purchasing.

We also have increased two streams of purchasing over the past several years that are heavily supported by Internet acquisitions. First, we are building in special collections, notably materials about our region or written by authors from our region. Prior to the advent of the used book networks, it was very difficult to even find this older material. Now we find it, and even monitor periodically the various vendor bases looking for materials on wish lists. Wilmington was not the center of the antiquarian or used book market, but now everyone is at the center of most materials markets with the Internet. A second major format change for us has been the increased need to buy media. The expansion of our film studies program, jazz music program, and the faculty member's desire for teaching materials in various media in general has shifted resources to nonbook formats. The Internet vendors that have specialized in these formats primarily for the general market offer us new avenues to find needed materials. Try buying 60 DVDs and videotapes of Indian films from Bollywood using traditional paper vendor sources!

4. *Internet vendors 1:* We also changed because the Internet world around us changed dramatically. The Internet vendors in books and media came of age. I am not sure they came of age to serve libraries, but they are present and available as new vendors. Amazon.com created the concept of the giant one-stop bookstore on the Net. For those materials that were popular in nature, Amazon, the Internet, and a credit card gave us the ability to "buy now" and track the complete transaction using e-mail and the Internet. Other traditional bookselling outlets have quickly added an electronic component to their sales mix.

5. *Internet vendors 2:* With the Internet, particularly the used book networks, we now have access to never before identifiable materials. The materials were out there somewhere, but what library could afford to find them? While this new vendor access for used materials is similar to number 4 (new outlets for new publications), I give it a separate category because it really not only used the technology to improve access, it literally created new markets that we couldn't even use before the Internet.

6. *Credit cards:* Finally, we get to the mighty credit card. The state of North Carolina gave our university and many other agencies within the state the ability to charge materials to selected accounts. Fortunately, book and media purchases were acceptable to buy with the credit card. This has made the use of Internet purchases quick and easy. The transaction is transparent and quickly completed to the satisfaction of the vendor, so that shipping is not delayed by accounting transaction time. With all of these changes come pluses and minuses. We think mainly pluses, but if you talk with our accounting technician you will find that her life has drastically changed from paper purchase orders to detailed entry of long credit card purchase records. The credit card gives us instant access to the small vendor, a problem in the past. The vendor doesn't care who you are if you have a credit card!

7. *Speed/delivery costs:* In 1996/1997 our normal delivery time on materials was five to six weeks. We weren't happy about it, but that was the industry norm. Today every vendor is faster! Most of our credit card purchases in media come within a week, and books are under two weeks. If we see an item is going to be delayed significantly due to notification of "out of stock" or "delayed stock," we just look at a competing vendor and select a better delivery time, always keeping the cost benefit (price) versus speed of delivery in mind in the decision-making process. Most of our major Internet vendors provide reduced or even free shipping. This is not an insignificant part of the cost of acquisitions. Shipping is a key part of the cost/benefit decision.

We are doing more ordering and receiving, yet have the same or even less direct acquisition staff than in the past. Some of the efficiency comes with use of computing and the Internet. Some comes by shifting much of the detailed work of the acquisition process to the accounting technician, away from the ordering technician. Whenever there is a crunch, the need to spend on projects or at peak periods of the budget year, the credit card allows several librarians to become acquisitions specialists, supplementing acquisitions services. This is another form of shifting work. Yes, even the university librarian (that's me) is competent enough to order special materials using Powells, Secondspin, Barnes & Noble, and many other vendors on the Web. Our associate university librarian of technical services/collections finds that she has added ordering as part of her duties in this new Internet world. Several years ago we lost one of our technical positions, and the associate university librarian has been forced to take on more ordering. In a particularly heavy year, she may place as many as 20% of the value of orders made. We are hoping to reduce this load over time, but expect the model to continue at some lower level because it is highly efficient for her to order as she selects in specialized projects and purchasing replacement materials. Why prepare an order form, when you can place the order directly?

Questions that we are asking ourselves, and would ask you, the reader, are:

1. If we all use the used book networks, will we run out of used books?

2. Can the publishers survive if the standard discount for any new book becomes more than 50%?

3. Is it efficient to use eBay as a buying tool for used materials?

4. Should our libraries become vendor nodes on the Internet, selling used materials that we do not keep?

5. What would happen if we lost our ability to use the credit card (heaven forbid)? Should we consider PayPal as an alternative to the credit card?

6. Will the Internet/credit card world allow us to do a better job buying internationally?

7. Do we have an obligation to help the local book and materials vendor?

8. Since the "tap dancing" seems to get more frantic each year, will we ever have time to change our shoes?

Our experience is that in this area, as in many areas of library service, we are reactors to non-library stimuli and movements. This revolutionary change in how we acquire book and media material is another example. The library world did not create the Internet. The library world did not create the electronic used book networks or the electronic bookstore. The academic library has not voluntarily created the pressures of journal pricing practices. Our library did not create the state use of credit cards for efficient purchasing. All of the factors listed above (our needs for better pricing and changing collection initiatives, as well as industry changes) have combined to alter radically how we do business at UNCW. We are now looking for even better and different ways to keep an acquisitions efficiency edge. I don't know what the next set of "opportunities" will be, but I assume there will be many coming in the near future.

INTERNET BUYING OF BOOKS

Nancy Gibbs, Head, Acquisitions Department, Duke University, Durham, North Carolina

Libraries have found many advantages to purchasing books over the Internet, but there are definitely tradeoffs.

I think it is important to distinguish the Barnes and Noble.com and Amazon.com type of companies from companies that offer eBay-type transactions. We use the former as just another vendor, reserving the latter for more specialized material. Most of my comments are aimed at this latter type of transaction.

Corporate accounts are easy for us. This is particularly true of BarnesandNoble.com because they reconcile our accounts title-by-title, unlike Amazon, which reconciles only to the bottom line invoice totals. Duke University Libraries reconciles all transactions in the integrated library system (ILS) and, when using the procurement card, must reconcile in the university's transactional system as well. As you can see, the ease of buying materials with the university procurement card is undermined by the double reconciliation process.

In the past three months we ordered 261 titles from Internet sites, with an average cost of $70.00.

Advantages to Purchasing Directly from an Internet Site

The Internet has made the buying of materials easier, especially for out-of-print or "hard-to-find" materials (e.g., Chinese/Japanese/Korean videos; hard-to-find DVDs), unusual titles, and materials that we seek for the Hartman Center for Advertising.

Purchases are made quickly and usually received quickly, making this a particularly good avenue for getting materials into the Libraries that are needed at the last minute.

We can do comparison shopping for many materials. We often are offered options for how material is to be shipped. We are able to locate many more out-of-print materials than we could in the past, with less effort on our part. Specifically, Internet purchasing has eliminated the need to send wish lists to vendors to research and locate materials for us.

Most vendor information, including the tax ID, is available on the Web site, making vendor setup easy.

The university purchasing card provider absorbs dispute fees and bank charges. It also converts foreign currency purchases to U.S. dollars, if needed, and these are recorded on the monthly statement.

Disadvantages to Purchasing Directly from an Internet Site

Shipping is expensive, as we usually buy and have shipped only one item at a time from a specific site.

These suppliers provide no statistics about purchases (number of orders placed and filled, types of materials, formats, prices, etc.). I depend on my vendors to run interference as I place orders, and they do a good job of this. I don't want to lose that service, and I certainly don't have the staff in-house to do all that.

As mentioned previously, Internet purchasing with procurement cards means that a second reconciliation with the procurement card database at the university is necessary.

We set up each of these Internet sites as a vendor in our ILS system, which means many more vendors to set up.

Many sellers have not adopted the ABA standards of description for their materials, resulting in inconsistent and misleading descriptions. Bibliographic information on the vendor Web site is sometimes less than adequate. Library purchases can turn out to be of poorer quality than expected because of such practices.

Trolling the Internet in a search for desired titles can be very time consuming.

Perhaps one of our biggest challenges comes from vendors who don't keep their stock information refreshed. Several times we have bought something only to be told later that it really was not available but the bookseller just didn't update the Web site. We have found this is especially true for some smaller antiquarian booksellers. When this occurs, the whole search process must begin again!

Internet purchases seem prone to unique anomalies. There are problems with PayPal, including requests for the university's bank information, provision of which is against university regulations. PayPal has been sued over this issue.

Odd things happen. Recently we received a $1.00 bill in the mail along with one of our purchases with no explanation about this windfall. What do I do with this? The cost to redeposit that dollar is more than $50.00. The university does not want to handle these types of transactions for such small amounts of money. Of course we deposited this in our "petty cash" fund, but it just struck me as an odd way to do business.

Summary

I'm sure this type of purchasing will continue to flourish, and each of us will have to decide whether to participate, based on our own institutional situation. At Duke, we will continue to use the Internet for purchasing library materials, but we will be selective in what we buy, from which online vendors, and how we use our procurement cards.

I see my next hurdle as convincing the university that buying books over the Internet from many book vendors using our procurement card is perhaps different from the usual purchases made with procurement cards by other staff on campus. Most of those other purchases are for services at conferences, travel expenses, meals, etc., and not esoteric videos from a province in China.

Since giving this talk at Charleston we have had a real problem with a procurement/purchasing card account being used illegally. We discovered this when we reconciled our accounts in November. Working with the University Procurement Card office, the GE credit card company (issuer of the cards), and our campus police department, we were able to put our procurement card procedures and training into place quickly and effectively.

Unfortunately, the person who used our procurement card fraudulently is still out there, SO BE CAREFUL! We thought we used only secure sites, but there must be a problem with one of those sites; we just don't know where the problem occurred. But it certainly was helpful to have all those resources available to us when we uncovered the fraud.

I believe there are places in our industry for both the traditional book vendors like Yankee and Blackwell's and those that sell almost exclusively over the Internet. Our task is to be able to delineate our needs and distinguish between the types of vendors that will best permit us to acquire a wide variety of materials. This will give us the confidence and knowledge to most appropriately place each order, whether by traditional methods or via the Internet.

BOOKS AND THE INTERNET: BUYING, SELLING, AND LIBRARIES

Rhonda Herman, McFarland& Co., Jefferson, North Carolina

McFarland was founded to serve the library market, and in 2004 it celebrates 25 years of publishing books for academic, public, and high school libraries. The Internet has become an important selling tool to libraries and our non-library customers. The following is one publisher's perspective on the phenomenon of libraries buying books on the Internet.

The publishing environment continues to be challenging, and worthwhile books that were viable publishing propositions just a few years ago may have very slim prospects today. In some cases libraries now share collections within a region or use inter-library loan instead of expending funds for optional purchases. Libraries are thinking of ways to buy fewer books or spend fewer dollars buying books. Many publishers are responding to the resulting erosion in single title sales by doing more with the same amount of staff (as librarians are also doing). There isn't much time to strategize about changing library buying procedures. Frankly, we depend on vendors to keep up with how libraries are changing. We are busy producing books! (McFarland publishes 270 new titles per year.)

Around five years ago, through discussion at the Charleston conference, I became aware that some libraries were purchasing our books through Amazon, challenging a perception that libraries almost always order through vendors that offer valuable services librarians have to have. At Charleston I also learned that libraries were buying McFarland books from our Web site using credit cards, a new phenomenon that enabled libraries to buy books using the Internet (for the first time?). As I understood it, this was a popular purchasing option when availability and a need for speed made regular channels less desirable.

When I got the e-mail inviting me to participate in a panel at Charleston this past fall, I realized that now some libraries were buying directly through the Internet as the *purchase strategy of choice*. It was a surprise but not an altogether pleasant one.

We have all learned to accept change, and an ever-quickening pace of change. But the kinds of changes that hurt companies with long histories of service to libraries are not easy to swallow. The long process of vendor consolidation has been painful to observe. It is not good for publishers. How can it be good for libraries? The traditional point of view of a publisher like McFarland is that vendors provide services to libraries that the publisher cannot reasonably provide and doesn't really want to provide. Do some libraries no longer need cataloging; approval plans that save on acquisitions personnel; or order aggregation that cuts down on invoicing, purchase orders, and shipping?

We intend to thrive in whatever environment develops. Publishers have benefited from good relationships with vendors, and an aggressive strategy to cut vendors out seems ill-advised. I hope there is enough business for all to survive.

How about book sales at McFarland from libraries directly through the Internet?

Because the method of payment for Internet bookselling is a credit card, this business is not really able to be tracked; that is, an Internet order from a library versus an Internet order from an individual is indistinguishable. Our orders through our Web site continue to grow each year, but it is not possible to track orders from libraries at this time.

Our traditional orders direct to libraries are a little over 1% of sales. This percentage does not include sales to high school libraries. Traditional orders to all wholesalers are 68% of sales.

Marketing to libraries through the Internet has been a totally natural progression. With our last Web site enhancement, we have a special component for libraries. We are using an e-mail title notification strategy that allows a library to receive upon request an e-mail message when a particular title is published or any title in a particular subject is published.

We are experimenting with allowing libraries to receive PDFs or links to PDFs of our catalog instead of or in addition to print catalogs. This may offer some positives for the environment as well as the librarian's work life.

From our point of view the pros of libraries using the Internet to order directly from McFarland are that:

1. The order is prepaid instead of having to wait 60 days or longer for payment.

2. Availability time might be improved for the customer; that is, if the book is out of stock at the vendor, we would get the books into the hands of the customer faster.

3. It can be a little disconcerting to have so much of our accounts receivable tied up with a few companies, particularly if important accounts don't pay on time. Significant activity in prepaid sales would improve accounts receivable.

4. Since there is a discount involved in books sold for resale, the dollars taken in per order would be increased.

The cons of libraries using the Internet to order directly from McFarland from our point of view are that:

1. Our invoice administration goes way up when we fill many small orders as opposed to a large vendor order.

2. Our shipping/handling efforts go way up when we fill many small orders as opposed to a large vendor order.

3. We lose a small percentage of the order to credit card fees.

Issues to consider related to Internet bookselling include the following:

1. *Updating inventory information:* We currently update once a week. It would be ideal to have real-time inventory information, but in our case it would expose our data systems to additional risk that we do not judge to be worthwhile at this time.

2. *Buyers of books:* If you need a book quickly, there is a chance that the vendor would have stock when the publisher is out of stock, and vice versa. This might determine the most advantageous purchasing option.

In sum, McFarland will continue to publish books and sell them through whatever sales channels libraries decide they want.

BOOKS AND THE INTERNET—BUYING, SELLING, AND LIBRARIES: A BRIEF, HIGHLY SELECTIVE, IDIOSYNCRATIC BIBLIOGRAPHY

Heather S. Miller, State University of New York at Albany

Hennessey, Anita. "Online Bookselling.." *Publishing Research Quarterly* 16, no. 2 (summer 2000): 34–51.

An overview of online bookselling for the seller.

Hundie, Kebede. "Library Operations and Internet Resources." *Electronic Library* 21, no. 6 (2003): 555–64.

Buying books is only one of the library operations described here that can benefit from using the Internet.

Matos, Jodie, et al. "Saving Money by Using Online Bookstores." *Computers in Libraries* 20, no. 5 (May 1, 2000): 42–47.

The title says it all.

Miller, Heather S., with Sydney K. Allen. "Libraries on the Book Buying Merry-Go-Round: Internet Book Seller vs. Library Book Vendor." *Against the Grain* 12, no. 2 (April 2000):1, 16, 18, 22.

Prices and other factors from general online booksellers are compared with those from traditional library vendor Web sites.

————."The Merry-Go-Round Revisited: Libraries Buying Books Online." *Against the Grain* 15, no. 4 (September 2003): 58, 60, 62.

Updates the previous article, with similar conclusions.

Movahedi-Lankarani, Stephanie Jakle. "E-commerce: Resources for Doing Business on the Internet." *Reference & User Services Quarterly* 41, no. 4 (summer 2002): 316–25.

A how-to guide for selling via the Internet.

Nikam, Khaiser, and M. V. Sunil. "Effective Book Buying Through a (sic) E-book Store." *SRELS Journal of Information Management* 37, no. 4 (December 2000): 245–50.

Describes India's answer to amazon.com.

Online Bookselling Resource Center. onlinebookselling.net.

More than you will ever want to know about selling books online.

Windwalker, Stephen. *Buying Books Online*. Belmont, Mass.: Harvard Perspectives Press, 2002.

A highly personal but useful guide for purchasers of books via the Internet.

We all hear a lot about the "Big Deal" and the pros and cons of consortial buying. This has become quite a controversial topic at the Conference. What can work to one library's advantage might not help another because we are all different in size, vision, and nature. The contributors in this section talk us through these issues and focus on the advantages and disadvantages of consortial purchasing, based on honest assessment.

Buying Books Consortially

BUYING SERIALS CONSORTIALLY: FROM THE BIG DEAL TO OPEN ACCESS

Yvonne Lev, Associate University Librarian, Towson University, Maryland (Moderator)

Introduction

At the conference session, three speakers represented three consortia: Ralph Alberico for VIVA, the Virtual Library of Virginia; Rick Burke for SCELC, the Statewide California Electronic Library Consortium; and Betty Day for MDL, the Maryland Digital Library and USMAI, the University System of Maryland and Affiliated Institutions. The session considered questions:

1. How are the consortia organized to meet the journal needs of different-sized libraries with different missions? In Maryland's USMAI consortium, we include a medical library, two law libraries, a small liberal arts college, several comprehensive universities, a special academic library that serves 150 FTE students, and a large research university that serves about 35,000 students. When selecting journal packages, is there a conflict between the common good and what is good for an individual campus? How does a consortium minimize those differences?

2. What are the advantages and disadvantages of buying journals through a consortium? At Towson University, a medium-sized comprehensive university, we now purchase more journals in electronic form than in print form, and that does not include journals in the aggregator databases. This increase is partly due to the consortium buying and the Big Deal. Our students have access to more online journal content every year. That is an important advantage. One negative aspect of the Big Deal is that when the economy has a downturn and we are forced to cut journals, the Big Deal licenses give us little flexibility. Another disadvantage is that in spite of the variety of institutions in our consortium, there is a great deal of overlap in the titles we buy. We have talked about canceling the extra copies and purchasing new titles, but for the most part that doesn't happen. Few libraries are willing to risk loss of ownership for their core titles.

3. What support are the consortia giving to open access (OA) journals? Why would a consortium spend money to buy journals that are free on the Internet? If the OA model becomes prevalent for journals or even primarily STM, what impact will that have on consortia?

E-JOURNALS AND SCELC

Rick Burke, Executive Director, SCELC, Los Angeles, California

I. What Is SCELC?

- Statewide California Electronic Library Consortium

- Membership is limited to private, nonprofit accredited academic institutions and non-profit research institutions in California.

- 82 members currently [2004]

- Nearly 350 different databases licensed

II. SCELC's Unique Issues

- We never license a particular product for the entire membership; for all offers any library can opt in or out.

- SCELC does not represent a systemwide set of similar institutions.

- Diverse membership:

  - Very large, like USC

  - Medium–sized residential liberal arts institutions (2001–9000 FTE)

  - Small residential liberal arts institutions (1000–2000 FTE)

  - Very small residential (or non–residential) colleges with less than 1000 students

  - Several small, graduate-only, distance learning only institutions

  - Smaller institutions, with mainly undergraduate populations (< 2000 FTE) constitute nearly 70% of the group!

III. Academic Areas Covered by SCELC

- The academic focus of SCELC institutions runs the gamut:

  - Science/medicine

  - Psychology, graduate programs in particular

  - Liberal arts

  - Sectarian religious institutions, particularly many small Christian colleges

  - Art institutions

  - Non-academic museum libraries, such as Getty Research Institute and the Huntington Library

  - Research think tanks with graduate programs, such as RAND Corp.

○ The complete membership roster can be viewed at our Web site at http://scelc.org.

IV. SCELC's E-Journal Experience

- It is difficult to choose offers with the broadest appeal.

- We have licensed five different e-journal packages to date.

- Each has garnered a decent base of subscribers, but in no instance has it exceeded 25 libraries.

V. An Overview of SCELC E-Journal Packages

Vendor A

Vendor A originally offered a three-year package, under which:

- Subject collections were provided based on the vendor's usage stats for a given library's collection.

- Usage stats were established after one year of providing access to the entire list of titles to each library.

- Upon renewal of the three-year contract, subscribing libraries began the process of attempting to build, via cooperative collection development among similar libraries, unique title lists to replace or supplement subject collections.

- Collaborative title selection for the lists, based on usage statistics, was a very tedious and labor-intensive process.

- Vendor usage stats were not accurate in many instances or were not trusted by the selectors.

- The vendor proposed a "unique title list" that librarians determined did not meet the needs of any one library, and whose cost was prohibitive for the smaller libraries.

The vendor has now accepted SCELC's attempt to construct "subcore title lists" (STL) that meet the need of different types of libraries. These are viewed as a feasible and flexible alternative and provide a means for pooling shared titles among libraries. This was an original goal with this vendor more than six years ago, when it first contacted SCELC.

Our goals now include

- the creation of a smaller, focused STL for smaller libraries that would keep costs within their budget, based on past subject collections usage;

- a second larger, but still reasonably-priced, STL for the larger liberal arts institutions;

- basing the title lists only on use of subject collections (subscribed titles usage was removed)

- requesting an "out" clause for two years for STL adopters (back to current subject collections at current rate + inflation);

- two tailored subcore title lists, one small—55 titles @ $3000ish for smaller schools based on their use; and a larger subcore title list, which came in at about 300 titles @ $11,000 after pulling out high cost per use titles (especially those used significantly by just one school)

The major advantages of the STL are the ability to adjust the list in future on a title by title basis, access to a wider range of well-used titles, and credit for overlap among subscriptions.

We are currently having trouble with two schools wanting to add back many high-priced titles while others want to keep the list smaller to keep costs down. We will attempt to compromise, and as a last resort suggest reanalysis with greater data for an STL for 2006.

Pluses

The principal advantage of this approach, if negotiations are successful, is that for the smaller libraries the net cost of their STL will be less than the print cost of a single title or a few titles than just a few years ago. Relative to cost per title, the libraries feel they are getting more value for their dollar.

For the larger libraries, they also benefit by getting the titles they need the most for the least cost, replacing less-effective subject collection holdings.

The very reasonable price cap provides budget predictability and savings over the course of the contract.

Minuses

The vendor's license states that if the net content holdings of a library fall below a certain amount, then archives cost a four-figure additional fee, which could be a deal breaker for many small schools, and the annual archival access could exceed the cost of the STL itself. Thus, this is still being negotiated.

The vendor has a rather intractable approach to the issue of cancellations, which are only allowed if titles of equal value are swapped for the canceled titles.

Vendor B

The terms of vendor B's offer were very attractive to libraries, and even in a time of budget contraction, this offer attracted a good level of participation. The offer included the following provisions:

- If a library holds print subscriptions, it can add online access for only 8% more. The regular rate is 20%, so the library saves 12% per journal.

- If a library holds online only subscriptions, it can join the consortium automatically in the current year. The library can purchase print titles at 8% of the subscription price. This reduces subscription costs while providing print subscriptions for selected titles.

- All members have electronic access to the shared collection at no extra charge.

- Free access is provided to backfiles to 1997 for a library's subscriptions and the shared collection. Compare this to when a library purchases an electronic journal through non-consortial channels, where it receives only the current year without backfiles.

- Flexibility. Although this is a three-year deal, each library can treat it as a one-year renewable contract. Should severe cuts in a library's budget occur, there is an "out" clause.

- A price cap of 7% will be applied in subsequent years for renewals.

- There is a low minimum participation fee for SCELC members:

  ○ Bring at least $2,500 in current holdings to share with the group or, if you have no holdings, join for $2,500.

Pluses

- Sufficient participation resulted in reaching the vendor's revenue goal, at which point the entire collection, including non-subscribed titles, was shared collectively among all the subscribing libraries.

- Archival access is provided and is very reasonable. In addition, the vendor supports LOCKKS— the "Lots of Copies Keep Knowledge Safe" initiative now in use in places such as Stanford's Digital Repository.

- For SCELC, what was key was the vendor's flexibility in providing a low entry level fee for smaller libraries.

- The vendor was also flexible in allowing print cancellations by individual libraries without that having a negative impact on the entire group package.

- The vendor gave credit for duplicate subscriptions, helping reduce costs for the group.

Minuses

The vendor does not provide MARC records, which is seen as problematic by some of our subscribing libraries.

Vendor C

This offer, implemented in early 2004, also provides similar advantages to Vendor B's offer:

- It is a three-year license.

- It includes electronic access to the shared titles of participating SCELC members, including our largest journal holdings, held by the University of Southern California.

- It provides full text journal content from 1997 for the majority of the journals.

- It provides for archiving rights: In the event of termination of the license, the contract reads that the "Vendor will provide SCELC with access to the full text of the electronic journals published during the term of the License, either by continuing online access to the same material on Vendor's server, or by means of an archival copy in the electronic medium selected by Vendor, at a cost-based fee agreed to by both parties."

- It allows for inter-library loan, whereby library staff may print out and send single paper copies of articles.

- It grants deep discounts on print to those institutions that wish to maintain print subscriptions. The cost for print copies will be 10% of the current year list price.

- It offers a 6.5% price increase cap for a multi-year license.

- It allows those SCELC members with journal holdings of less than $2,500 to enter into the license agreement for a minimum annual fee of $2,500.

Pluses

- There is a low entry level fee for smaller libraries

- Archival access is provided and is reasonable.

- The offer shares titles among the entire set of subscribers.

- The offer allows for substitution of titles, so libraries can collectively substitute to obtain the most desirable titles and eliminate unused titles.

Minuses

The vendor instituted a system of "tokens" to provide access to full text for unsubscribed titles, but the system was difficult to understand and implement, according to some of the participating libraries. However, libraries did appreciate that the vendor was making an attempt to allow access to articles in non-subscribed titles as part of the consortial package

The biggest problem was an accounting/distribution issue. The subscription agents wanted to handle the e-journal subscriptions, and the vendor also wanted to have the libraries pay directly to them, and, in the first year, invoiced the libraries directly rather than going through consortium billing channels. The consequence was that SCELC got calls from subscription agents, and libraries asked SCELC what they should do, while SCELC, not being the invoicing agent, had no clear idea of what was happening! This situation was resolved this year by:

- centralizing invoicing through SCELC, and

- a vendor offer of a 1.5% early renewal discount that was applicable if a library renewed direct with the vendor via SCELC.

Communication between the library and the vendor was clarified, with SCELC acting as an informed intermediary when necessary. Subscription agents still handle any print subscriptions, but the billing of the electronic titles is handled by the consortium in most instances.

Vendor D

This offer was initially a three-year offer based on print subscription costs. The offer included:

- access to the vendor's entire title list regardless of individual library holdings, and

- an entry level cost of only $1,500 for those with few or no title holdings.

Libraries liked the offer because it brought down print costs for some and allowed small libraries to get in a very low entry fee if they lacked print holdings.

Renewal Offer

Upon renewal of the three-year offer, pricing became based on electronic costs, with print available for an additional percentage similar to other offers. The entry level cost for libraries doubled with the renewal, in theory because of the value of titles added to the package. Greater future price increases for new subscribers in coming years will likely put this package out of reach for most libraries, although the vendor has indicated that current subscribers' price increases will be reasonable and not linked to the new pricing.

Pluses

- The low entry cost helped small libraries.

- Access to the entire title list was attractive.

- It lowered print costs for libraries.

Minuses

The issue resulting in the most complaints was that new titles added by the publisher in the course of the initial three-year contract resulted in those titles appearing when the database was accessed, even though they were actually inaccessible. These new titles were flagged with asterisks, designed to indicate that these titles were not accessible, but this was not clear to the end-users or the librarians. New titles added during the contract should not have appeared when searching, so as to minimize confusion.

In moving from a print-based to an electronic-based pricing model, extreme price increases for e-only in the future do not bode well for this offer

VI. Summary

What are the critical issues that SCELC has learned to look for in obtaining an e-journal package?

1. Archival access is important, as is the issue of lost content and how to replace that content (in those instances where a vendor is licensing titles from a third party).

2. The trend toward separate publishers' journal packages is creating headaches for serials librarians, who need to keep up with new interfaces and collections.

3. Vendors have consistently had incorrect subscription lists for the libraries, which prolongs and complicates the process of determining which titles can be shared, billed, etc. Libraries have received other library's lists, lists with wrong start dates, and multiple subscriptions to the same journal where only one exists.

4. There are problems with inconsistent license language: e-access fees versus content fees, technology fees, etc. There is no standardization among contracts.

5. Libraries overall like e-journals because of improved access as compared to print. Usage is perceived to have gone up.

6. Publishers or vendors need to be very clear about what are subscribed versus non-subscribed titles when that distinction exists, and, if titles are not available, they need to be masked to avoid confusion.

7. It is unclear how to resolve the issue of direct ordering of e-journals versus subscription agents handling these as they have done with print in the past. Possible collaboration between consortia and subscription agents in this arena needs to be explored further.

THE USMAI/MARYLAND DIGITAL LIBRARY, CONSORTIAL E-JOURNALS, AND OPEN ACCESS

Betty Day, Manager, E-Content Management and Delivery, University of Maryland, College Park

The consortial acquisition of electronic journals poses a number of challenges to academic libraries in terms of evolving price models, distribution of costs among consortial members, relationships with electronic publishers, and appropriate responses to developments in the arena of scholarly communication. These challenges become even complex when the consortium is a gathering of multiple types of libraries. I am writing from my perspective as the manager of electronic resources for the University System of Maryland and Affiliated Institutions (USMAI) and the Maryland Digital Library.

In most instances, when a group of libraries forms an alliance to provide services and build collections in a cost-effective way, they also share some basic characteristics and purposes beyond simply the desire to save money. The University System of Maryland and Affiliated Institutions is a consortium of the 14 state-funded four-year colleges and universities in the state of Maryland. The 16 libraries at these 14 universities have recognized for many years the importance of sharing the library collections that had been built using state funds. Since 1992, most of these libraries have shared an integrated online catalog that facilitated direct patron borrowing of library books no matter at which campus the patron was located. These 16 libraries include one ARL (College Park), a medical school, two law libraries, an environmental sciences library supporting several research labs scattered across the state, a state-funded four-year liberal arts college, and 10 other libraries supporting a diverse range of undergraduate and graduate programs. In addition to the diverse teaching and research programs that need to be supported by the 16 libraries, there has also been a history of disparate levels of funding for the libraries. As a consortium, USMAI needs to balance the inequities in library funding and competing campus needs.

Maryland Digital Library (MDL) is a statewide library consortium of more than 50 college and university libraries—libraries in all areas of higher education, from the USNA and Johns Hopkins, to religious seminaries, to community colleges, private colleges, and of course the University System of Maryland and Affiliated Institutions. The MDL started in 2000 with money from the state of Maryland. These funds were used to acquire a common set of electronic resources to support the research needs of all Maryland undergraduate students. Unfortunately the financial support for MDL was based on soft monies, and after 18 months the consortium moved to a self-funded model. Most of the MDL consortial buying has focused on bibliographic databases and electronic reference tools, but the wider academic community of the Maryland Digital Library does have some involvement in the consortial e-journal subscriptions pursued by the University System of Maryland and Affiliated Institutions.

I have highlighted the competing teaching and research needs faced by the participating institutions and the divergent patterns of funding and ability to build adequate library collections in order to give some context to the challenges we have faced as a consortium trying to work together to build a shared collection of electronic journals. There are almost no subject or curriculum areas that are common to all of our 16 libraries except the most general and multidisciplinary areas. Because of this, it is more difficult for us to gather sufficient muscle to negotiate terms. In this situation, we cannot operate at the same level as NERL (all ARL libraries) or the CIC. Also, because the USMAI libraries support different curricula and have been funded at different levels, we do not bring equivalent collections of print journals, an important factor in determining pricing for electronic journal subscriptions. At the same time that we are dealing with these challenges, we are also able to approach the consortial acquisition of electronic journals as an opportunity to create an important virtual collection of titles common to all the libraries that chose to (and can afford to) participate in the program. These virtual collections of electronic journals become resource sharing in the best sense.

It is also much easier for a consortium of multiple types of libraries to find common ground in terms of collection decisions when there is a source of centralized funding. State-wide consortia such as OhioLink and Galileo, which are largely funded by a central pool of state resources, find it easier to reach consensus. We have had only limited opportunities to develop shared electronic journal collections funded by central state monies, an opportunity that arose at the initial stage of the Maryland Digital Library.

In creating that original collection, we were looking to build a collection rich in full text electronic journals and e-books. Much of the e-journal content was selected through several aggregator databases, but the MDL directors wished to fund Project Muse or at least the Johns Hopkins University (JHU) Press titles as a political gesture of support to a regional electronic publisher. As I mentioned, the state funds disappeared after 18 months, but the USMAI library directors decided to use a portion of a shared pool of funds to continue access to some of the electronic resources that had been funded by MDL; this included the JHU titles from Project Muse. This pool of USM resources was also used to centrally fund the original collection of Berkeley Electronic Press titles (an investment in alternative scholarly publishing) and the *New England Journal of Medicine* for all 16 libraries. All of our other consortial e-journal acquisitions have been funded by the individual libraries and have, as a result, more complex histories.

In the following discussion I briefly describe our experiences with two publishers, situations in which we have been able to leverage existing print subscriptions to create electronic collections available to all who elected to participate. For over five years, we have had a consortial subscription to the American Chemical Society (ACS) e-journals that was based on College Park's subscription to the entire package of ACS print journals. Other campuses in the consortium (including two Maryland Digital Library institutions outside USMAI) were given access to the full ACS e-journal collection. The surcharge for consortial electronic access was distributed proportionately to the participating libraries by enrollment. The other instance is our ScienceDirect consortial subscription—a situation in which we were able build a shared collection of titles that leveraged the print collections of a number of our libraries. This "unique title collection" was available to all participants regardless of the number of individual print subscriptions held, for a "cross access" fee. This cross access fee provided access to a collection worth hundreds of thousands of dollars. There were duplicate subscriptions in this collection of course, but several libraries took advantage of the option to cancel duplicate titles and replace the duplicates with an equivalent value of new titles. Those libraries were able to add titles that were new and unique to the consortial collection—enriching the collection for the entire consortium.

The consortial packages just described were organized a number of years ago, and while not necessarily perfect, at least established a norm with which our libraries seemed comfortable. Events in the realm of electronic publishing and the continuing budget difficulties of our state-funded institutions have created situations in which we are having to reinvent the way we are doing business as a consortium with electronic journals. E-publishers are buying each other (or their content) up; they are creating new price models. As vendors move from offering electronic access as an add-on (either free or for a small fee) to current print subscriptions or to e-only, or to the reverse model of adding print on as the option to print, we have had to re-evaluate each of the consortial subscriptions I've just mentioned.

Project Muse became a particular issue because this subscription had been centrally funded for the JHU titles. Five of the schools had added their own funds to get the complete Project Muse. After much study, Project Muse announced new models and pricing for 2005. The USMAI faced an immediate quandary because the package to which we had originally subscribed was no longer available. The collection closest to our original subscription was the basic undergraduate collection, but this much larger collection had a higher price tag. In addition, Muse greatly reduced the amount of discount that consortia could apply to their subscriptions. With lower consortial discounts and tiers that also incorporated usage, the USMAI's potential costs increased beyond what our budget could handle. The USMAI directors agreed to fund only the exact number of dollars they had spent in 2004. Each campus then had to analyze the content of the new collections being offered by Project Muse and to determine how much additional money they would need to supply from their own budgets to obtain a collection appropriate for their users. The libraries have now made their decisions. Two of the libraries have decided not to continue Project Muse, five are selecting the basic undergraduate collection, five are going for the complete collection, and two are choosing individual Muse titles equivalent to the number of dollars centrally funded. For example, the Center for Environmental Science has selected a set of environmental titles. In addition, four of the libraries will follow the lost Duke content to Duke University Press.

The other two examples were complicated in that the consortial subscriptions were either entirely or heavily based on the historic print subscriptions of the University of Maryland College Park. The College Park collection librarians, faced with soaring serials costs and budget cuts, have been working for several years, together with their faculty, to determine a set of principles by which the libraries would decide to move journal subscriptions from print to e-only.[1] College Park also wanted to maintain the right to manage its own collections, to be able to cancel individual titles as its budget and evolving collection priorities dictated and in reaction to subscription price increases.

As a result, as we moved the consortial ScienceDirect subscription into its second three-year contract, College Park opted out of the consortial subscription and moved all of its Elsevier subscriptions to e-only. After much negotiation, we were able to maintain a Maryland Digital Library consortial subscription whereby the consortial partners continued to have access to the "unique title list" for a slightly increased fee. This shared title list included College Park's content, but because College Park had opted out, its patrons no longer have access to titles from the medical school or any of the other campuses.

For the 2005 MDL renewal of the ACS package, we are also faced with the results of College Park's migration to e-only. ACS had been offering us a consortial package for several years that was a reverse of our current model, but we could not take advantage of this reverse model until College Park was ready to move e-only. The new price model has been an initial shock to the individual participants because it is now based on the historic print subscription cost and so the costs for individual libraries to get e-access to the ACS journals have greatly changed. Many of the consortial participants are following College Park's lead and moving to e-only, a move that realizes some savings for them. A major concern is that, under the terms of the original consortial license, no campus was allowed to cancel print subscriptions in recent years. A few of the smaller campuses had been maintaining a large number of the ACS titles because of their local needs, needs that were obviated by the complete electronic collection. Now the costs for those historic print collections are penalties. The libraries have come to terms with this year's price model and cost distribution, but we are already in negotiation with ACS to come up with a more equitable model for next year that takes into account factors such as usage data and the size of chemistry departments and programs.

The USMAI directors strongly want to expand the number and scope of consortial electronic journal acquisitions. For 2005, though, beyond dealing with the changes in current subscriptions, we will only be expanding our consortial purchasing to one additional publisher—the Springer family of e-journals. In addition to the complexities created by shifting publisher models, we are also confronted with a number of other issues that have prevented us from expanding our efforts. Many of the journal publishers do not have accurate or current lists of the titles and holdings to which our individual libraries subscribe. If we cannot get accurate lists of print subscriptions, we cannot analyze the possibilities for consortial collection building. Since the libraries in our consortium use multiple serials jobbers, we cannot rely on support from a serials jobber for the work involved in creating accurate title lists for consortial holdings. An added difficulty is timing. Serials publishers often do not know their new price models in sufficient time for the individual libraries to review their holdings and make decisions on whether or not to participate in a consortial offering. A third area of difficulty comes in the loss of content. Difficult as it is for an individual library to track what company has bought what society or what individual titles, it multiplies out exponentially for a consortium.

At the same time that the University System of Maryland and Affiliated Institutions pursue the traditional path to building a virtual e-journal collection, we are also actively working to support alternate methods of scholarly publication. In the past year, our Council of Library Directors has issued "The Future of Scholarly Communication: A Proposal for Consideration by the University System of Maryland and Affiliated Institutions."[2] This document outlines the issues related to the "crisis in scholarly communication" and proposes that the "USMAI institutions develop and commit to a new, shared vision where: (1) USMAI research is 'published' first on institutional or disciplinary repositories in draft form, (2) peer review and editing, resulting in a final version that is published with adherence to the principle of widest distribution at the lowest cost, preferably in not-for-profit scholarly vehicles rather than commercial presses, (3) copyright is retained by the institution or researcher (or both), and (4) faculty promotional review through alternative publication formats will be recognized and rewards." This proposal was presented to the USM Provosts' Academic Affairs Advisory Council on October 19 and endorsed by the Council. Next steps will include similar presentations to the administrations of the two affiliated institutions, Morgan State and St. Mary's College of Maryland, to build full institutional commitment. The directors are also planning a USM forum on scholarly communication for their faculty in fall 2005. College Park has already established an institutional repository, and the other campuses have begun explorations.

The Council of Library Directors also decided to subsidize faculty at the participating institutions to encourage them to submit their research to open access (OA) journals by joining both BioMedCentral (BMC) and the Public Library of Science (PLoS) as a consortium. These consortial memberships mean that our faculty either pay no fees or pay reduced fees to submit their articles. In addition, both BMC and PloS have given us promotional materials. BioMedCentral distributed a press release on the USMAI. Staff at the 16 libraries are promoting these memberships in conjunction with the CLD white paper to the faculty at their campuses. The consortium has created a Web site[3] that gathers individual USM Web sites as well as other resources on scholarly communication.

In addition to these strategic activities, the USMAI has been pursuing technical activities to increase access to OA journals through our SFX implementation. The 16 libraries have implemented 16 instances of SFX. We are configuring OA journals as SFX targets as the titles are identified. To date, we have enabled all OpenURL-compliant OA journals available through the Directory of Open Access Journals and SciELO (the Scientific Electronic Library Online) (1,108 and 235 titles—some overlap). Integrating these OA journals through SFX accomplishes several strategies. Our users are no longer reliant on finding publisher Web sites to locate e-journal articles; the full text of the article is linked immediately to the exact bibliographic citation for which they are looking. Because our A-to-Z serials list is generated from the SFX database, the OA titles are included with subscription titles. Also, one concern raised about OA journals is that libraries will not have vendor-supplied usage statistics by which we can evaluate our collections. With SFX, we will have our own local means of monitoring usage statistics.

In order for the OA titles to be accessed through SFX, they need to be indexed by the bibliographic databases. As a consortium, we can work with our database vendors to encourage them to include OA journals in the body of scholarly publishing that they index. We are also in initial stages of working with our portal developer, Ex Libris, to explore the possibilities of using metadata harvesting software to create "metaindexes" of open archive materials. This metadata harvesting would enable us to gather scholarly publications from institutional repositories, again breaking the lock that the traditional STM publishers have on the presentation of scholarly publication.

Notes

1. These principles can be found at http://www.lib.umd.edu/CLMD/e-verpol.html.
2. http://usmai.umd.edu/schocomm_051304.doc
3. http://usmai.umd.edu/SCHOLAR.htm

BUYING SERIALS CONSORTIALLY: THE VIVA EXPERIENCE

Ralph Alberico, Dean of Libraries and Ed Technology, James Madison University, Harrisonburg, Virginia

This chapter examines the policies, procedures, and decision processes employed within the Virtual Library of Virginia (VIVA) with regard to review, selection, and licensing of electronic serials. I also provide a brief profile of the collection characteristics associated with the approach to collection development taken by VIVA.

VIVA Background

VIVA is a large consortium of academic libraries at public and non-profit, independent higher education institutions within the Commonwealth of Virginia. VIVA members include

- 15 public colleges and universities,

- 24 public two-year colleges,

- 31 private non-profit colleges, and

- The Library of Virginia (the state library).

Decision making within VIVA reflects the diverse institutions that comprise its membership, a reliance on legislative appropriations for revenue, a highly decentralized organizational structure, and adherence to fundamental principles agreed upon by all members. The first principle that guides VIVA is a belief that one of the most important roles of the consortium is to level the playing field for libraries at all member institutions. VIVA strives to ensure that every student and faculty member will have access to a common core of high-quality resources, whether they are affiliated with a major research university, a small liberal arts institution, or a community college. A second fundamental principle involves sharing. VIVA members agree to share items from their collections with other members by providing priority inter-library loan service. The sharing principle is also reflected in willingness of administrators at member libraries to offer substantial amounts of unpaid staff time and expertise to contribute to the work of the consortium. The third fundamental principle underlying VIVA's success is value. VIVA's mission stresses cost beneficial service. The consortium is much more than a buying club, but that does not mean that delivering value to higher education in Virginia is not among VIVA's priorities. These principles inform all of the activities of VIVA, including collection development decision making.

In December 2004 VIVA collections included more than 150 abstracting and indexing (A&I) services. Those services cover a broad range of disciplines, with an emphasis on those that are included in the curricula of more than a few member schools. In addition to A&I services, VIVA licenses more than 20 online journal collections and aggregator services, including more than 6,000 journal titles and million of articles. VIVA online offerings also include full text reference collections, historical documents, poetry and drama collections, reports, and statistical data.[1] While a few of the VIVA collections are loaded on servers at member institutions, most VIVA resources are accessible to students and faculty on Web sites hosted by vendors and publishers.

VIVA services include expedited support for inter-library loan. Inter-library loan is supported by providing reimbursement to VIVA lending libraries for expenses those libraries absorb as part of inter-library loan operations. VIVA also acquires Ariel software for use by member libraries and sponsors training and technical support for inter-library loan activities. Other training and professional development activities that VIVA sponsors focus on use of online collections, information literacy, and emerging technologies. And VIVA sponsors the Virginia Heritage Project, an effort initially funded by the National Endowment for the Humanities to develop finding aids to items in Virginia libraries' special collections related to the African American experience.

VIVA Governance

Much of the work of VIVA is done by librarians at member institutions. A steering committee composed of library directors who represent the different types of academic institutions that belong to VIVA is responsible for governance and must approve all expenditures of VIVA funds. The only full-time professional employee of VIVA is a project director, who is responsible for overseeing the operations of the consortium. The project director is assisted by 1.5 FTE classified employees, who handle procurement and other administrative functions. The director reports to the steering committee. Thus VIVA follows the familiar corporate model, with a CEO reporting to a board of directors. When VIVA was established in 1997 a decision was made to streamline administrative structure (and by extension, administrative costs) to the fullest extent possible.

In addition to the steering committee three standing committees handle all of the work of VIVA. An outreach committee manages public relations and advocacy activities. A resource-sharing committee oversees inter-library loan and other resource-sharing activities. And the resources for users committee is responsible for collection development. Ad hoc committees are appointed on an occasional basis by the steering committee to handle tasks that fall outside the purview of the three standing committees. The membership of the standing committees is also representative, with members drawn from public doctoral and comprehensive institutions, the state community college system, and private, non-profit colleges. All committees are staffed by librarians employed by member schools; the work of the consortium and the authority for collection development decision making are highly distributed.

VIVA Budget

The estimated VIVA budget from all sources for the 2004–2006 biennium is approximately $13.3 million. The vast majority of that funding comes from legislative appropriations. All public higher education institutions benefit equally from those appropriations, and all are VIVA members by default. Other funds come from member contributions and from non-profit, independent schools that opt to join VIVA. Non-profit, independent schools receive some matching funds for shared online collections, and individual independent schools can also take advantage of consortial discounts.

One of the remarkable aspects of VIVA is the ability of the consortium to manage large sums of money and intense collection development activity with such a small administrative staff. VIVA budget allocations reflect the priorities of the consortium. More than 88% of the budget is reserved for information resources, 7% is allocated to support inter-library loan and other resource-sharing activities, 1% is allocated for travel and training, and less than 4% is used for administration. As these numbers indicate, collection development is the highest priority activity within VIVA.

VIVA Collection Development Principles

The VIVA resources for users and steering committees strive for consensus with regard to collection decisions. During the course of our 10-year history VIVA collection expenditures have shifted from general A&I services and aggregators suitable for lower division undergraduates to more specialized services and electronic journal collections. In the early years of VIVA, when budgets were lower and choices were more limited, it was easier to go after the proverbial low-hanging fruit, licensing collections that provide roughly equal benefit to each of the diverse categories of institutions that comprise VIVA. In the current environment, collection decisions are more complex.

The fundamental principles that VIVA employs stress equitable, cooperative, and cost beneficial decision making. Decisions are also driven by data. Much effort is devoted to compiling and analyzing data that are used to determine usefulness, usability, and cost effectiveness of resources under consideration for initial licensing or renewal. Priority is given to resources that provide broad support for academic programs at member institutions. The Big Deal is important, but so is the big audience. VIVA serves approximately 400,000 students and faculty in Virginia, so there is a tendency to seek license agreements that represent the interests of different types of schools and offer lowest common denominator solutions. VIVA licenses are Big Deals by default. And VIVA licenses tend to involve big publishers or vendors offering multiple journal titles rather than smaller publishers or vendors offering single titles.

At the same time, priorities for higher education at the state level must be taken into account. The fact that the state has identified enrollment growth as a priority bolsters the case for a centrally funded consortium like VIVA. When supporting high priority areas such as nursing education, where there are numerous programs in place, achieving consensus is relatively easy. However, when the state also establishes a priority to increase sponsored research funding at state institutions and identifies target areas such as biotechnology, IT, and engineering, challenges arise. VIVA revenue is not sufficient to absorb the total cost of STM collections and collections that support lower division programs.

Political considerations also factor into collection decisions. Almost all VIVA funding comes from legislative appropriations. Legislators recognize that VIVA is a partnership involving different sizes and types of higher education institutions. Advocacy work with funding agencies places an emphasis on leveling the playing field and low administrative overhead. Thus it is critical for VIVA to demonstrate value to multiple constituencies. And as information provided through VIVA increases in size and scope, the need for administrative support also increases.

VIVA Selection Process

Requests for e-journals and other resources to be considered for consortial licensing originate from VIVA members. Items under consideration are referred to a resources for users committee (RUC), whose members represent the different types of VIVA schools. Members of that committee are assigned to work with specific vendors and subject specialties. This practice allows RUC members to establish ongoing relationships with publishers and to develop expertise with specific product categories. RUC members handle the first contact with vendors in their portfolio and ensure continuity of communication as the selection and license negotiation process unfolds. Trial subscriptions are the norm, and input is solicited from all interested parties at VIVA institutions who can exchange views on a restricted listserv. Final license negotiations are handled by the VIVA director, whose office is located at George Mason University, and procurements are handled by the procurement office at James Madison University. Recommendations pass from the RUC to the steering committee, which must approve all contracts and expenditures of appropriated funds.

Licensing Considerations

Decisions about new subscriptions and renewals are based on a number of factors, including programmatic need, congruence with the VIVA mission, and usage data. Publishers must be willing and able to deal with a consortium. The ability of a publisher to supply usage data is a critical consideration. Another important criterion is support for OpenURL and other technical standards. VIVA aims for simple, straightforward contracts; licensing terms and conditions must apply equally to all consortium members. Financial benefits associated with consortial licensing must exceed the benefit that would accrue to members if they negotiated their own individual licenses. RFPs are often used to ensure competitive pricing. In summary, the selection process used in VIVA is utilitarian and pragmatic. There is an emphasis on the consortium providing measurable financial benefits in a way that achieves the greatest good for the greatest number of its members. Open access (OA) licensing arrangements are generally not pursued by VIVA because there is no added benefit to individual institutions that is associated with a consortial rather than an individual subscription. Furthermore, some (OA) publishers, like some commercial publishers, refuse to deal with consortia. Within VIVA (OA) journals are handled by individual schools rather than by the consortium.

Consortia often develop models for allocating costs to members. Just as publishers use many factors to establish a price, consortia use different factors to establish the financial obligations of members to the consortium. Financial arrangements in VIVA include:

- Consortial discount; consortium pays for license.

- Consortial discount; members pay for individual licenses.

- Consortial discount; consortium and members share cost of license.

- Consortial discount; private, non-profit schools can take advantage of cost sharing and pay for their own licenses under consortial discounts.

Since the bulk of VIVA funding is allocated centrally, the model that is used most frequently for the public institutions, which comprise most of the membership, is the model in which the consortium pays for the total cost of the license on behalf of all members. Such a model emphasizes consensus with regard to collection decisions. Other cost-sharing models are used especially for non-profit independent members, but the majority of procurements are handled and funded totally by the consortium.

Consortia of Convenience

There have been cases when an e-journal collection was either too expensive or too specialized to be considered for a centrally funded VIVA license. For example, an expensive collection of scientific research journals might not appeal to small liberal arts colleges or community colleges. Yet the collection might appeal to the larger research institutions in VIVA. On a number of occasions a subset of the VIVA membership have come together as an ad hoc consortium to negotiate a license that falls outside the VIVA mission. Such consortia of convenience have involved various combinations of members and occur outside the VIVA consortial framework. Nevertheless, the ability of VIVA members to participate effectively in such consortia of convenience is made possible by trust and working relationships established within the VIVA consortium.

When a group of VIVA member institutions agree to pursue a license outside the context of VIVA, the group follows practices that are similar to those employed in VIVA. For example, participating institutions agree to be represented by a team that crosses institutional boundaries and that is empowered to negotiate with a single voice. And the team for the biggest licenses has included an attorney, a collection development librarian, and a library director, each from a different institution. Directors of member libraries also agree to desired terms, conditions, and outcomes before entering into negotiations with vendors. Consortia of convenience formed outside of VIVA have resulted in group licenses for a number of large e-journal collections from publishers such as Elsevier, Wiley, and Kluwer. The substantial number of journal titles available to many VIVA schools through such arrangements is not reflected in VIVA statistics.

Consortium E-Journal Characteristics

Like many consortia, VIVA operates in a unique financial, political, and institutional milieu. The environment in which VIVA exists is quite different from the environment in which its individual members operate. The consortium must be sensitive to broader inter-institutional issues. And the political context for VIVA, which is centrally funded by the state, drives the decision-making processes of the consortium. It is reasonable to assume that the nature of a journal collection developed under the auspices of a consortium will reflect the milieu in which the consortium exists. This chapter ends with a brief, unscientific analysis of the characteristics of VIVA e-journal collections.

One issue worth examining is the extent to which VIVA's mission and selection processes shape VIVA journal collections. I also want to look at usage patterns within VIVA for articles from different categories of journals. In order to understand whether the approach taken by VIVA results in an emphasis on a specific publishing model, it was necessary to categorize VIVA journal collections to reflect the publishing models in place. As indicated earlier, true OA as a publishing model is generally not consistent with the selection processes used within VIVA. However, there are a number of other non-profit publishing models that do apply. For the purposes of this quick, unscientific analysis the following publishing entities were identified:

- Learned societies (e.g., American Association for the Advancement of Science)

- University presses (e.g., Oxford University Press)

- Commercial trade publishers (e.g., Lippincott, Williams and Wilkins)

- Non-profit publishing Cooperatives (e.g., BioOne, Project Muse)

- Commercial aggregator services (e.g., Gale InfoTrac)

It is important to note that any analysis based on this categorization scheme is rough at best and that results are not generalizable in any sense. There are many possible ways to categorize suppliers of online journals, and placing individual journals and journal collections into appropriate categories is not as simple a task as it might seem. There is considerable overlap in journal titles available from different vendors, publishers, and aggregators; the same titles are available from different sources though often with different levels of coverage. Thus it is possible that one title might belong to multiple categories. There is also overlap within categories. For example, Project Muse, which I categorized as a non-profit publishing cooperative, includes titles from both learned societies and university presses. And there are complex ownership and business relationships among publishers and distributors. It is not uncommon for a journal from a learned society to be distributed by a trade publisher; nor is it unusual for one trade publisher to be a subsidiary of another. For example, Lippincott is a subsidiary of Kluwer, and Lippincott journals as well as journals from the American Psychological Association (APA) licensed by VIVA are distributed by Ovid. For the purposes of this analysis, APA was counted as a learned society, and Lippincott was treated as a trade publisher.

Further complicating the situation are the link resolution services implemented by many VIVA libraries. From the perspective of the user, such services blur the distinction between journal collections and abstracting and indexing (A&I) services. Meta-search services used in some of our libraries also make it difficult to count searches and article downloads. Finally, many A&I services (e.g., Ulrich's, Ovid, Cambridge Scientific Abstracts) available from VIVA provide direct links to OA titles. In some sense, by subscribing to those A&I services VIVA is offering OA titles. Open access is also enabled by the interlinking that occurs between articles in journals licensed by VIVA (e.g., titles from Highwire Press) and articles available under OA.

In this arena, counting is at least as problematic as categorizing. Journal title counts are a moving target, especially for aggregated titles. For the purpose of this analysis, in order to get an accurate count of the journal titles available from different aggregation services from one vendor, it was necessary to de-duplicate titles offered in common by more than one of the services. And for another aggregator, it was not possible to get a count at all. Journals available from aggregators play an important role in VIVA, but journal title counts do not reflect the content that is really available from each title; backfile availability varies widely, and coverage of specific titles comes and goes. Trying to make sense of data on articles downloaded is even more challenging than getting a bead on which journal titles VIVA offers. Clearly, in a world of stable URLs, link resolvers, e-reserves, and course management systems, each request for an article from a VIVA is not created equal.

VIVA has been diligent about collecting and maintaining usage data. Nevertheless, our knowledge about which resources we have access to and how we use those resources is inconsistent and incomplete, and in some cases, the accuracy of the information we receive from vendors is questionable. Usage statistics supplied by publishers and vendors are not as reliable as we would like them to be. This is especially the case for consortia. The situation is improving; VIVA is part of a working group with Project COUNTER that is seeking to improve the quality of data available to consortia. Maybe someday we will have trustworthy, standardized usage and collection data that will enable us to do a reliable analysis of our e-journal collections.

In the meantime, the data presented in tables 1 and 2 and in the PowerPoint used for the panel discussion indicate a journal collection that represents a wide variety of publisher and vendor types and a large number of e-journals. Usage is also relatively high, but the nature of the use is hard to ascertain. Finally, the number of journal titles available and the relatively low cost per use for article downloads seem to indicate that VIVA is achieving its mission of leveling the playing field for higher education in Virginia by providing equitable, cost-effective information service.

Table 1. VIVA E-Journals by Publisher or Vendor Category, FY 2005.

Category	E-Journal Titles	% of Total VIVA Journal Titles	No. of Publishers or Vendors	% of Total VIVA E-Journal Vendors	% of Total E-Journal Titles Excluding Aggregators
Learned Society	135	2.03%	6	33.33%	11.77%
University Press	387	5.83%	3	16.67%	33.74%
Trade Journal Publisher	292	4.40%	4	22.22%	25.46%
Non-profit Collaborative	333	5.02%	4	22.22%	29.03%
Trade Aggregator Service	5,490	82.72%	1	5.56%	NA
Total	6,637	100.00%	18	100.00%	100.00%

The data show that VIVA selection practices result in more business relationships with non-profit vendors or publishers than with commercial enterprises. However, that does not necessarily mean that the level of overall investment or the number of titles and articles available is greater in the non-profit sector. The largest single category in terms of number of vendors is learned societies, and those vendors typically offer fewer titles per vendor than the other categories. The largest number of e-journal titles is associated with the single aggregator vendor, for which data were available. It should be noted that the availability of journal content from an aggregator service is not equivalent to the content that would be available from a subscription. When commercial aggregator services are factored out, the distribution of e-journal titles across categories is relatively balanced, with vendors in each category responsible for an average of between 50 and 100 journal titles.

Table 2. VIVA Journal Article Downloads by Publisher or Vendor Category, FY 2004.

Category	Total Expenditures	Total Article Downloads	Average Cost per Article Download	% of Total VIVA Article Downloads
Learned Society	$ 673,221	357,194	$ 1.88	9.78%
University Press	$ 391,720	140,171	$ 2.79	3.84%
Trade Journal Publisher	$ 219,610	419,688	$ .52	11.49%
Non-profit Collaborative	$ 265,646	239,995	$ 1.11	6.57%
Trade Aggregator Service	$ 466,151	2,496,984	$ .19	68.34%
Total	$2,016,348	3,654,032	$ .55	100.00%

Usage data can be problematic. It is not certain that the types of use reported by vendors are consistent with one another. And there are a number of important e-journal vendors from whom usage data are not available. Most significantly, we do not have a clear understanding of how e-journals are being used. For the purposes of this analysis each article download is treated equally, yet the impact of the articles on readers varies considerably. For VIVA it is clearly more cost effective to license access to e-journal articles on a consortial basis than it would be for individual libraries to negotiate their own separate contracts. Consortial use is also more cost effective than document delivery. The relatively low cost per article download from trade publishers was somewhat of a surprise. The low cost, along with the relatively small number of trade publishers and e-journal titles from trade publishers, probably reflects VIVA's selectivity. VIVA is providing value by selecting publishers and vendors that are able to best meet demand for cost-effective access to scholarly information from the higher education community in Virginia. VIVA's business practices tend to favor vendors that offer information that serves large numbers of students and faculty. For example, the relatively high cost for e-journals from learned societies and commercial aggregators is counterbalanced by high use. Such usage patterns, along with distribution of use across multiple institutions, clearly indicates that VIVA is leveling the playing field and expanding access to new populations. As arbitrary and unreliable as the data are, I hesitate to read too much into them, but they do seem to indicate that the decision-making processes employed within the VIVA consortium have been successful in developing information services that are valuable to members.

As VIVA matures as a consortium it will be necessary to evolve in response to changes in the political, economic, and information environments. Scalability has become an issue within VIVA. Much of the low-hanging fruit has already been picked, and if VIVA is to respond to demands for information in support of statewide research agendas, members will have to develop cost allocation models that provide for research collections in addition to supporting broad-based demand. As the scope of VIVA collections expands and the financial relationships between individual members and the consortium grow more complex, it will also become necessary to increase central administrative support. At the current time VIVA is conducting a review of core journals held by institutions in the state based on a union report from Ulrich's Serials Analysis software, which was licensed on behalf of the state by VIVA. It is likely that the analysis of journal subscriptions among VIVA members will result in new business practices and expanded access to resources. Buying serials has become one of the most important activities pursued by VIVA. As the serials landscape has changed, VIVA has adapted. Finally, even if VIVA does not become directly involved in OA publishing ventures, there is certainly a role for the consortium to play in educating its members about OA issues and opportunities.

Note

1. More information on VIVA collections may be found at http://www.vivalib.org/collect/.

THE CAROLINA CONSORTIUM: BUILDING AN INTERSTATE GRASSROOTS BUYER'S CLUB

Tim Bucknall, Assistant Director, University of North Carolina at Greensboro

Introduction

The Carolina Consortium comprises 38 libraries working together to share access to over 2,000 academic journals. The emergence of yet another library consortium is usually of little note, but the Carolina Consortium has several features that might make it of special interest. It is a multitype, multistate, "opt in," grassroots, special purpose consortium—perhaps the only one in the country. As such, it may serve as a possible model for the creation of similar consortia in areas with similar needs.

Although all of the current participants are academic libraries, the group is *multitype* within that context. It includes small private colleges with less than a thousand students, large public research universities with ARL libraries, and everything in between (even including a large community college). It is also *multistate*, with 21 North Carolina members and 17 from South Carolina. The Carolina Consortium allows any participating school to *opt in* (or out) of any specific deal. The development of the consortium was a *grassroots* effort involving the active participation of librarians from all the schools—primarily department heads from serials or collection development. There were no centralized resources whatsoever dedicated to the establishment of the consortium; it grew organically from the labors of its participants. The Carolina Consortium was created with the sole intent of fulfilling a single, *special purpose*—the sharing of high-quality research journals among the participating institutions.

Why Create a New Consortium?

Few, if any, libraries have adequate funding to support subscriptions to all of the research journals needed by their faculty and students, yet the demand for immediate access to these materials continues to increase at many institutions. Several publishers are willing to allow consortia to pool and share their journal title sets, and others offer bulk access to their entire stable of journals. Under both models, the increase in the number of accessible titles can greatly surpass the nominal increase in cost to the participating institutions.

Although interest in these large, academic journal deals was high at a number of schools in North Carolina, we lacked an effective mechanism to pursue them. Our statewide consortium, NC LIVE, has historically been an extremely egalitarian operation, purchasing only those resources that receive significant interest from the state's public libraries, community colleges, independent colleges and universities, and the 16 UNC system schools. Although this "all for one, and one for all" philosophy is highly laudable and was very helpful in procuring funding from the state legislature for basic resources, it did mean that expensive, highly specialized academic journals were very unlikely candidates for NC LIVE. In some states, an alternative venue for statewide cooperation among academic libraries is the state university system. But in North Carolina, the UNC system is quite decentralized. That makes it easier for each school to tailor its services and resources to its own clientele, but it can make cooperation a bit tricky. Compounding the complexity of the consortial environment within the UNC system, the two large ARL UNC libraries (North Carolina State and UNC-Chapel Hill) have historically cooperated primarily with Duke as part of the Triangle Research Libraries Network. This small, research-focused consortium had previously implemented Wiley, Springer, and Blackwell title-sharing deals of its own, but had never offered to expand those deals statewide.

So, given the policies and histories of NC LIVE and the UNC system, there was no effective avenue for establishing large, shared academic journal title packages using extant consortia. The schools interested in such publisher deals had to face the fact that in order to take advantage of some wonderful deals involving lots of high-demand serials, we would need to establish our own consortium.

Building a Grassroots Consortium

The deals deemed to be the most appealing to potential members were Blackwell, Wiley, and Springer. The Wiley and Springer deals were similar "title-sharing" deals. If a library agreed to retain its current subscriptions throughout the term of the contract, then that library would be able to share access to any of the publisher's other journals to which any school in the consortium subscribes. Under the Blackwell deal, schools that agreed to maintain their current subscription levels plus pay a surcharge gained access to all of Blackwell's online titles (as well as ownership of all titles for that publication year). All three of the deals included six to eight years of backfiles for most titles. The multi-year contracts (Wiley and Springer) also included attractive inflation price caps and a "bail out" clause in case of financial emergency.

Once the specific deals were identified, the publishers were able to provide spreadsheets identifying which schools in North Carolina carried current subscriptions. The schools were then contacted and the potential deals described. Although many of the schools that were called had evinced interest in participating in these deals in theory, it wasn't known how many might step up when specific deals were on the table. Given that the devil is in the details, it was somewhat surprising that nearly all the schools that were contacted agreed to attend a meeting in Greensboro, North Carolina, to discuss the particulars of these deals with the publishers.

The meeting was quite successful. Despite the lack of (or perhaps due to the absence of) any centralized authority, any elected or appointed leaders, and any bylaws, policies, or rules, librarians with widely differing experience and representing highly varied institutions worked collegially to hammer out agreements that benefited everyone. Specifically, we agreed that there was sufficient interest to pursue all three deals, and the group established some specific negotiating points to which the publishers must agree if the deals were to be consummated.

After the meeting, South Carolina libraries were contacted and invited to participate, and the license negotiations began in earnest. Throughout the negotiation period, the publishers were quite eager to work with us and, for the most part, were willing and able to accommodate our consortium's needs. In fact, in some cases the publishers even exceeded their contractual responsibilities. For example, although the contracts stipulated a start date of January 1, 2005, all three publishers allowed the consortium to access their materials weeks before that date.

Benefits of the Consortial Deals

Now that the deals are formally in place, 38 schools have online access to up to 2,175 academic journals. Because each school can opt in or out of any specific deals, the degree of participation varies. The shared-title deals proved to be the most popular, with 36 schools choosing Wiley and 35 selecting Springer. Only nine wanted to participate in the Blackwell deal, reflecting the fact that for most institutions, it required the highest increase in expenditures.

The three deals certainly benefit the consortium as a whole. If we look at the subscription costs of the journals in each package and multiply that by the number of institutions participating, we end up with a book value of $65 million dollars. The actual Carolina Consortium costs for 2005, including serials renewals and all other consortium costs, were about $2.5 million. That's a pretty steep discount.

Consortial membership also benefits individual institutions. Let's examine the case of Meredith College, one of the largest private colleges for women in the Southeast. Meredith has a total enrollment of around 2,400 and is located in Raleigh, North Carolina. In 2003 the Library's collection included about 150,000 volumes and 840 periodical subscriptions, including three from Wiley and eleven from Springer (including Springer's Kluwer and Brill imprints). The 2004 subscription prices for those 14 journals totaled approximately $9,950. Because Meredith elected to join these two publisher deals via the Carolina Consortium, it is committed to retaining those subscriptions, plus paying a relatively small premium for the expanded access. Aside from the normal inflationary increases, Meredith needed to pay only about $200 additional for the consortial access in 2005—a tiny 2% increase in their expenditures. But the number of accessible Wiley and Springer titles rose from 14 to 1,461, a phenomenal increase in titles. The students and faculty of Meredith now have access to as many (and in some cases more) titles as the students and faculty of the major ARL libraries in the state that declined to participate in the consortium.

The University of North Carolina at Greensboro provides a somewhat different example. Prior to consortial participation, UNCG was already making available to its faculty and students nearly all of the titles included in the three publisher deals. But joining the consortium enabled the university to gain free access to many titles it had previously been getting through pay-per-view, allowed UNCG to drop its costly Solinet Springer deal, and allowed it to realize a significantly reduced inflationary increase on subscriptions. In total, UNCG's real savings will amount to approximately $140,000 over the life of the three contracts.

The benefits to the schools, then, are obvious. Most schools, like Meredith, get many more titles at nominal additional cost. Schools like UNCG, which already offered virtually all the titles, realize a significant actual savings.

The benefits for publishers are perhaps less obvious but are no less real. After all, these for-profit companies are highly unlikely to pursue a business model that they believe hurts them financially. In aggregate, the 2005 income derived from the Carolina Consortium deals is approximately equivalent to what they would have received if they had dealt with each of the 38 schools separately. They aren't losing any money on the deal, and it costs them little to have their Webmaster turn on additional titles for Meredith, UNCG, or the other participants. So, while the publishers only break even on income for 2005, their actual costs stay fairly static. The real benefits for these companies are happier customers and improved income stability over several years. By locking schools into their current levels of subscription expenditures, the publishers are guaranteeing their income stream during a time of high volatility in the academic journal market. This buys time for these companies to evaluate and respond to emerging trends such as open access and makes it much less likely that their journals will be the ones on the chopping block if universities initiate yet another round of serials cuts. And by offering their customers more titles for basically the same price, they build brand loyalty and foster improved customer relations. In addition, the contractual requirement that all consortially shared title subscriptions be in electronic format (although an additional print copy is still available for a surcharge) will no doubt hasten the transition of library subscriptions from print to electronic, which will in the long term reduce publisher print and distribution costs.

Conclusion

The Carolina Consortium came into being with the express purpose of concluding deals with Wiley, Blackwell, and Springer. Without any central authority or funding, librarians from 38 schools cooperated and forged mutually beneficial resource-sharing deals over the course of a few months. The resultant deals now provide greatly enhanced journal access at little or no extra cost. Many journal publishers seem receptive to such grassroots initiatives and are currently offering attractive consortial models. Now is an excellent time for libraries to investigate the sharing of scholarly journals. And if an appropriate consortium doesn't exist that meets your needs, you can always create your own!

The Carolina Consortium—Participants

Appalachian State University

Belmont Abbey College

Campbell University

Central Piedmont Community College

Chowan College

The Citadel

Clemson

Coastal Carolina University

College of Charleston

East Carolina University

Elizabeth City State University

Elon University

Fayetteville State University

Francis Marion

Furman

Guilford College

Lenoir-Rhyne College

Medical University of SC

Meredith College

North Carolina Ag & Tech State University

North Carolina Central University

UNC Asheville

UNC Charlotte

UNC Greensboro

UNC Pembroke

UNC Wilmington

University of SC—Aiken

University of SC—Beaufort

University of SC—Columbia

University of SC—Lancaster

University of SC—Salkehatchie

University of SC—Sumter

University of SC—Union

University of SC—Upstate

Wake Forest University

Western Carolina University

Winthrop

Wofford

The Carolina Consortium—Contacts

Tim Bucknall—UNCG
    Convener—Carolina Consortium
    bucknall@uncg.edu
    336-256-1216

Jan Cambre—USC
    Chair—PASCAL Consortium Purchasing Committee
    jan@gwm.sc.edu
    803-777-3041

Sylvia Bonadio
    Kluwer/Springer/Brill Representative
    sylvia.bonadio@springer-sbm.com
    866-269-9527x646

Diane Conroy
    Blackwell Representative
    dconroy@bos.blackwellpublishing.com
    781-388-8354

Mike Phillips
    Wiley Representative
    MiPhilli@wiley.com
    773-631-4001

The chapters in this section focus on the importance of MARC records for e-journals. For quite a while, librarians have pondered the issue of putting everything in their OPACs or simply providing links from all resources through a single search box. Our speakers focused on the need to incorporate these records in the OPAC, but we were all informed as they walked us through varying scenarios.

MARC Records for E-Journals

MARC RECORDS FOR E-JOURNALS

Heather S. Miller, Assistant Director for Technical Services and Systems, State University of New York at Albany

Introduction

When e-journals first appeared, the reaction of catalogers was often "we can't handle them," leaving it to Web sites to offer lists of e-journals. Time has proven these lists to be flawed, ponderous, and incomplete. Meanwhile, librarians have found ways of adding catalog records for e-journals to library catalogs. "MARC Records for E-Journals" brought together six librarians who have found different ways of obtaining MARC records for e-journals and incorporating them into OPACs. They briefly explained their methods for doing so and why representing e-journals in the OPAC is advantageous, so that others may follow in their footsteps. Time limitations necessitated very brief comments by the panelists, with the expectation that interested persons would follow up individually for specific advice.

The panelists all believe that using MARC records for e-journals is essential if libraries are to provide useful means of access to them. Omitting from the OPAC a whole class of resources that is becoming increasingly essential to library users does those users a great disservice. Yes, doing so is not a simple task. Aside from the mechanics of obtaining and incorporating such records, there are questions of whether to add the e-journal to a record for the print version, eliminate Web lists, or run parallel systems (OPAC and Web list), and if so, whether to generate the Web list from the OPAC, among others. The panelists have taken different routes to answer these questions; most have tried several approaches, and they will very likely try something else in the future. None declared his or her solution the final word on the subject, and all admitted to something less than perfection. Nevertheless, all have put a great deal of work into providing MARC records for e-journals and are committed to continuing while at the same time trying to find more efficient means of doing so. They spoke to an audience that was eager to learn about ways to utilize MARC records for e-journals, indicating that there is considerable interest in this topic.

The comments of the speakers follow.

E-JOURNALS IN THE OPAC—UNIVERSITY OF ROCHESTER

Helen Anderson, Head, Collection Development, University of Rochester, New York

Introduction

At the University of Rochester, we now use the multiple record approach and Endeavor's Voyager as our ILS. We have contracted with Serials Solutions for MARC records. We do maintain a separate list of e-journals on the Web, which is generated from two sources: the OPAC and a spreadsheet from Serials Solutions (see figure 1).

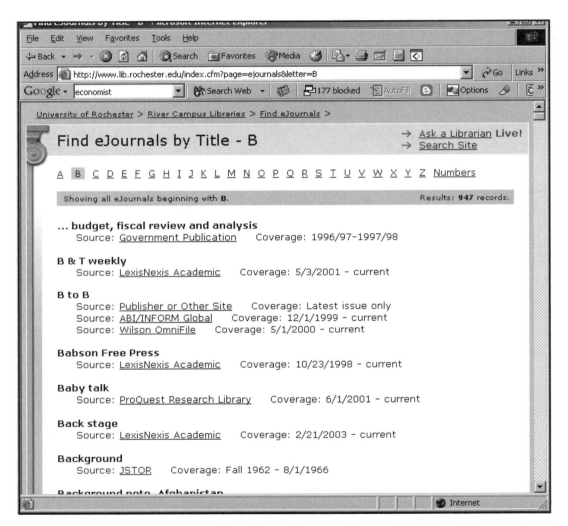

Figure 1. Page from the E-Journals List (http://www.library.rochester.edu/index.cfm?page=ejournals).
For details regarding the e-journals list, contact Jeff Suszczynski Library Systems Analyst,
Digital Initiatives, at jeffs@library.rochester.edu.

Then

We made our first proposal for cataloging e-journals in the OPAC in 1996. We undertook a study that recommended single records for each title, with a holdings record for each link in the same record.

There were many new and emerging products and collections in 1997. Project Muse had 40 titles, JSTOR, and Academic Press brought out new products, and ScienceDirect was in beta testing.

Between 1998 and 2000 we cataloged manually on single records, placing the link in the holdings record in Voyager for Project Muse, JSTOR, Academic Ideal, and individual titles from 16 publishers.

In 2000 we abandoned the single record approach in order to have any kind of records in the OPAC for aggregator titles. We used records from various sources such as Yale for ScienceDirect titles, we subscribed to records from Proquest, we used OCLC records, and we created records in-house for some aggregators using a program from the University of Tennessee at Knoxville.

These are our results:

- Some titles had four, five, or more records each. WE had to be persistent to find what we wanted, but it was there—somewhere (see figure 2).

- At one point we had some 30,000 records for e-journals in the OPAC.

- We had no good way of keeping the links up to date, although there was a report of broken URLs.

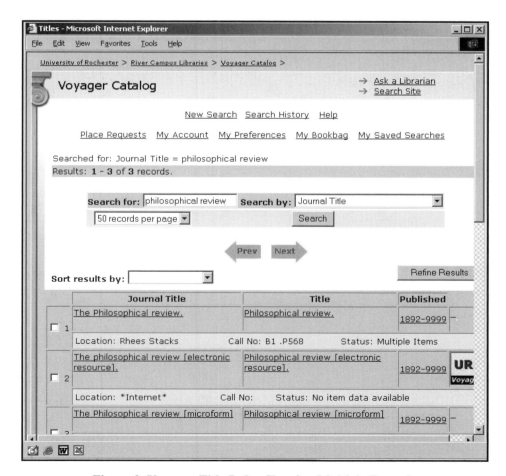

Figure 2. Voyager Title Index Showing Multiple Records.

In 2001 we began our Web-based e-journals list, drawing titles from the OPAC. Subject librarians continued to maintain separate e-journals lists for their disciplines.

Now

In May 2004 we contracted with Serials Solutions for MARC records. These are the challenges we asked Serials Solutions to deal with:

- Due to a bug in our Voyager system, we couldn't load records with multiple URLs and copy all URLs into the holdings record automatically. There was a problem with the length of the URLs and the method we had originally employed: placing the links in the holdings records came back to haunt us. Serials Solutions kindly helped us around this by creating intermediate pages for each title where all the links are seen together, with no scrolling down. (See figures 3 and 4.) Serials Solutions maintains these pages, but we designed them to look like part of our site.

- We have many records to undo. Some sets were easy to pull and discard, but manual records done in the early days are time-consuming to identify and discard, especially where print and electronic are included in the same record. We are working on this gradually

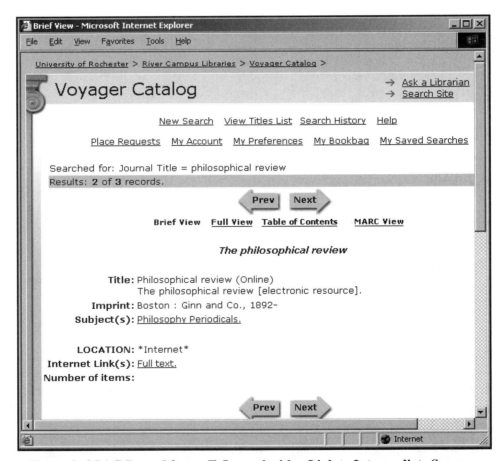

Figure 3. OPAC Record for an E-Journal with a Link to Intermediate Screen.

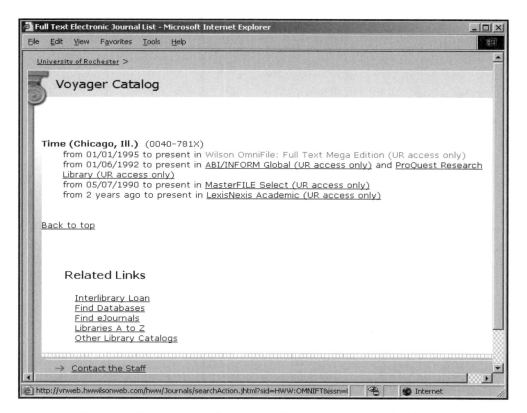

Figure 4. Intermediate Screen Holdings and Links to Full Text.

These are the benefits we have seen from contracting with Serials Solutions:

• We have reduced the number of records that appear in our OPAC, meaning less confusion for the user when searching the title index; we now have about 12,000 e-journal records in the OPAC.

• Serials Solutions monitors and updates broken or changing links—we don't have to do it.

• The e-journals list is compiled from two sources. We use Perl scripting to pull the catalog records from Voyager on a nightly basis, and once a month we run the program against a spreadsheet provided by SerSol to incorporate the holdings of the titles we process through them. It's usually the second or third most accessed page on our site and is always in the top five. Subject librarians continue to maintain their own subject lists.

Future

These are our plans going forward:

• We will process more and more titles through Serials Solutions.

• We will keep cleaning up earlier records as time allows.

• How many people are using the OPAC to find e-journals, anyway? Who are they, and what are the circumstances under which they're doing this?

- Aren't most people really using e-journals lists, Google, bookmarks, A&I publisher pages, or metasearch products to access journal content?

- To what extent can we expect to improve the OPAC itself so that the e-journal content is a snap to access? Is this possible or realistic or even desirable?

- Think of the OPAC as a back-end or source for other applications such as the e-journals list, metasearch, etc.

- Let people who still want to search the OPAC for journals do it; don't take it away, but concentrate on developing other applications that provide access in ways that are natural and useful for people. Example: We'll be working on adding subject access for the e-journals list and will have to grapple with the issue of which subject headings to use.

- Some subject librarians will probably continue to maintain their individual Web lists of e-journals for some time.

THE GUMBERG LIBRARY'S EXPERIENCE WITH E-JOURNALS AND MARC RECORDS

Carmel Yurochko, Serials/Electronic Resources Librarian, Duquesne University, Pittsburgh, Pennsylvania

In April 2000, the Gumberg Library at Duquesne University made the decision to catalog our electronic journals into our online public access catalog (OPAC) because we believed our e-journal collections were being underused. We also wanted our online catalog to be a one-stop shop for our users' needs. At the time, we did not have an external A-to-Z list of e-journals.

The two-person serials unit staff developed a process wherein we would pull in a separate OCLC e-journal MARC record for individual titles in our electronic resource databases and include a link to each database from which the journal could be found. The OCLC records would be edited accordingly and, in addition, we would include a holdings statement for each database. Cataloging began in January 2001. The two-person staff quickly found this to be a cumbersome and complicated project. Add to the mix the fact that certain electronic databases routinely dropped or added titles, and that holdings also routinely changed, and we quickly found ourselves unable to keep up.

In approximately two and a half years, the two-person team cataloged, and attempted to maintain, approximately 3,700 e-journals in our OPAC. Usage certainly increased. But many e-journals were still not cataloged. To expedite the process and make the remainder of our e-journals known to our users, we decided to look into electronic journal management products.

A number of electronic journal management vendors visited and demonstrated their products, all of which would produce an external A-to-Z list of e-journals. Production of an A-to-Z list would mean that all of our e-journals would be made available to our users quickly and easily. In addition, management of e-journal links and updates would now be out of our hands.

After careful consideration, in July 2003 we decided to go with Ex Libris and its product, SFX. What tipped the scales in its favor was Ex Libris's development of MarcIT, a collection of MARC records that could be purchased and batch downloaded into an OPAC. Utilizing this product, our OPAC could still serve as a one-stop shop and we would also gain access to an external A-to-Z list as well.

After our two-day training session in August 2003, the two-person team produced an external A-to-Z list of electronic journal titles. By November 2003, the two-person team had become a three-person team by the inclusion of our IT director. Because our users had become accustomed to our e-journals presenting in a particular manner in our OPAC, we wanted to replicate this look if at all possible. With the help of MarcEdit, the Ex Libris MARC records were edited to our standards before being batch downloaded. Within a few minutes, we had batch downloaded approximately 5,400 Ex Libris MARC records into our OPAC.

Now, changes to databases and holdings are managed by SFX; new databases or individual titles are quickly and easily added to the A-to-Z list and to our OPAC by a routine batch downloading procedure. All in all, our users are better served.

In September 2004, while refreshing the A-to-Z title list, the system took an inordinately long time to complete the process. A phone call to the reference staff let me know that the

A-to-Z title list was down but that the e-journals could still be accessed via our OPAC. While I had previously believed that our decision to include the e-journals in our OPAC was a sound one, after the glitch in the refresh, I knew this for a fact. Not only is it generally useful to have the records in our OPAC, it saved the public service staff a lot of headaches, and with just a few words of direction, our users continued to work without interruption.

Our future plans include exploring federated searching possibilities and products as well as looking at other ways to employ SFX to our benefit. Only time will tell what else is in store for us, electronically speaking.

My advice to others would be to use an electronic journal management product if at all possible, for either an A-to-Z title list or for MARC records. With the September list refresh experience still fresh in my mind, I would certainly recommend the inclusion of MARC records in an OPAC. Although this feat can be accomplished in many ways, batch downloading from a vendor produced the best results for us. I recommend the same procedure to others. The benefits are well worth the cost of the product and the time saved. The Gumberg Library learned this valuable lesson firsthand.

BIBLIOGRAPHIC CONTROL OF DIGITAL RESOURCES AT RENSSELAER POLYTECHNIC INSTITUTE

D. Ellen Bonner, Coordinator, Technical Services, Rensselaer Polytechnic Institute, Troy, New York

Introduction

When I arrived at Rensselaer Polytechnic Institute over four years ago, the library, like everyone else, was struggling to enable effective and timely bibliographic access to electronic resources. The staff had already reached consensus on a preference for webPAC access, a decision informed in part by the limited staffing available to create and maintain a separate list or database.

Shortly after my arrival I gathered cataloging production statistics and determined that at the existing cataloging treatment level (full-level OCLC records, or—more likely at the time—original cataloging), it would have taken 14 years to get all of Rensselaer's accessible digital resources into the webPAC.[1]

Consequently, my approach to solving this dilemma was informed by practicality and outsourcing. Initially I implemented basic bibliographic control over e-journals by contracting with Serials Solutions. We subsequently moved to EBSCO A-to-Z, but have adhered to the following three principles since the summer of 2001:

- Generate a publicly accessible HTML file of searchable e-serial titles from EBSCO A-to-Z data.

- Export text data from A-to-Z and use them to create corresponding brief bibliographic records in the webPAC.

- Regularly replace all webPAC brief bibliographic records for all products.

Record Production

Producing brief records from EBSCO Excel data is fairly straightforward and is based on a process developed by Jon Jiras at RIT several years ago.[2] Microsoft Word mail merge functions enable data massaged in Excel to be plugged into a text-based MARC template. We convert the resulting formatted text file into proper MARC records using MARCEdit,[3] then load them into our ILS.

Although our expressed goal is to grant equivalent access to e-serials from our vendor-produced HTML list as well as from our webPAC, there are some situations in which that is not feasible. For those resources where direct title-level access is not available, we do not generate brief records. For instance, e-serials included in Gale, Lexis-Nexis, and some OCLC databases appear in our e-journals list, but we do not add them to the catalog. Only if we can link directly to the title described by the record do we include it in our webPAC.

Record Characteristics

In their HTML products, e-serials management vendors most often provide a list of unique titles with multiple associated URLs (see figure 1).

Pacific Affairs
Academic Search Premier 2002 to present
JSTOR Arts & Sciences I Collection 1928 - 1999 (Embargo: 5 years)
ProQuest Research Library Complete 1994 to present
ISSN: 0030-851X Online ISSN: (unknown)
Publisher: University of British Columbia
Subject: History: Oceania (South Seas)

Figure 1. Sample of Rensselaer's HTML E-Journal List from EBSCO A-to-Z.

Yet in the vendor's control database itself—from which the text data for our brief records are drawn—the same serial title is repeated within the title list of each appropriate aggregator's managed content (see figure 2).

	A	B	C	D	E
1	Title	Source	Publisher	PrintISSN	ManagedCoverage
2	Pacific Affairs	Academic Search Premier	University of British Columbia	0030-851X	2002 to present
3	Pacific Affairs	JSTOR Arts & Sciences I Collection	University of British Columbia	0030-851X	1928 - 1999
4	Pacific Affairs	ProQuest Research Library Complete	University of British Columbia	0030-851X	1994 to present

Figure 2. Extract from Rensselaer's E-Journal Data from EBSCO A-to-Z.

Thus, using text data exported from this source dictates that we include multiple records for individual titles in our catalog—one record for each vendor or aggregator through which we access any portion of a given title (see figure 3).

Pacific Affairs		
1	☐	**Pacific Affairs** [Electronic Resource]
		Web Resource (Troy); JSTOR Arts & Sciences I Collection
2	☐	**Pacific Affairs** [Electronic Resource]
		Web Resource (Troy); ProQuest Research Library Complete
3	☐	**Pacific Affairs** [Electronic Resource]
		Web Resource (Troy); EBSCO Academic Search Premier

Figure 3. Browse Display from Rensselaer webPAC.

Recently, e-serial management services have begun to provide MARC record subscriptions that present multiple URLs on single bibliographic records, but as yet Rensselaer has not opted into such services.

Record Content and Maintenance

We also enter data into our brief records in accordance with III webPAC display parameters designed to help clarify search results. For instance, we use a consistent 099 tag as a collocation device for all titles accessed via the same interface. That 099 call tag appears in the results display for users and distinguishes otherwise identical titles in browse displays. (See the example above, with JSTOR, ProQuest, and EBSCO all showing in the second line of the extended results display.)

In addition, we include as much EBSCO-supplied information as possible in brief serial records, including publisher, a generic subject heading, ISSN, a textual holdings statement, and (of course) the URL (see figure 4).

Location	Web Resource (Troy)
Call #	JSTOR Arts & Sciences I Collection
Title	**Pacific Affairs [electronic resource]**
Published	University of British Columbia

Click on the following to:
Connect from Troy (restricted access)

Holdings	Electronic Materials / 1928-1999
Subject	**History: Oceania (South Seas).**
ISSN	0030-851X
Note	Full-text not available for the current 5 years.

Figure 4. Typical Brief Record Viewed in Rensselaer webPAC.

Using the 099 tag and other embedded identifiers, we regularly extract and replace all brief records, thus ensuring that our webPAC accurately reflects the sometimes volatile content of aggregated databases.

This approach has worked extremely well at Rensselaer—users have access to all e-serials, either through the HTML list or via the catalog. Although the process of extraction and replacement is somewhat time consuming, it is an effective tool for maintaining webPAC title and URL accuracy.

E-Books

Although e-books present a slightly different set of problems, we have established a similar routine for dealing with them. Since EBSCO A-to-Z and related services are limited to the control of e-serials, the sources for e-book record data can vary. Most of our e-book purchases to date have been publisher or aggregator specific—for example, Safari or Books24x7. Most such vendors provide MARC records, which we edit for display and identification coding, then load directly into our system.

On a case-by-case basis we determine if bulk extraction and replacement is required for a specific e-book aggregator/provider. Depending on the nature of their MARC records and the level of control a given vendor is able to exert over its record provision service, we often opt for record management by adding and deleting groups of specific records incrementally. There are some sets of e-books for which we download text or Excel data from a Web site and generate brief records using the same process as with e-serials. For the most part, these tend to be groups of open access titles such as the University of California Press eScholarship Editions.

Thus far I have had no reason to regret my choice never to combine electronic record attributes with bibliographic records descriptive of printed materials—the classic "single record approach."[4] When I first implemented our current process, I spent most of a summer unbundling the hundreds of hybrid and mixed records that had already crept into our system during the era of cataloging indecision. The benefits we have reaped from my summer of toil have been tremendous—improved user access, accurate staff access (a very useful feature for our ILL department), and much more precise statistical counts of accessible digital resources.

Future Developments

As a technical services librarian, however, I have come to accept as truth the adage that nothing remains constant except change itself. To wit, I am anticipating a drastic change in our approach to managing digital resources in the not-too-distant future.

When we implemented SFX, I began to think about using that service to resolve electronic serial holdings from our catalog using one record for each title, without regard to aggregator. No longer would we have to replicate a title endlessly in order to represent each aggregator and its respective holdings for a particular title. Instead, I envisioned loading one unique brief title record and using the SFX menu to display multiple links to specific aggregators along with their individual holdings. The potential advantages seemed clear:

- less time spent manipulating multiple titles for the same record;

- better access to unique titles, without the complicating factor of aggregator duplication;

- less complex search results screens;

- no URL maintenance issues; and

- no payment for e-serial MARC record services.

Unfortunately, our ILS system restricts interactivity with SFX to ISSN metadata only, and not all serial titles in EBSCO's A-to-Z list have ISSNs. I have considered using the knowledge base from SFX to replace our EBSCO service, but at the moment the content of the two is significantly different. SFX contains title information only for those items that have consistent URL structures—the attribute of a viable SFX target. The contents of aggregated packages that do not fall into this SFX-parsable subset of the universe of electronic serials would require manual creation and maintenance. Thus, we would find ourselves replacing the routines we currently use to maintain the catalog with a functionally similar set of routines tailored to SFX knowledge-base maintenance. Those routines, in turn, would replicate the services we now pay EBSCO to perform—package content management. The conclusion seems unfortunately obvious—don't bother.

Still, I haven't entirely abandoned this line of inquiry. With the advent of ILS modules for managing digital content (specifically Ex Libris's Verde), I am hoping that a new solution will come to light that will allow us to include in our webPAC one record for each unique electronic title to which we have access—thereby simplifying our digital resource management routines, while still maintaining the productivity and service levels we have sustained over the last three years.

Notes

1. Of course, subsequently, the number of e-serials and e-books to which we subscribe (or to which we now *know* we subscribe, basic bibliographic control having been the issue initially) has increased almost exponentially. By 2004 that original 14-year projection would have become even more ludicrous.

2. See Jon Jiras, "Creating MARC Records from E-Journal Title Lists" (paper presented at IUG 2000), http://www.innopacusers.org/iug2000/proceedings/j1.html.

3. This program is made available by Terry Reese. See http://oregonstate.edu/~reeset/marcedit/html/downloads.html.

4. The most notable exception to this policy is our collection of government documents, for which Rensselaer is a selective housing site for the Troy Public Library depository. Since we contract with Marcive for this subset of resources, we have opted not to alter the national level "single record" versions they distribute.

MARC RECORDS FOR E-JOURNALS: SUNY ALBANY'S EXPERIENCE

Daniel McShane, Electronic Resources Librarian, State University of New York at Albany

Like many other libraries, SUNY Albany has found no easy route to providing access to e-journals, but we have been committed to cataloging them using the single record approach so that the OPAC includes links to electronic full text, along with all the other formats represented therein.

Past Procedures

Prior to 2002, the Library created brief records (using MARC Maker) for all titles provided by Serials Solutions and loaded those records into the OPAC. These brief records mirrored the fields provided by Serials Solutions, with the addition of a 516 and a 710 for the aggregator. No attempt was made to add information to already existent records.

Present Procedures

Shortly after my arrival in 2002, we purchased Ex Libris's SFX product. Our methodology changed accordingly. Because at the time the SFX database was (and to a great degree still is) populated only with records that have ISSNs, we were forced to provide two methods of access; one for titles that have ISSNs *and are* activated in the SFX database, and one for titles that do not have ISSNs *and are not* activated in the SFX database.

Our current policy regarding access to electronic resources in the OPAC is to follow the single record approach. In cases where we own the print version of a resource, we attach electronic holdings information to the print record and add several fields to the bibliographic record (i.e. 007, 530) to reflect the additional format. In cases where we do not own the print version, the policy is a bit less consistent. In some cases, a bibliographic record exists for both a print and an electronic version,. while in others, a bibliographic record exists for only the electronic version. Practice regarding which records should be downloaded varies greatly.

Processing

The path from acquisition to access in the OPAC is elaborate but is mostly governed by one thing: the presence or non-presence of the ISSN. In essence, there are three separate processes at work—one for the Serials Solutions list, one for activating titles in the SFX database, and one for all of the aggregators/major publishers not included in the Serials Solutions profile.

Serials Solutions

Our current Serials Solutions profile accounts for 23,965 journals from the following aggregators:

Ebsco Academic Search Premier and Business Source Premier

Contemporary Women's Issues

Gale InfoTrac OneFile and Expanded Academic ASAP

LexisNexis Academic and LexisNexis Academic (selected full text only)

International Index to the Performing Arts Full Text

International Index to Black Periodicals Full Text

The process for these titles begins with the receipt of the bimonthly list of titles. The list is sorted and separated into tab-delimited files based on aggregator. Each of the files is loaded into an Access database and compared to its counterpart from the previous update. Separate lists of additions and deletions are derived from this comparison for each aggregator. The addition and deletion lists are further processed into lists for titles with ISSNs and titles without ISSNs.

A master ISSN file is constructed from the addition files. For titles that have ISSNs, the processed Serial Solutions lists are used to construct the SFX target activation list and are run against the OPAC to identify new additions or deletions. A list of ISSNs that were not found in the catalog is used for downloading records from OCLC. The downloaded records are then processed using the MARC.pm Perl module to strip out unwanted fields and to add needed fields (i.e. 530, 866, 911). Upon completion of this processing, the file is loaded into the catalog. Holdings are then added to these records manually, in a local 956 field (as a backup access point should the SFX server go down).

For those titles that match a record in the catalog, holdings information is added to the record manually and the bib record is revised (if necessary). For the titles without ISSNs, title searches are performed in the catalog and holdings added when appropriate. When a title is not found, a brief record is created.

Titles that do not have ISSNs are searched in OCLC. MARC records for the print version, if available, are downloaded, "neutralized" via several MARC.pm scripts, and holdings are manually attached to the records after they have been loaded into the OPAC. The holdings, in these cases, utilize an 856 instead of a 956 so that patrons will know that access is not provided via SFX but rather directly via the aggregator.

SFX

The SFX database is populated with records derived from the Serials Solutions list as well as lists from other major publishers like JSTOR, BioOne, Project Muse, Ingenta Select, ScienceDirect, etc. Currently there are 21,866 titles activated in the database. Although Ex Libris has stated their intent to include titles in the database without ISSNs, only 23 exist to date, and these titles have alternate index keys like LCCNs. For all practical purposes only titles with ISSNs are included in the database.

The mechanism used to activate the titles in SFX is a fairly simple one. A tab-delimited file is created for each aggregator/publisher that includes two fields, the ISSN and Availability (either ACTIVE or INACTIVE). This file is used in the SFX Data Loader module as an input file for a program that automatically activates or deactivates all titles defined in the file for the respective aggregator. This mechanism is used for both aggregators/publishers included in the Serials Solutions profile and those that are not included. In the case of non-Serials Solutions aggregators/publishers, title lists are developed by the vendors themselves or constructed manually.

The SFX record for any given title also provides for customization of the date threshold (holdings). Currently, we use the global (default) date threshold for all titles. This is due to the unique syntax that is used to construct these thresholds, which is not compatible with the Serials Solutions provided holdings format. Customizations to these thresholds are performed when discrepancies are reported on REFPROB, an internal discussion list used to communicate issues of importance to public service personnel.

Major Publishers

Titles lists from other major publishers including ScienceDirect, Emerald Full-text, Springer-Link, IEE, IOP, APA Prola, Ingenta Select, JSTOR, Haworth Press, and Ovid are reviewed on a biannual basis. All of the processing procedures described above are performed on these lists as well. The lists are reviewed for additions/deletions, holdings changes, etc. OCLC records are downloaded and added to the system and changes to already existent records are made as necessary. These lists tend to be less volatile than the aggregator lists, and hence are reviewed less frequently.

Free E-Resources

Free electronic resources are cataloged by request from bibliographers via an online request form. The requests are received and acted upon by the electronic resources librarian. In most cases, the request is fulfilled via the addition of a URL to an already existent record. In other cases, an OCLC record is downloaded, revised, and added to the OPAC. These requests are sporadic and are not as statistically significant as our purchased resources.

Choices

1. *Abandon the single record approach:* Most of the time spent on processing electronic resources occurs in identifying additions and deletions to the database and holdings maintenance. We do not yet have a way of automating either procedure, and we are still in the process of refining batch record loaders and overlay procedures in the new system. Processing these resources could be accelerated if we abandon the single record approach, expand the Serials Solution profile to include as many aggregators/publishers as possible, and take advantage of Serials Solutions' MARC records service. By customizing the records to include a field that identifies the records as being provided by Serials Solutions, we could provide a mechanism by which we could "refresh" our records by deleting records from previous lists prior to loading the new ones. Customization of our holdings records would also become possible thereby making "up-to-date" and "accurate" holdings a reality. Taking this action would enable us to update all or most of our e-resource records upon receipt of the bi-monthly list, and may even have the added benefit of reducing any need for the SFX service. Although we would lose the functionality of being able to refine a journal request by year, volume, or issue number, many of the URLs provided by Serials Solutions and the major publishers result in the user being directed to a browse screen

from which the exact resource can easily be found. In addition, the holdings record will display each of the available destinations for any one resource, thus obviating the need for SFX to serve as a "meta-aggregator." However, public service personnel continue to prefer using a single record, believing that multiple records confuse users.

There are budgetary ramifications of this approach. The consortial price quote for our current Serials Solutions profile is $6,311.39. If we were to revise our profile to include most/all of our aggregators/publishers we could expect to have to pay somewhere in the vicinity of $12,436.84. It is important to keep in mind that no additional costs would be incurred in processing and loading these records into the database, and that some of the additional Serials Solutions subscription costs could be absorbed by cancellation of the SFX service.

2. *Maintain the single record approach:* Under this scenario, as we grow our electronic resources collection, more manpower will have to be devoted to processing it. Currently, with the assistance of two students spending on average 16 hours per week performing holdings maintenance, the lists are usually completed two weeks before the arrival of the next one. Prior to holdings maintenance, the electronic resources librarian is responsible for the downloading, enhancement, addition, and deletion of catalog records, as well as the activation of titles in the SFX database. The timely completion of this process will be affected by the addition of ScienceDirect titles as well as any other future acquisitions.

The non–Serials Solutions aggregator title lists are not as volatile. Periodic updates are provided electronically for JSTOR, MUSE, and BioOne titles, and are processed as needed. Comprehensive reviews of the other aggregators are done biannually.

There are budgetary ramifications. Prior to migration to the ALEPH 500 system, I was spending approximately 65% to 70% of my time processing e-resources (this included processing the SS/publisher lists, downloading OCLC records, and holdings maintenance). Sixteen hours of student labor was also committed to holdings maintenance. As our collections increase, more time (and consequently more money) will have to be spent on processing the resources. If the ultimate goal is to maintain timely processing of our e-collections, the question remains about which method will prove to be most cost effective: purchasing MARC records for automated processing or continuing to hire and train students to process the collections.

Future Directions

Logical Bases

The Ex Libris ALEPH system provides many customization options which will make the discovery of electronic resources easier. One of these options is the use of logical bases which are essentially preset searches already done for the user in order to present a subset of the entire database for the user to search. Presently, logical bases can limit the search universe by format, collection, or location. We have already implemented logical bases for journals and DVDs. There are many other possibilities. It is a matter of deciding which segments of the collections are of sufficient interest to this library's users to warrant creating logical bases for them.

A-to-Z Browse Lists for Journals and Databases

There has been renewed interest in using A-to-Z browse lists for both journals and databases. This could be easily implemented within the confines of the OPAC itself. Each of the search screens for the logical bases for journals and databases could be customized to display an A-to-Z list in addition to the browse and search functionality that exist now.

Holdings Maintenance

We migrated to the Ex Libris ALEPH system in July 2004 and are in the process of examining how the ALEPH system will affect our procedures. We are unsure of the use of the 956 field as the backup access point, as we have yet to test the ease of making the subfield u in the 956 field a live link, and have yet to test whether they can be expanded from the holdings record. We are investigating alternative "fall-back" methodologies.

We are curious to see if ProQuest's purchase of Serial Solutions will have an effect on data quality.

We are also investigating methods by which automatic updating of holdings can be achieved. Currently these are done manually, but we'd like to develop a Perl script that will enable us to batch load holdings records into ALEPH. An automated method would greatly reduce the amount of time needed to process our electronic resources.

E-JOURNAL MARC RECORDS AT THE SIMON FRASER UNIVERSITY LIBRARY

Don Taylor, Electronic Resources Librarian, Simon Fraser University, Burnaby, British Columbia

The Simon Fraser University (SFU) Library automatically generates aggregator neutral MARC records for the online catalog from the records in the Library's electronic journals database. The electronic journals database includes e-journals from all sources—full text article databases, journals directly from publishers, open access, etc. This model was developed in 2000, when the Library decided to create an electronic journals database to manage e-journals.

The MARC records (see figure 1) contain the following fields: 005 (created when MARC record generated), 022, 110, 245, 246, 590 (local holdings), 690, 710 and 856. The reason that 690 is used rather than 650 is to prevent e-journal MARC records being subjected to subject authority control. However, the 110 and 710 are subjected to authority control.

```
LEADER 00000nms 22001577a 4500t
005 20040922030503.0
022 00703370; 15337790
035 |sEJDB1179
245 00 Demography|h[electronic resource]
299 00 Demography|h[electronic resource]
590 Available full text from Project Muse (Johns Hopkins):
 v.37 (2000)—onwards
590 Available full text from ABI/Inform Global: v.32 (1995)—
 onwards
590 Available full text from JSTOR Arts & Sciences I
 Collection: Vol. 1 (1964)- three years ago
690 Demography|vPeriodicals
710 Population Association of America
856 4 |uhttp://www.lib.sfu.ca/researchtools/electronicjournals/
 ejdb.htm?Display=JournalID1179
```

Figure 1. E-Journal MARC Record.

The MARC records are created from what are called the "version records" in the electronic journals database. A version is a combination of an e-journal bib record and the source/supplier record. The source/supplier is the vendor providing the e-journal. For example, SFU has access to the journal *Demography* from three different sources—JSTOR, Project Muse and ABI/Inform. Consequently there are three different version records for *Demography*, one for each vendor. The version record has the holdings information, URL for the journal, and any pertinent notes regarding that version (e.g., embargo information).

Using MARC.pm tools, the SFU Library Systems division developed a Perl to MARC utility to combine the bibliographic data from the electronic journals database bib records and the holdings and source information from the version records to create MARC records. The utility also creates a leader and 005 field and also inserts |h[electronic resource] into the 245 and |vPeriodicals into the 690 of the MARC records. The records are aggregator neutral.

As can be seen in figure 1 there is only one URL in each MARC record, even if there are multiple versions of the journal. The 856 URL links to the display screen for the journal in the electronic journals database (see figure 2). Consequently, all link management can be done in the electronic journals database and any transient notes about access, downtime, etc are also done through the electronic journals database and viewed on the electronic journals database's journal display screen. This allows for easier maintenance of journal URLs and avoids the need to make any changes to the e-journal records in the library's catalog. Consequently, the e-journal records in the library's catalog depend upon the electronic journals database not just as the source of MARC records, but also as the access point to the electronic journals themselves.

Electronic Journals

Browse | Keyword search | Subject categories | About | Help

The Library provides access to selected issues of:

Demography (ISSN 00703370; 15337790)

which are available from the following suppliers. Choose a link below to gain access:

ABI/Inform Global from ProQuestDirect v.32 (1995)—onwards

To find journals in ProQuest, click on the 'Publication Search' tab on the ProQuest toolbar. Because of agreements with publishers, ABI/Inform from ProQuestDirect does not always provide access to the most current issues of journals. **In *some* cases 3-12 months of the most current full text is excluded.**

Project Muse (Johns Hopkins) v.37 (2000)—onwards

JSTOR Arts & Sciences I Collection Vol. 1 (1964)- three years ago

---

Figure 2. Electronic Journals Database Display.

To facilitate the creation of MARC records, the data entry fields in the electronic journals database records are tagged as MARC fields and MARC coding is used when entering data into the fields. For example, the journal *Physical review B. Condensed matter and materials physics* is entered as Physical review B. |pCondensed matter and materials physics.

Every Wednesday at 3:00 A.M. the Perl-to-MARC utility is run automatically and MARC records are created for each e-journal in the electronic journals database. The utility takes about 10 minutes to run. Currently SFU has approximately 10,000 unique e-journal titles in the electronic journals database. At 6:00 A.M. *all* e-journal MARC records are deleted from the catalog and replaced with the MARC records recently created by the perl to MARC utility. Figure 3 shows the workflow for the creation of the MARC records and loading into the catalog.

Since the creation of e-journal MARC records is a weekly activity, the catalog will not reflect the very latest e-journal additions/deletions. However, to date this has never been an issue with patrons.

Patrons are encouraged to search for e-journals using the catalog because of ease of searching and since they will also be able to view print holdings. For example, the electronic journals database requires exact punctuation, so that searching for *Physical Review (series 1)* as *Physical Review series 1* would result in zero hits in the electronic journals database. The catalog, however, omits punctuation and would allow retrieval of the journal using the above search.

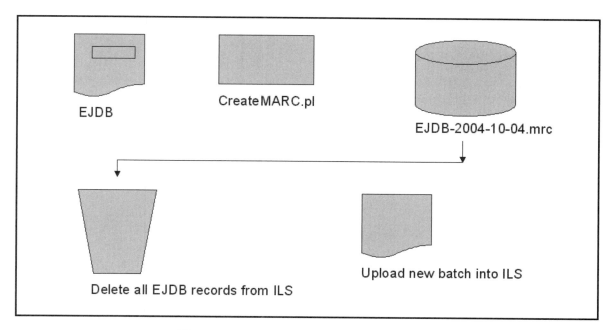

Figure 3. MARC Record Creation Workflow.

Unlike with an ILS, there was no way to automatically download records into the electronic journals' database—all record addition was done by hand keying the records. This can be a daunting task when the Library signs onto a Big Deal giving us hundreds of new e-journals in one fell swoop. Therefore, in summer 2002 SFU Library Systems developed a "harvester" software program (named Massey after the tractor manufacturer Massey Ferguson) to automatically create electronic journals database records for Big Deal packages and a "loader" to load the records into the database and create version records. Prior to this, each e-journal record for a Big Deal was hand keyed into the electronic journals database and then version records created manually. This was a very time-consuming process and delayed providing OPAC access to the new journals available via a Big Deal. This all changed with Massey.

Massey allows the library to harvest MARC records from consenting libraries using Z39.50 and turn these records into e-journal bib records for the electronic journals database. Using the ISSN of a journal, Massey searches library catalogs for the journal MARC records, harvests the MARC records, and stores them in a MARC file. The software then extracts data from the 022, 110, 245, 246, 650 (deletes the |v periodical subfield) and 710 fields and creates e-journal bib records for the electronic journals database. At this point another locally developed software program, called a "loader," is used. The loader takes the holdings information and URL for each journal (contained in a spreadsheet put together by the electronic resources librarian), matches them with the relevant electronic journals database e-journal bib record, and creates version records for each of the new e-journals. These version records are loaded into an offline version of the electronic journals database, analyzed for any obvious flaws, and then loaded into the regular electronic journals database. Massey does not manage to harvest

100% of all required titles, so between 5% and 10% of e-journal records for Big Deals are still created manually. The lengthiest part of the process is the preparation of the spreadsheet containing the URLs and holdings information for the journals. After the spreadsheet has been created the process of running Massey and the loader takes only a couple of hours.

Massey and the loader allow the SFU Library to create electronic journals database records for Big Deals in a very short period of time. The following Wednesday the records are converted to MARC records and loaded into the catalog so that patrons have access to the new resources via the catalog.

Massey and the loader software have also been used to convert vendor supplied MARC records into electronic journals database records, thus enabling the Library to easily load records for full text journals found in full text article databases.

Finally, the SFU Library has developed CUFTS (the successor to SFU Jake),[1] which includes a MARC record-creating utility that allows libraries to create MARC records for any of the e-journals provided by one of the 245 separate sources in the CUFTS knowledgebase.

Note

1. http://cufts.lib.sfu.ca/tools.shtml

MARC RECORDS FOR E-JOURNALS—CONSORTIUM PERSPECTIVE

Christopher Thornton, Coordinator, Bibliographic Services, Case Western Reserve University, Cleveland, Ohio

Case Western Reserve University is in a somewhat unique position in regard to e-journals and their management. Of the roughly 5,300 titles that Case has access to, at least 4,500 are made available by OhioLINK consortium through its Electronic Journal Center. As a result, decisions made on the state level have a profound effect on how we and other local libraries list their e-journals in the library catalog. The basic design of the OhioLINK consortium also effects how ejournal cataloging decisions are made statewide. The OhioLINK consortium is based on a model in which local catalogs feed into a larger central catalog. Therefore, some degree of statewide coordination is needed. This coordination is provided through the Database Management & Standards Committee, which consists of representatives from the various member libraries. The recommendations of the DMS Committee are directed primarily at issues that affect the central catalog. However, the implications are statewide.

In regard to MARC records for e-journals the committee made recommendations for "separate" MARC records for the central catalog. Since OhioLINK has no cataloging staff per say and the MARC records are contracted through OCLC TechPro, this makes a lot of sense. As new publishers are added to EJC, MARC records are contracted for through TechPro and batch loaded into the local catalogs which in turn feed into the central catalog. The DMS standards "allow" for the single record approach for local libraries that wish to follow that option. However, since OhioLINK makes the TechPro records available to local libraries, it makes a lot of sense for the local libraries to use separate records in their own catalogs. Besides, it is just much easier (and cheaper) for catalog departments to deal in batch adds and deletes for eresource MARC records.

The public service concerns for having "multiple" records for a title in the catalog have not been an issue here at Case. Displaying journal holdings seems to be complicated no matter how you format them.

The numbers provided in the first paragraph are for "stand-alone" type e-journals and not those e-journals included in aggregator databases. OhioLINK does make available MARC records to represent the full text journals in the EBSCO research databases that the consortium subscribes to. This amounts to several thousand more titles. At Case, we have decided NOT to include MARC records in our catalog for these titles. It was felt that even with the records being available in batch, it would be difficult for us to accurately maintain those records, especially in that the titles tend to be somewhat volatile. This is strictly a local decision that other OhioLINK libraries other than Case do not necessarily follow.

Several months ago the Case libraries (Main, Law, Medical, and Applied Social Sciences) got together and decided to go with a commercial vendor to maintain a separate Web list of e-journals. We chose EBSCO's A-to-Z product mainly for economic/price reasons but also because EBSCO is the primary journal vendor on campus and it made sense for us to have that sort of "seamless" connection for many of our journals. The A-to-Z list is not generated from the OPAC database. Rather it is generated from a customized list of accessible titles. With regard to OhioLINK e-journals, EBSCO agreed to include these in its A-to-Z product as "managed" titles. As with the library catalog, Case decided against listing aggregator database type e-journals to the list. Recently, we decided to add the MARC record component to the A-to-Z service. EBSCO will now supply us with full MARC records for our non-OhioLINK e-journals.

We may decide to change in the future, but for now are just including stand-alone full text e-journals in or library catalog and on our A-to-Z Web page list. Rather than opting for a comprehensive one-stop shopping type of access, we have tried to make e-journals manageable and easy to use.

Index

5726 C06